W0186072

# Welcome to Context 21 • Starter

- Are you learning English because you want a good job when you leave school? (▸ p. 62)
- Or because you enjoy meeting, talking and chatting to young people from all over the world? (▸ p. 24)
- Or just because you like English as a subject and hope it will help you to get a good Abitur grade? (▸ p. 145)

*Context 21 • Starter*, with many new features, will enable you to further **improve your ability to communicate in English. Check it out:**

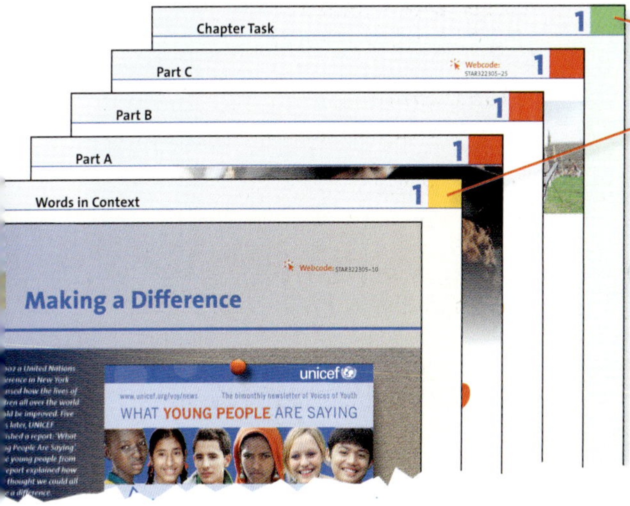


- **Chapter Tasks** will let you practise skills you need for exams as well as for day-to-day survival.
- **Words in Context** will help you to improve your vocabulary and use it better.
- **Language help** will start you off on answers, discussions, essays, ...

> **Language help**
> - (The stylistic device) ... makes you think / gives you the impression that ...

- **Trouble spots** will point out 'false friends', tricky spellings, common mistakes, ...

> ⚠ **Trouble spot**
> **eventually** = schließlich, irgendwann
> eventuell = **perhaps**
> ▸ LP 28 False Friends (p. 121)

**Right now you'll be learning new skills and techniques** in English. And, of course, you'll be getting ready for your Abitur and for the world after school. This book will make all that easier by introducing you to and giving you practice in the skills you will need, for example:

- Reading and talking about novels (▸ p. 82), poems (▸ p. 17) and short stories (▸ p. 18)
- Understanding and commenting on newspaper articles (▸ p. 73), sound files (▸ p. 57 CD) and videos (▸ p. 34 DVD)
- Doing research with English sources (▸ p. 40)
- Being creative in English (▸ p. 60)
- Coping with common situations in English (▸ p. 39)

**At the back of the book there's a reference section** which you can turn to whenever you're unsure about something you've learned:

- **Language Practice (LP)** (pp. 105–131) gives you the chance to do extra work in the field of grammar, vocabulary and communication skills.
- The **Skills File (SF)** (pp. 132–157) summarizes the key aspects of all the skills you've learned.
- The **Glossary** (pp. 158–165) explains all the terms you need for text analysis.
- **Language for Tasks** (pp. 168–169) helps you to understand and get used to the wording of your Abitur tasks.

## Chapter 1: Making a Difference

A look at how different people from all walks of life get involved to make the world a better place

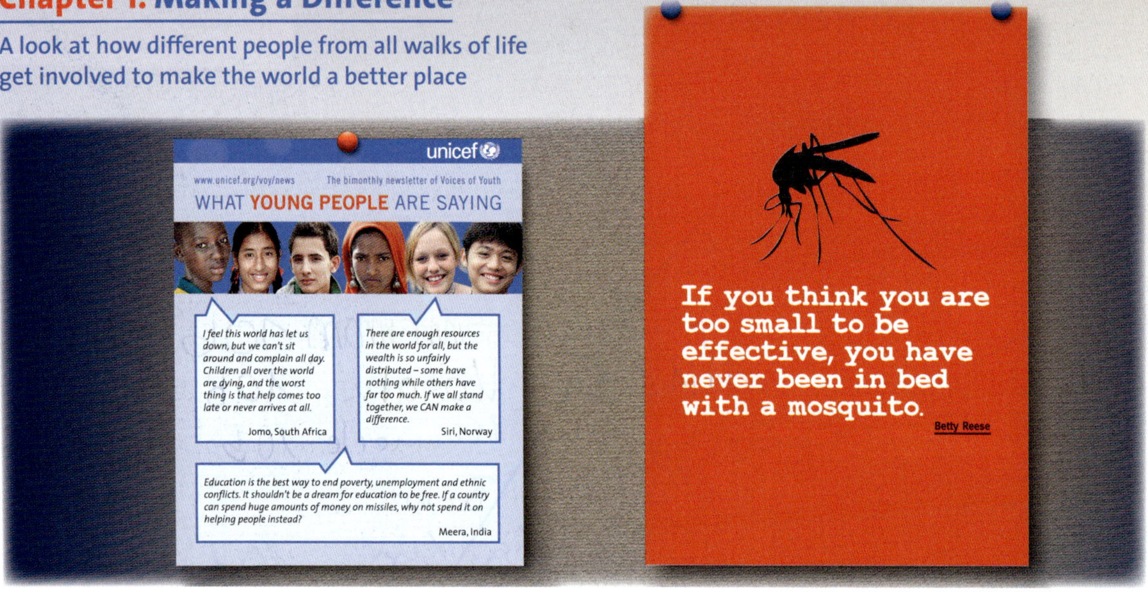



| | | | |
|---|---|---|---|
| 10 | **Lead-In** | | |
| 12 | **Words in Context:** Getting Involved | | |
| | ▪ Ways of getting involved<br>▪ Analysing a poster<br>▪ Word families<br>▪ Activating your passive vocabulary<br>▪ Problem area: *to*-infinitive or *-ing* form?<br>▪ Writing | | |
| 14 | **Part A:** It's Your Turn | | |
| 14 | **A1** Take a Chance | ▪ Commencement address given by Barack Obama at the University of Massachusetts Boston, June 2006 | CD I.02–03 |
| 16 | **A2** Cutting through the Complexities | ▪ Commencement address given by Bill Gates at Harvard University, June 2007 | CD I.04–05 |
| 17 | **Part B:** Can I Help? | | |
| 17 | **B1** If I Can Stop One Heart from Breaking | ▪ Poem by Emily Dickinson | |
| 18 | **B2** Bread on the Water | ▪ Short story by David Lubar<br>▪ Mediation | CD I.06–07 |
| 25 | **Part C:** Nothing's Impossible | | |
| 25 | EXTRA<br>**C1** Kierra Box | ▪ Magazine article by Alice O'Keeffe in *New Statesman* | |
| 26 | **C2** Be the Change | ▪ CNN website<br>▪ CNN video logs | DVD 01–03 |
| 27 | **Chapter Task:** Applying for Volunteer Work | | |
| | ▪ Understanding a job description: What are they looking for?<br>▪ Introducing yourself<br>▪ Correcting common mistakes<br>▪ Writing a personal statement | | |


▸ The chapters can be done in any order, which means you don't have to start with Chapter 1. There is no vocabulary progression in the book.

## Chapter 2: Our Changing Planet

A look at the causes and effects of global warming and what we can do to slow it down and protect nature and the environment

| | | | |
|---|---|---|---|
| 30 | **Lead-In** | | |
| 32 | **Words in Context:** People and the Planet | | |
| | ▪ Sustainable consumption<br>▪ Our carbon footprint<br>▪ Word formation<br>▪ Interpreting charts and graphs | | |
| 34 | **Part A:** The Scientist's View | | |
| 34 | **A1** What Is Global Warming? | ▪ 'Is the Earth Getting Hotter?' by Glenn Murphy, from *Why Is Snot Green?*<br>▪ 'The Science of Climate Change' by Terence Wood, from a discussion paper on *The Science behind the News* | |
| 36 | **A2** 'There Goes Our Warm Climate' | ▪ Film clips from *The Day After Tomorrow* | DVD 04–05 |
| 37 | **Part B:** The Artist's View | | |
| 37 | **B1** Countdown for Our Planet | ▪ 'Earth's Clock' – poem by Pat Moon<br>▪ 'River Runs Red' – song by Midnight Oil | DVD 06 |
| 38 | **B2** Climate Change | ▪ 'Global Warming' – painting by Paul Cumes<br>▪ 'Positive proof of global warming' – poster | |
| 40 | **Part C:** Solutions | | |
| 40 | **C1** The Healthy Climate Pledge | ▪ 'Healthy Climate Pledge Statement' | |
| 41 | **C2** Buy Local! | ▪ Article from *Change the World 9 to 5* | |
| 42 | **C3** Greener Travel | ▪ Table of statistics from *50 Ways to Greener Travel* | |
| 43 | **Chapter Task:** Discussing a Current Affairs Topic | | |
| | ▪ Preparing and conducting a group discussion<br>▪ Reporting what you have read or heard<br>▪ Mediation<br>▪ Species extinction and human activity<br>▪ Listening to people's opinions | | CD I.08<br>CD I.09–10<br>CD I.11–12 |

## Chapter 3: The Web of Communication

A look at the various aspects of communication and how we present ourselves: what we say, how we say it and through which media

| | | | |
|---|---|---|---|
| 46 | **Lead-In** | | |
| 48 | **Words in Context:** You Can't Not Communicate | | |
| | ▪ A communication model<br>▪ Matching nouns and verbs<br>▪ Matching nouns and adjectives<br>▪ Activating your passive vocabulary | | |
| 50 | **Part A:** Connecting through the Internet | | |
| 50 | **A1** Online Pressure | ▪ Extract from a newspaper article in *The New York Times* | |
| 52 | **A2** An Online Hoax | ▪ Extract from a newspaper article in *The New York Times* | |
| 53 | **A3** Risky Behaviour | ▪ Radio interview on the risks involved with social networking websites | CD I.13 |
| 54 | **Part B:** To Talk or Not to Talk? | | |
| 54 | **B1** Meeting the Stepmother | ▪ Extract from the novel *Black Swan Green* by David Mitchell | |
| 57 | **B2** A New Kind of Connectedness? | ▪ Radio interview on the effect of modern media on family togetherness | CD I.14 |
| 58 | **Part C:** Rhythm Is It | | |
| 58 | **C1** Expressing Yourself through Music | ▪ Film clips from *Rhythm Is It!*<br>▪ Mediation | DVD 07–08<br>DVD 09 |
| 60 | **C2** Expressing Yourself through Poetry | ▪ 'How to Eat a Poem' – poem by Eve Merriam<br>▪ Poem skeleton / Biography poem / Rondo<br>▪ Contribution to the 11th International Youth Poetry Slam Festival in Washington, D.C. | CD I.15 |
| 62 | **Chapter Task:** Presenting Yourself Creatively | | |
| | ▪ Getting it right<br>▪ Being creative<br>▪ Putting together an application | | DVD 10 |

## Chapter 4: Migrants and Minorities

A look at how migration is changing the face of Europe in general and how the UK and Ireland in particular are responding to new ethnic minorities in their societies

| | | | |
|---|---|---|---|
| 64 | **Lead-In** | | CD I.16 |
| 66 | **Words in Context:** On the Move<br>▪ Word families<br>▪ Word power<br>▪ Activating your passive vocabulary<br>▪ Analysing a photo | | |
| 68 | **Part A:** Westward Bound? | | |
| 68 | **A1** Warsaw on the Thames | ▪ Extract from a magazine article in *Newsweek* | |
| 70 | **A2** From Kiev to Kent | ▪ Extract from the novel *Two Caravans* by Marina Lewycka | |
| 73 | **A3** The Pendulum Effect | ▪ Extract from a newspaper article in *The Scotsman* | |
| 74 | **Part B:** Migrants as Minority Groups | | |
| 74 | **B1** 'It's not all Take, Take, Take' | ▪ Radio report on immigration | CD I.17–18 |
| 76 | **B2** The Changing Face of Ireland | ▪ TV report on immigration to Ireland | DVD 11–12 |
| 77 | **Part C:** The Downside of Migration | | |
| 77 | **C1** Black Hoodie | ▪ Text puzzle from the short story 'Black Hoodie' by Roddy Doyle | |
| 79 | **C2** It's a Free World | ▪ Film clip from *It's a Free World* by Ken Loach<br>▪ Mediation | DVD 13–14 |
| 80 | **Chapter Task:** Writing an Essay<br>▪ Preparing your essay<br>▪ Writing a first draft<br>▪ Preparing a final draft<br>▪ Using participle constructions to link sentences<br>▪ Writing the final draft | | |

## Chapter 5: A Good Read

A look at young-adult fiction: preparing students for reading full-length novels in English that deal with the joy and pains of growing up

| | | | |
|---|---|---|---|
| 82 | **Lead-In** | | |
| 84 | **Words in Context:** The World of Books | | |
| | ▪ Word power<br>▪ Activating your vocabulary<br>▪ Evaluating a chart | ▪ Teenage reading habits<br>▪ What is reading?<br>▪ Classroom discussion: The future of books | CD II.02–03 |
| 86 | **Part A: For Starters: Opening Lines** | | |
| 86 | **A1** The Curious Incident of the Dog in the Night-Time | ▪ Opening lines of the novel *The Curious Incident of the Dog in the Night-Time* by Mark Haddon | |
| 87 | **A2** The Absolutely True Diary of a Part-Time Indian | ▪ Opening lines of the novel *The Absolutely True Diary of a Part-Time Indian* by Sherman Alexie | |
| 88 | **Part B: Who Is Telling the Story?** | | |
| 88 | **B1** The Curious Incident ... | ▪ Extract from the novel by Mark Haddon<br>▪ Interview with Mark Haddon | CD II.04–05 |
| 90 | **B2** Looking for Alaska | ▪ Extract from the novel *Looking for Alaska* by John Green | |
| 92 | **Part C: Presenting the Characters** | | |
| 92 | **C1** Junior and Penelope | ▪ Panel discussion with Sherman Alexie<br>▪ Extract from the novel by Sherman Alexie | DVD 15 |
| 95 | **C2** Miles and Alaska | ▪ Extract from the audiobook of *Looking for Alaska* | CD II.06 |
| 96 | **Part D: Turning a Book into a Film** | | |
| 96 | EXTRA<br>**D1** About a Boy | ▪ Extracts from the novel *About a Boy* by Nick Hornby<br>▪ Clip from the film adaptation | DVD 16 |
| 98 | **D2** Twilight | ▪ Audience reviews of the film adaptation of the novel *Twilight* by Stephenie Meyer<br>▪ Mediation | |
| 99 | **Chapter Task:** Keeping a Reading Journal | | |
| | ▪ Read and Recap<br>▪ Reflect and React<br>▪ Review and Report | | |

| | | |
|---|---|---|
| 102 | **Partner B Pages** | |
| 102 | ▪ Chapter 1 | |
| 103 | ▪ Chapter 3 | |
| 104 | ▪ Chapter 5 | |

## Reference Section

| | | |
|---|---|---|
| 105 | **Language Practice** | |
| 105 | ▪ Grammar | |
| 118 | ▪ Vocabulary | CD II.07–10 |
| 128 | ▪ Communication Skills | |
| 128 | – Expressing Opinions | CD II.11–13 |
| 129 | – Persuading People | CD II.14–16 |
| 130 | – Agreeing and Disagreeing | CD II.17–19 |
| 131 | – Making Comparisons | CD II.20 |
| 132 | **Skills File** | |
| 132 | ▪ Study and Language Skills | |
| 145 | ▪ Exam Skills | |
| 146 | ▪ Listening and Viewing Skills | |
| 148 | ▪ Speaking Skills | |
| 150 | ▪ Reading Skills | |
| 152 | ▪ Writing Skills | |
| 158 | **Glossary** | |
| 158 | ▪ Fiction | |
| 161 | ▪ Non-Fiction | |
| 163 | ▪ Style | |
| 165 | ▪ Stylistic Devices | |
| 166 | Acknowledgements | |
| 168 | **Language for Tasks ('Operatoren')** | |


## Abbreviations and symbols used in Context 21 • Starter

| | |
|---|---|
| **abbr** | abbreviation |
| **adj** | adjective |
| **adv** | adverb |
| **AE/BE** | American English / British English |
| **cf.** | confer, see |
| **e.g.** | (Latin) exempli gratia = for example |
| **esp.** | especially |
| **etc.** | (Latin) et cetera = and so on |
| **ff.** | and the following lines/pages |
| **fig** | figurative(ly) |
| **fml/infml** | formal / informal |
| **i.e.** | (Latin) id est = that is, in other words |
| **jdm./jdn.** | jemandem / jemanden |
| **l./ll.** | line / lines |
| **► LP** | Language Practice (pp. 105–131) |
| **n** | noun |
| **p./pp.** | page / pages |
| **pl** | plural |
| **sb./sth.** | somebody / something |
| **► SF** | Skills File (pp. 132–157) |
| **usu.** | usually |
| **v** | verb |

| | |
|---|---|
| **CD I.04** | indicates that the sound file can be found on the accompanying audio CD (CD I, Track 4). |
| **DVD 07** | indicates that the film or video clip can be found on the accompanying video DVD (Track 7). |
| **EXTRA** | marks additional (optional) material and tasks. |
| * | indicates that the word or expression is explained in the Glossary on pp. 158–165. |

**Webcode:**
STAR322305-25

is found at the top of some pages. It can be entered in the search box at www.cornelsen.de. This connects you directly to a specific website or download (e.g. vocabulary lists) related to a section of the textbook.

Webcode: STAR322305-10

# 1 Making a Difference

*In 2002 a United Nations conference in New York discussed how the lives of children all over the world should be improved. Five years later, UNICEF published a report: 'What Young People Are Saying'. Three young people from the report explained how they thought we could all make a difference.*

unicef

www.unicef.org/voy/news    The bimonthly newsletter of Voices of Youth

## WHAT YOUNG PEOPLE ARE SAYING

*I feel this world has let us down, but we can't sit around and complain all day. Children all over the world are dying, and the worst thing is that help comes too late or never arrives at all.*

Jomo, South Africa

*There are enough resources in the world for all, but the wealth is so unfairly distributed – some have nothing while others have far too much. If we all stand together, we CAN make a difference.*

Siri, Norway

*Education is the best way to end poverty, unemployment and ethnic conflicts. It shouldn't be a dream for education to be free. If a country can spend huge amounts of money on missiles, why not spend it on helping people instead?*

Meera, India

**let sb. down** jdn. im Stich lassen
**complain** say you are unhappy about the way things are
**distribute sth.** [dɪ'strɪbjuːt] *here:* divide sth.
**poverty** ['pɒvəti] state of being very poor
**unemployment** state of not having a job
**huge amounts of** a lot of
**missile** [*BE*: 'mɪsaɪl; *AE*: 'mɪsl] rocket

### 1 Young people's worries

**a** Work in groups of three. Each study one of the statements above and identify what the person is worried about. What do you already know about that person's country? Which of these issues might play a role: famine, health, war, education, racial conflicts, pollution, the gap between rich and poor?

**b** What issues are you worried about – in your town, your country or abroad? Make a list.

**c** Are Siri, Meera and Jomo's worries different from or the same as yours? Discuss and explain. ■ **Language help**

**Language help**

- I think the worst problem in Siri's country is ..., so ...
- Jomo is angry because ...
- I think it's difficult for us to ..., but we should ...

▶ LP 36 Expressing Opinions (p. 128)

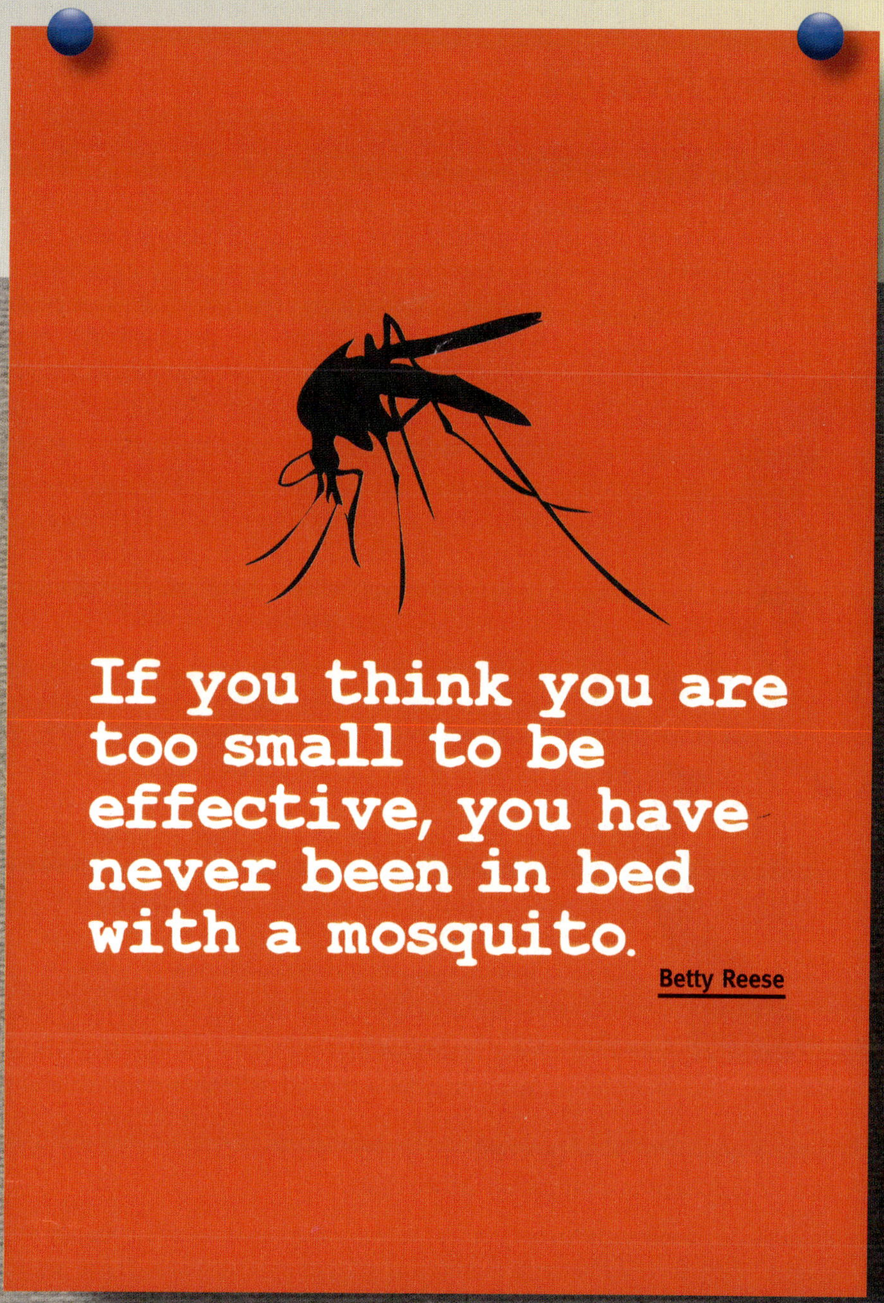


**2 Working with posters**

a Explain what you think this poster means.

b Is the poster effective? How does it get its message across? Think about the drawing of the mosquito, the colours, ...

c Discuss your list from **1b** with a partner. Decide on one issue that you would like to draw people's attention to with an English poster like the one above. Write a description of the poster you would make and read it to the class.

d EXTRA Make your poster. Display it in the classroom. Walk round and discuss the posters.

► SF 12 Working with Pictures (p. 140)

# Getting Involved

▸ LP 25 Increase Your Word Power Online (p. 118)

Schools in English-speaking countries usually offer extra-curricular activities, and they encourage kids to 'get involved'. Students join school clubs and participate in school sports, and as they get older, they often join voluntary organizations. These groups perform a service to the community, like cleaning up a park, doing the shopping for an elderly person, or raising money for a homeless shelter; or they may get involved in more political activity, like making and putting up posters to promote a particular cause – a campaign to stop smoking, for example.

*Anita Roddick, founder of The Body Shop and lifelong activist*

When they leave school, many young people take time off before starting university. This is known as a gap year. While some 'gappers' use this time to travel or to pursue their hobbies, many enjoy doing volunteer work during this time, often abroad.

Young international volunteers mostly spend their time working in developing countries. There they do social work (e.g. helping to bring health care to rural areas or teaching children to read) or help on construction projects (e.g. building schools or clinics, or bringing clean water to poor communities) or ecological projects (e.g. planting trees or showing local farmers how to save water). Some serve in places that have been hit by natural disasters such as earthquakes, tsunamis or tropical storms.

While most volunteers work quietly to make a difference in their small corner of the world, activists want to change the world – or at least people's thinking and/or behaviour. Activists hope to achieve social or political change. To do so, they lobby politicians, advertise for their cause or stage protests to draw people's attention to their cause.

But why do people want to help others by volunteering or donating money to a charity? Well, there are rewards for this sort of commitment. Research has proved that when we help other people, we feel better ourselves: do good, feel good!

**1 Ways of getting involved**

**a Think:** Collect different ways of getting involved that are mentioned in the text. Add your own ideas.

**b Pair:** Compare notes with a partner. Discuss which ways of getting involved would be practical for people your age in Germany.

**c Share:** With another pair, agree on the three most practical ways of getting involved and report to the class.

▸ SF 12 Working with Pictures (p. 140)

**2 Analysing a poster**

Analyse the three main elements of the poster above: the photo, the drawing, the words. Comment on the effectiveness of the poster.

## 3 Word families

**a** Add the missing words to a copy of the chart below. Some of the words you need are in the text on p. 12; you can find the others in a dictionary.

► LP 32–33 Word Formation (p. 124)
► LP 34 Word Stress (p. 126)
► SF 8 Using a Dictionary (p. 136)

| Abstract noun | Noun: person | Verb | Adjective |
|---|---|---|---|
| *activity* | ... | ... | *active* |
| ... | ... | *advertise* | ——— |
| *campaign* | ... | ... | ——— |
| *charity* | ——— | ——— | ... |
| ... | *politician* | ——— | ... |
| *thought* | ... | ... | ... |
| ——— | *volunteer* | ... | ... |

**b** Make sentences with five of the words you have added to the chart, but leave a gap for the words. Swap papers with a partner. Can he/she complete your sentences with the correct words?

## 4 Activating your passive vocabulary

► LP 26 Collocations (p. 120)

When reading the text on p. 12, you probably understood a lot of English expressions that you may not have seen before. But will you remember them if you need to use them?
Translate the following sentences. Pay special attention to the underlined expressions. Look at the text again if necessary.

1 Viele Jugendliche machen ehrenamtliche Arbeit.
2 Sie gehen ihren Hobbys nach.
3 Sie wollen auf ihre Sache aufmerksam machen.
4 Einige spenden Geld an eine Wohltätigkeitsorganisation.
5 Das nennt man ein „gap year“.
6 Sie nehmen eine Auszeit, bevor sie mit dem Studium beginnen.

## 5 Problem area: *to*-infinitive or *-ing* form?

► LP 19 *To*-infinitive and Gerund after Verbs (p. 115)
► LP 20 Gerund after Prepositions (p. 115)

**a** Complete the sentences with a *to*-infinitive or an *-ing* form. Scanning the text on p. 12 for the underlined words in each phrase may help you.

1 The poster is supposed to encourage people (get) involved in political activities.
2 Before you start a charitable organization, you need to be clear about what you hope (achieve).
3 Would you rather spend your time (play) video games or (help) people?
4 Would you enjoy (take part) in volunteer work?
5 I'd like to teach immigrants (speak) our language.
6 Many schools run clubs which get involved in (raise) money for charity.

**b** EXTRA Note down the underlined words from **a** in the way that best suits you for learning new vocabulary. You might like to use the form you would find in a dictionary, e.g. *encourage sb. to do sth.*

## 6 Writing

► SF 31 The Stages of Writing (p. 152)
► SF 33 Structuring a Text (p. 153)

Discuss one of the following topics in 250–300 words. Use expressions from pp. 12–13.

1 Gap year – a practical alternative for German students?
2 Should employers consider volunteer work when choosing applicants for jobs?
3 Volunteering at home or abroad – is one more valuable than the other?

# It's Your Turn

## A1 Take a Chance Barack Obama CD I.02–03

*The following extract is taken from the Commencement Address given by Barack Obama at the University of Massachusetts Boston on 2 June 2006.*

America is an unlikely place – it's a country built on defiance of the odds; on a belief in the impossible. And I remind you of this because as you set off on your own lives of success and achievement, it's now your turn to help keep it this way.

It's your turn to keep this daringly radical but unfailingly simple notion of America alive – that no matter where you're born or how much your parents have; no matter what you look like or what you believe in, you can still rise to become whatever you want; still go on to achieve great things; still pursue the happiness that you hope for. [...]

Now, there may be some who doubt that much has changed – those who doubt that things are better today than they were yesterday. For those who believe that, take a look at this class of 2006.

More than half represent the very first members of their family ever to attend college. In the most diverse university in New England, I look out at a sea of faces that are African-American and Hispanic-American and Asian-American and Arab-American and Anglo-American. I see students who've come here from over 100 different countries, believing like those first settlers that they too could find a home in that City on a Hill – that they too could find success in the unlikeliest of places.

All this has occurred in the midst of a city where *No Irish Need Apply* signs once hung from stores. All of this in a city where, just thirty years ago, buses of black students were pelted with rocks as they pulled into schools in South Boston, where the Red Sox were once the team who refused to sign the great Jackie Robinson.

But the problem isn't that we haven't made progress – we have. The problem is that the progress still isn't good enough. There is more work to be done, more justice to be had, there are more barriers to break down. And now it's your generation's turn to bring those changes about.

The last century was undoubtedly the American century. Our victory over Fascism and Communism liberated millions. At home, we built a shared prosperity that created the largest middle-class in history. Ours was a nation of liberators; of free people; of prosperous people – and the world took notice.

But today, just a few years into the twenty-first century, we've already found ourselves in a different and sometimes precarious position. As revolutions in communications and technology have broken down barriers across the world, it's given more power to both our competitors and to our enemies.

No longer can we assume that a high-school education in Boston is enough to compete for a job that can easily go to the college-educated in Bangalore or in Beijing. No more can we count on employers to provide health care and pensions and job training when their bottom lines know no borders. Never again can we expect the oceans that surround America to keep us safe from attacks on our own soil.

**Commencement Address** [kə'mensmənt] speech at a US university ceremony where students are given their diplomas
2 **built on defiance of the odds** [dɪ'faɪəns] darauf gegründet, widrigen Umständen zu trotzen
5 **set off** start
9 **daring** gewagt
10 **unfailingly simple notion** always simple idea
14 **pursue sth.** etwas verfolgen
15 **doubt sth.** [daʊt] not believe sth.
18 **attend college** go to college
19 **diverse** [daɪ'vɜːs] mixed
23 **City on a Hill** *(biblical)* a place that is easily seen and, figuratively, a shining example
**unlikely** unwahrscheinlich
24 **occur** [ə'kɜː] happen
**No Irish Need Apply** Irish people not wanted for a job
26 **pelt sb. with rocks** jdn. mit Steinen bewerfen
27 **Red Sox** Boston's baseball team
**sign sb.** arrange for sb. to sign a contract
**Jackie Robinson** first famous African American baseball player
31 **bring sth. about** make sth. happen
33 **liberate sb.** free sb.
**prosperity** Wohlstand
39 **competitor** [kəm'petɪtə] Konkurrent/in
40 **assume sth.** [ə'sjuːm] etwas annehmen
41 **compete for sth.** [kəm'piːt] try to be the one chosen for sth.
42 **provide sth.** give sth., offer sth.
**pension** ['penʃn] Rente
43 **bottom line** Betriebsergebnis
44 **soil** Erde, Land

So what does this mean for you? What role will you play in meeting these challenges?

I do not pretend to have all the answers. Each of you are going to have to discover those on your own. But perhaps I can offer a few suggestions that may be useful along the way. [...]

First: take risks [...]. When I was on the brink of graduating from college, I had this crazy idea that I wanted to be a community organizer and work in low-income neighborhoods. [...]

My mother and grandparents thought that I should go to law school, and my friends, they were all busy applying for jobs on Wall Street. But I went ahead and I wrote, it must have been 200 letters, to every organization in the country that I thought was trying to do something good in their neighborhoods. And finally, there was this small group of churches on the south side of Chicago who wrote back and offered me a job helping them deal with the consequences of steel plants that had closed and put thousands out of work.

The churches didn't have a lot of money – so they offered me the grand sum of $12,000 a year plus $1,000 car expense. So I bought an old beat-up car for $800, and I packed up my belongings, and I got out a map, and I started driving west to Chicago – a place where I had never been and where I didn't know a single living soul.

And about halfway between New York City and Chicago, I stopped for the night at a small town in Pennsylvania whose name I can't remember anymore. I found a motel that looked cheap and clean, I pulled into the driveway and went to the counter, where there was this old guy doing crossword puzzles. I asked him for a room, and as he was filling out the information, he looked up and he asked me where I was headed. I explained to him I was going to Chicago, because I was going to be a community organizer. [...] And he said to me, 'You know, you look like a nice clean-cut young man, and you've got a nice voice,' he said. 'So let me give you a piece of advice – forget about this community organizing business. You cannot change the world, and people will not appreciate you trying. What you should do is go into television broadcasting. I am telling you, you can make a name for yourself there.'

Now, I could have taken my mother's advice and I could have taken my grandparents' advice. I could have followed the same path that my friends were traveling. I could have taken the words of wisdom from that old man in Pennsylvania. Objectively speaking, he made some sense. But I knew that there was something in me that wanted to try for something bigger.

So don't let people talk you out of doing what you think is that bigger thing. Listen to what's in you, decide what you care so much about that you are willing to risk everything for.

From: *University of Massachusetts at Boston Commencement Address*, 2 June 2006

***"It's your generation's turn to bring those changes about."***

47 **challenge** Herausforderung
48 **pretend** so tun, als ob
55 **on the brink of** an der Schwelle zu
57 **community organizer** *etwa:* Bürgeraktivist/in
58 **low-income neighborhood** *(AE)* sozial schwaches Viertel
61 **law school** Jurafakultät an einer Hochschule
63 **Wall Street** New Yorker Finanzviertel
68 **deal with sth.** mit etwas fertig werden
69 **steel plant** Stahlwerk
72 **beat-up** *(infml)* zerbeult
74 **living soul** Menschenseele

**Trouble spot**
**a piece of advice** = ein Ratschlag
Not: ~~an advice~~

► LP 21 Uncountable Nouns (p. 116)

84 **appreciate sth.** [ə'pri:ʃieɪt] etwas zu schätzen wissen
88 **words of wisdom** weise Worte
91 **talk sb. out of doing sth.** persuade sb. not to do sth.

### 1 Comprehension

a In a few words, say what Obama's *speech is about. Identify at least two topics.

b In his presidential election campaign Obama's theme was 'change'. List the changes mentioned in his speech that have taken place in America so far (ll. 15–23).

c Explain why Obama says that the last century was 'the American century' (l. 32).

d One phrase that Obama regularly used in his campaign speeches was 'Yes, we can'. Find passages from the speech that illustrate this attitude.

### 2 Looking at stylistic devices

▸ LP 10 Emphasis: Inversion (p. 110)

a Look at these common *stylistic devices which Obama uses in his speech:
- speaking to the audience directly (using 'you' or imperatives)
- inversion (putting the auxiliary before the subject in a statement)
- repetition (using a word or phrase several times for effect)

Find passages in the speech to illustrate them.

b What effect do the devices have on you? Which are most effective in the speech and why? ▪ **Language help**

**Language help**
- (The stylistic device) ... makes you think / gives you the impression that ...
- The effect/purpose of ... is to ...
- By using ..., the speaker captures the audience's attention.
- In my opinion, the most effective device is ... because ...

## A2 Cutting through the Complexities Bill Gates CD I.04–05

*On 7 June 2007, Bill Gates, founder of Microsoft, gave a speech at Harvard University's Commencement Ceremony. In it he explained how we can 'turn caring into action' and why, as a rule, we don't.*

*▪ impact ▪ revolting ▪ approach (n) ▪ inequity ▪ conscious effort ▪ determine sth.*

### 1 Comprehension

▸ SF 19 Listening for Gist (p. 146)
▸ SF 4 Taking Notes (p. 134)

a Make sure you know the meaning of the words on the left. Then listen to the extracts from Bill Gates's *speech and take notes on the topics he talks about. Summarize two of his main points.

b EXTRA Gates says, 'I believe we have more caring than we know what to do with.' Explain what he means. Do you agree with his view? Why (not)?

### 2 What would you do?

▸ LP 14 Conditional Sentences: Type II (p. 112)

Answer Bill Gates's question: If you had a few hours a week and a few dollars a month to donate to a cause, how would you spend them?

**⚠ Trouble spot**
spenden = **donate**
**spend** = *(Geld)* ausgeben, *(Zeit)* verbringen

▸ LP 28 False Friends (p. 121)

### 3 EXTRA Writing a speech

Write your own speech about something you would like to change. Use ideas you have collected so far in this chapter. Think about the occasion and the audience. You can use some of the *stylistic devices that Obama and Gates use in their speeches. Then present your speech to a partner.

# Can I Help?

## B1 If I Can Stop One Heart from Breaking Emily Dickinson

If I can stop one heart from breaking,
I shall not live in vain;
If I can ease one life the aching,
Or cool one pain,
Or help one lonely person
Into happiness again,
I shall not live in vain.

[2] **in vain** for nothing
[3] **ease the aching** ['eɪkɪŋ] den Schmerz lindern

1

2

3

4

### 1 Talking about the poem and pictures

**a** State the main idea of the *poem in one sentence. Read the poem again out loud.
**b** In groups of four, each describe one picture. What do you think the people might be saying?
**c** Choose your favourite picture. Look for a *line or phrase in the poem that fits it and explain why.
**d** EXTRA Write down the *rhyme scheme of the poem. Explain how it affects the way you read the poem. Read the poem out loud to illustrate your view.

## B2 Bread on the Water David Lubar

*Do you think people are born with the desire to do good? Or is it something we learn? And if we learn it, where do we learn it?*

'It's going to be a long sermon,' Andy whispered to me.

'Yeah, we're doomed.' I could tell we were in trouble all the way from the back pew. Pastor Donald had stuck so many little colored slips of paper in his Bible, it looked like a piñata. He wasn't the sort of preacher who'd share a couple short verses and set us free to enjoy the day. He really liked to hammer home his messages.

'Turn with me to Romans twelve,' Pastor Donald said.

Andy started to snicker. 'Romans twelve, Christians nothing,' he whispered.

'Ssshhh.' I gave him an elbow and looked around. Mrs. Skeffington, three pews ahead and over to the left, was glaring at us. So were Mr. and Mrs. Linden, over on the right. [...]

Pastor Donald started to read out loud. 'Verse twenty tells us, *if your enemy is hungry, feed him.*'

'Feed him some knuckles,' Andy said, lifting his face from his hands.

I checked out my parents, up front. They hadn't looked back. Not yet. Neither had Andy's parents. If I could just get Andy to calm down, everything would be okay. 'Just cut it out,' I said. 'All right?'

No such luck. Andy was on a roll. And Pastor Donald was about to hand him even better material to work with. After a brief visit with the Good Samaritan in Luke, and a short hop through Ecclesiastes, he landed squarely in James, chapter two, verse fifteen.

*'If a brother or sister be naked ...'*

'If a sister be naked, I'm staying,' Andy said. 'If a brother be naked, I'm splitting.'

*'... and destitute of daily food ...'*

'I thought destitutes made good money.' He scratched his head. 'Hold it. I think I got my 'tutes mixed up.'

*'And one of you say unto them, Depart in peace, be ye warmed and filled; notwithstanding ye give them not those things which are needful to the body; what doth it profit?'*

'Doth?' Andy said, stretching it out wetly like Daffy Duck. 'Doth who? Doth Vader?' He looked at me and raised one eyebrow. 'Be ye warm, Tommy?'

As I reached over to smack Andy, the shadow of Assistant Pastor John fell across us.

'Out,' he whispered, pointing at the door with one hand and clutching the edge of the pew with the other. I could almost hear the wood splintering beneath his grip.

'I wasn't doing anything,' I said.

His index finger curled in, joining the rest of his fist. 'Out. Both of you.'

Andy shrugged and slipped past me. I followed him toward the door, hoping nobody noticed that we'd just been banished from church. As I glanced back, I saw that Mrs. Skeffington was following our exodus with the gloating satisfaction of someone who has just seen her worst enemy caught stealing money from the collection plate. No doubt, she'd make sure that my parents didn't remain uninformed of my transgression.

1 **sermon** ['sɜːmən] Predigt
2 **be doomed** verloren sein
3 **pew** [pjuː] bench in a church
5 **piñata** [pɪn'jɑːtə] *(from Spanish)* figure decorated with coloured paper and filled with sweets
18 **feed sb. some knuckles** ['nʌklz] *etwa:* jdm. die Faust in den Mund schieben
22 **be on a roll** *(infml)* be in good form and unstoppable
27 **split** *(infml) here:* leave
28 **destitute of sth.** ['destɪtjuːt] *(fml)* completely without sth.

► LP 31 Phrasal Verbs (p. 123)

32 **be needful to sb.** *(old-fashioned)* be needed by sb.
33 **doth** [dʌθ] *(old-fashioned)* does
**Doth Vader** ['veɪdə] reference to Darth Vader, a character in the 'Star Wars' series of films
35 **smack sb.** hit sb.
41 **shrug** move the shoulders up and down
42 **banish sb. from a place** force sb. to leave a place
43 **exodus** *(biblical)* situation in which many people leave a place at the same time
46 **transgression** *(fml)* Sünde

My only consolation was the sight of Pastor Donald's Bible, which still had enough slips in it to fuel a small fire. I was going to miss a ton of Scripture.

I could still hear Pastor Donald as the door closed behind me, 'We are here to help others. Friend, enemy, brother, sister, neighbor, stranger – it doesn't matter.' [...]

It felt good to be free.

'So, whatcha want to do?' Andy asked when we'd walked down the steps to the street.

'I want to snap your head off,' I said.

'Now that's not very Christian.' Andy pointed over his shoulder. 'You should spend more time in church.'

'Look who's talking.' I wanted to be angry, but what the heck – it was a beautiful autumn day, cold and crisp, without a cloud in the sky. And my fate was at least an hour and a half away. Between the sermon and the singing, church wouldn't get out until eleven. I slipped into my jacket.

Andy was already walking toward the center of town. 'What do you feel like doing?' I asked when I'd caught up with him.

'I don't know. How much money you got?'

I looked through my wallet. 'Enough for a couple orders of fries and some shakes,' I said. 'But not enough for a cruise to the Bahamas.'

'Guess we'll have to settle for the fries.' Andy checked his own wallet. 'I think I can upgrade our meal in the direction of a couple burgers.'

We headed toward the Bridgeview Diner. When we were half a block away, I noticed a guy huddled in the entrance of a small office building across the street. He noticed me, too. He stood and headed toward us in a way that reminded me of how my cat acts when I open the fridge.

'Man, he's going to ask for spare change,' I said. His hand was already out. I hated dealing with bums.

'I never give them money,' Andy said.

I was glad to hear that. I figured they probably just spent it on booze.

Sure enough, the guy reached us before we could get to the door of the diner. I took a step back. He looked pretty grubby. His wool plaid jacket was so worn that the squares were all the same color. I dropped my gaze and found myself staring at shoes that had split on the sides and were now wrapped with twine.

'Could you boys spare some money? I haven't eaten in a while.' His voice was so quiet I almost couldn't make out the words.

Before I could tell him to leave us alone, Andy said, 'I'd be happy to buy you some food. You want a meal? Come with us.'

I glanced at Andy, surprised. But then I figured out what he was doing. He was calling the guy's bluff. That was brilliant. The bum didn't want food. He wanted our money so he could go buy a bottle of cheap wine. No way he'd come with us.

'After you,' Andy said, holding the door open.

The guy went in. Man, I'd have bet a million bucks he'd have walked away from the offer. I figured Andy would back off now, but he followed the man right in. I didn't. I was used to Andy doing what he wanted. I'd seen him do stuff at school – like talk with the kids who everyone else made fun of. But this was way over the top. Whoever the joke was on, it wasn't funny.

47 **consolation** Trost
48 **Scripture** ['skrɪptʃə] religious writings
58 **fate** Schicksal
73 **bum** *(AE, offensive)* homeless person
75 **booze** *(infml)* alcohol
77 **grubby** dirty
79 **twine** Paketschnur
85 **call sb.'s bluff** jdn. herausfordern

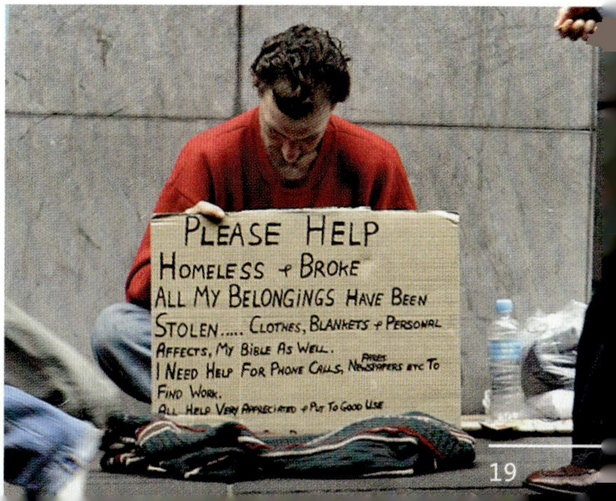

98 **ditch sb.** *(infml)* get rid of sb. you no longer want to be with
100 **appendix** Blinddarm
103 **fancy** elegant
107 **booth** Nischenplatz

I thought about splitting. No way I wanted to eat with this guy. I glanced at my watch. It was too early to go back to church. Besides, I couldn't ditch Andy. He'd stuck with me a couple times when it would have been more fun to take off. And he was the only one from our school who'd visited me back when I'd had my appendix out. On the other hand, I'd never made him share a meal with a bum. 'Let's just get it over with,' I muttered as I went through the door.

The place wasn't exactly fancy. Even so, the waitress gave all three of us the same sort of look I'd probably just given the guy myself. I guess she'd already figured she wasn't in for much of a tip from two kids and a bum. She turned away from us and fidgeted with the coffee pot, then started wiping the counter with a rag.

We grabbed a booth. I slid in next to Andy. I didn't really want to face the guy, but it beat sitting next to him.

Andy pointed to himself. 'I'm Andy. This is Tommy.'

The man nodded toward Andy, then toward me, but he kept his eyes down and didn't tell us his name. His left hand was shaking. After a minute, he put it on his lap.

The waitress finally came over. 'Ready?' she asked, her pad out and pencil poised. I guess she didn't want to invest too much effort in conversation.

'After you,' Andy said to our guest.

The guy looked at the menu, but didn't speak.

'Get whatever you want,' Andy said. 'It's our treat.'

Our treat? I shot Andy a look. He shrugged, as if he assumed I wouldn't mind. I guess there wasn't anything I could do about it right now. And he'd sprung for a movie last month when I was broke, so it sort of worked out.

The guy glanced up at the waitress, then back at the menu. I thought about the times when someone was treating me and I wasn't sure how much they wanted to spend. I always wrestled with what to get.

The waitress cleared her throat, then sighed. I didn't see why she was in such a rush. There weren't any other customers at the moment except for one guy at the counter, eating a donut.

'How about a steak and a salad?' Andy suggested.

The man nodded. In my head, I could hear the ka-ching of the cash register.

'Cokes for us,' Andy added. He glanced at me. 'Split some fries?'

I shook my head. 'I'm not hungry.'

The waitress scritched her pencil across the pad, then left.

'Thank you,' the man said.

'Our pleasure,' Andy said. 'Me and Tommy, we've known each other since we were little. I'm a jock. Tommy wants to be, but he's pretty uncoordinated. They let him on some of the teams because they feel sorry for him.' He glanced out the window. 'Nice day, today. Supposed to be sunny the rest of the week. I noticed they're tearing up part of Main Street for the new parking garage.'

Andy kept talking, stopping once in a while to allow the guy to say something if he wanted to, but not asking any questions. I guess Andy talked because that's what people do when they're waiting for their food. And I guess the guy didn't talk because it was hard enough just asking for the food. I wondered how many people had turned him down today. And I wondered how he'd ended up on the street. This close, beneath the whiskers and the dirt, he could pass for one of my uncles. Actually, I had an uncle who looked worse. For that matter, I had an aunt with more whiskers, too.

It was starting to sink in that this wasn't any kind of joke. This was just Andy being himself. Of course, if his act of kindness annoyed the waitress, I suspected that was just fine with him, too.

**Trouble spot**

**It's our treat.** = Wir bezahlen.
**treat sb.** = jdn. einladen (z. B. in einem Restaurant bezahlen)
**invite sb.** = jdn. einladen (z. B. zu einer Party)

► LP 27 One German Word, Two English Translations (p. 121)

118 **spring for sth.** *(AE, infml)* pay for sth.
119 **be broke** *(infml)* have no money
123 **sigh** seufzen
133 **jock** *(AE, infml)* boy or man who is good at sports
143 **whiskers** *(pl)* hair that grows on a man's face

**Trouble spot**

**wonder** ['wʌndə] = sich fragen
sich wundern = **be surprised**

► LP 28 False Friends (p. 121)

I could smell the steak before it came out of the kitchen. My stomach rumbled, even though I'd stuffed myself on pancakes at breakfast. A whole hour ago. Across the room, the donut eater tossed a couple of coins on the counter and headed up front to pay his bill.

A moment later, the waitress came out of the kitchen. She plopped down the thick white plate with a loud clack, then gave us our sodas.

The guy tore into the food, eating so fast at first, I was afraid he'd choke. He finally slowed after half the steak and all of the salad had vanished. No question, he'd been hungry. I sipped my soda and thought about how lucky I was to have a home and a family. Even a family that dragged me to church every Sunday.

Andy kept talking. I talked some, too. The guy didn't talk, but he looked at each of us now as we spoke. I didn't look away when he caught my eye. I tried to imagine who he'd been. Tried to really see him.

Lifting his right hand, he pointed to the pile of French fries on his plate.

'Hey, thanks, don't mind if I do,' Andy said. He reached out and grabbed a couple.

He nudged me. I took one and ate it. It didn't kill me. Actually, it tasted pretty good. The three of us sat there and shared the rest of the fries.

The waitress was back the instant the guy swallowed his last bite. I still hadn't finished my soda. 'Pay there,' she said, putting the bill down by Andy's glass and tilting her head toward the register. I gave him all my cash and he went up front.

'Thank you,' the guy said as he stood.

'You're welcome.'

He started to leave, then turned back and held out his hand. We shook. His grip was firmer than I expected. He headed out, stopping by Andy for a moment. They shook hands, too. Andy came back as I slurped the last of my drink. I saw he still had some money. He jammed a dollar in my shirt pocket. 'Can't let my best friend walk around flat broke.' Then he dropped the rest of the money on the table. Three dollars and eighty cents.

'What was that for?' I asked as we left the diner.

'Tip,' he said. 'She works hard. This place is open all night. She's probably been here since four.'

'She wasn't very friendly,' I said.

'Would a small tip make her more friendly?' he asked. I guess he had a point.

We walked back through town, reaching the church just as the crowd was coming out the door. I worked my way against the flow, hoping to hook up with my parents before they figured out I hadn't been there during the service.

'I'm toast,' I muttered to Andy as I caught sight of Mrs. Skeffington talking to my mom.

When my folks reached me, my dad didn't waste any time. 'I'm very disappointed with you,' he said.

'Sorry.'

'Getting thrown out of a church service. Of all the places to misbehave.' He went on for a while, and I nodded and made the proper noises to show how bad I felt. Out of the corner of my eye, I could see Andy dancing through the same routine with his mom and dad.

Finally, my dad turned to my mom and said, 'Let's go. I'm starving.'

I followed my parents to the car and got inside. Behind us, I saw old Mrs. Wilming hobbling slowly along the sidewalk. Mrs. Skeffington cruised past her, not offering a ride. On the church steps, the Lindens were pulling their little kid by the arms as he dragged his feet and screamed his head off, pleading for a Happy Meal. When they

162 **nudge sb.** jdn. anstupsen
173 **flat broke** *(infml)* completely broke
192 **be starving** *(infml)* be really hungry
194 **hobble** walk weakly and unsurely

197 **swat on the rear** Klaps auf den Hintern
200 **decent values** ['di:snt] anständige Wertvorstellungen
215 **tacky** *(infml)* cheap; showing bad taste

reached level ground, Mrs. Linden gave him a swat on the rear to speed him along. Through my open window, I heard her say, 'Just wait till I get you home.'

'We're trying to raise you the right way,' my mom said as Dad shot out of the parking lot. 'We want you to have some decent values. Not like that friend of yours.'

'But he's –'

'Drop it,' Dad warned before I could say anything to defend Andy.

I sighed and settled back in my seat. Dad cursed as he got caught in town by the long red light on Harmony Street. To my right, I saw the waitress from the diner. I guess she was on her way home. A guy in a long overcoat walked up to her, his hand out. She stopped and reached into her pocket.

The light changed and we drove off. I looked back, but I didn't get to see what happened. Maybe she gave him something. I'd like to think so.

In the front seats, my parents were playing Invisible Son, talking about me like I wasn't there.

'Tommy needs to show better judgment. That Andy kid is a bad influence,' my dad said.

My mom nodded. 'Teaching our son all the wrong things. Running around, getting into trouble. And his mother. Did you see the dress she was wearing? It was so tacky.'

'We'll straighten Tommy out,' my dad said. He floored the gas and tried to beat the next light. It was red by the time he went through it. 'I'm gonna make goddam sure he doesn't skip any more sermons. Somebody's got to teach him right from wrong. I'll tell you something else. Next Sunday, he's sitting up front with us. We'll see he doesn't miss anything.'

I reached into my shirt pocket and took out the dollar bill Andy had given me. As my parents continued to discuss the lessons I was going to learn, I held the bill near the window and let the breeze tug at it, then loosened my grip and watched it fly free.

From: Donald R. Gallo, ed., *Destination Unexpected – Short Stories*, 2006

► LP 6 Simple Past, Past Progressive and Past Perfect (p. 108)

## 1 Comprehension

Choose the best answer.

▸ SF 18 Answering Multiple-Choice Questions (p. 145)

1 The boys are thrown out of church because ...
**A** they think Pastor Donald's sermon is too long. **B** Andy was being rude to Mrs Skeffington. **C** Andy was making fun of Pastor Donald's sermon. **D** All of the above. **E** None of the above.

2 After they are told to leave the church, ...
**A** Tommy is a bit angry at Andy. **B** Tommy is glad to be outside. **C** Tommy is worried about what his parents will say. **D** All of the above. **E** None of the above.

3 When Tommy sees the homeless man, ...
**A** he is happy that he and his friend can help him. **B** he doesn't want to give him any money. **C** he wants to buy the man a meal. **D** All of the above. **E** None of the above.

4 When Andy offers to buy the homeless man a meal, ...
**A** Tommy thinks his friend is testing the man. **B** Tommy offers to help pay for the man's dinner. **C** Tommy is glad that he'll have the chance to talk to a homeless person. **D** All of the above. **E** None of the above.

5 Andy gives the waitress a large tip because ...
**A** she had provided a good service even though she wasn't happy to have a homeless person in the restaurant. **B** he wants to make her feel bad about the way she treated the homeless man. **C** he feels bad about bringing a homeless man into the restaurant. **D** All of the above. **E** None of the above.

## 2 Looking at the characters

a Read the quotes from Pastor Donald's sermon again (ll. 17, 26–32). What are they about? Summarize Pastor Donald's message in one sentence.

b Give each of the following *characters a mark: A ('excellent'), B, C, D or F ('fail') for how well they behaved according to the lesson of the sermon:
- Andy
- Tommy's mum
- other churchgoers (e.g. Mrs Skeffington)
- Tommy
- Tommy's dad

Be prepared to explain your marks with quotes from the story.

c Explain your marks to your partner. Try to agree on a mark for each character. Then report your results to the class. ▪ **Language help**

### Language help

- Do you really think Andy and Tommy should get the same mark? Andy was ...
- That's true. Let's mark ... up/down.
- I disagree. Tommy says in line ...
- OK, then we both have ... for Tommy.
- Well, then we'll have to agree to disagree.

▸ LP 38 Agreeing and Disagreeing (p. 130)

## 3 Looking at narrative technique

The story is told from a first-person *point of view. Choose a passage of about 20–30 lines and rewrite it using a third-person *narrator. Compare the effect of this type of narration with the original.

## 4 Close reading

Read ll. 131–141 again. Describe and comment on the way Andy communicates with the homeless man. Do you think Andy is right to act the way he does in the situation? Why (not)?

▸ SF 38 Writing a Characterization (p. 156)

## 5 EXTRA Writing

In no more than 300 words, discuss the *proverb 'Actions speak louder than words' in the context of the *short story.

▸ SF 31 The Stages of Writing (p. 152)

**THE FAR SIDE® By GARY LARSON**

The Far Side® by Gary Larson © 1991 FarWorks, Inc. All Rights Reserved. The Far Side® and the Larson® signature are registered trademarks of FarWorks, Inc. Used with permission.

**6 Communicating with strangers**

**a** When was the last time a complete stranger started talking to you? Describe the situation to your partner and try to remember what was said. Discuss whether your reactions were appropriate. Then try to think of more situations in which you might experience this sort of small talk.

**b** How could you react to the following typical small-talk questions? Think of a situation in which you might hear them. Remember that one- or two-word answers are not polite in English.

1 Excuse me, do you think you could take a photo of me and my friend?
2 Have you been here long?
3 Hey, how's it going?
4 Have you been to this club before?
5 The queues are always long when you're in a hurry, aren't they?
6 Excuse me, those are really cool glasses. Where did you get them?

**c** **Role-play:** The role cards your teacher will distribute describe a situation. Find the student/s with the same number as you and act out the situation. Try to keep the conversation going for at least two minutes.

► SF 15 Mediating (p. 144)

**7 Mediation: Helping a new friend at the hostel** CD I.06–07

**a** When mediating, you may need to paraphrase words or concepts you don't know in English. Do you know the English for the following words? If not, how would you paraphrase them? ▪ **Language help**

1 Spind | 3 Etagenbett | 5 Schließfach für Wertsachen
2 Zahlenschloss | 4 Sperrstunde

**Language help**

- It's something / somewhere / an object / a machine / a place / a type of ... that ...
- It helps/allows you to ...
- You can ... with/in/on this.
- When there's a ..., it means that you can/can't ...
- It's something that you use to ...
- You find this type of ... in ...

**b** Imagine you are staying at a youth hostel in England and are chatting with some new friends there. Three of you speak English, but the fourth person is a Russian who speaks almost no English but very good German. Help him in the following situation. Remember to give only important information.

*Russian:* Ich kann meinen Spind nicht abschließen. Ich hatte zwar ein Zahlenschloss mit, aber in London wollte das Ding nicht mehr aufgehen. Ich musste es aufbrechen, um meinen Rucksack wiederzubekommen. Kannst du mal die anderen fragen, ob einer ein Extra-Schloss dabeihat?

*You:* ...

*Paraguayan:* I haven't got a lock, but I think the hostel manager sells them. At least he did at the last hostel I stayed at.

*You:* ...

Continue with the *dialogue. You can find the rest on the CD. Then listen to Track 07 to hear the suggested answers.

# Nothing's Impossible

## C1 EXTRA Kierra Box Alice O'Keeffe

*Before you read the *feature story, discuss whether you think people your age should be able to influence politics, and why (not).*

I don't think of what I've done as amazing. I thought some things were wrong so I tried to do something about them – that's just a logical progression. I always find it much more surprising that people don't get involved in anything.'

It was 'Hands up for Peace', the organization Box founded with some friends in the run-up to the Iraq war, that established her as the unofficial spokesperson for British youth. The idea was a simple one: to collect paper handprints on which children wrote their feelings about the impending conflict, paste them on to sticks and 'plant' them in Parliament Square. 'It was only afterwards that someone told us the idea was a brilliant piece of marketing,' she says. 'We just thought it up in five minutes.'

With impressive determination and media savvy, Box and her friends collected nearly 3000 hands from young people across the world. They were displayed in both Parliament Square and Hyde Park, and the concept has since been copied by protest movements everywhere, from Brighton to Australia. And it didn't end there. 'We realized that we weren't just fighting against the war, we were protesting about the lack of structures through which we could express ourselves.' The group was renamed 'Hands up for ...' and launched as a web discussion forum where young people could access debates and information on a wide range of issues.

Since then Box has brought the same energy and creativity to a baffling number of projects. She devised her own curriculum for citizenship classes, which was piloted in several schools in London and Oxford. It is based around three areas – sustainability, politics and social issues – and is highly imaginative, using games to provoke children into thinking critically about issues around society and governance. Her current preoccupation is young people's sexual health, and she is conducting her own research into sex education with groups of primary-school children. [...]

Box passionately believes that children and young people have the right to have a say in the policies that affect them. 'Perhaps I do know too much now to really be "the young person on the ground",' she says. 'But I go along to every meeting and I think, I'm glad I'm here, there needs to be a young person here. So many things that affect us are decided with no consultation at all.' She sees herself going into youth work and campaigning, and aims eventually to become Commissioner for Children. I think they could safely give her the job straight away.

From: 'Kierra Box', *New Statesman*, 17 October 2005

*'Hands up for peace'*

5 **run-up to sth.** time just before sth.
**spokesperson** sb. who represents a group
7 **impending** about to happen
10 **impressive determination** beeindruckende Entschlossenheit
**savvy** ['sævi] *(infml)* knowledge, skill
14 **lack of** Mangel an
17 **access sth.** ['ækses] find sth., reach sth.
**wide range of issues** ['ɪʃuːz] a lot of different topics
18 **baffling** amazing
19 **devise sth.** [dɪ'vaɪz] invent sth.
**citizenship class** ['sɪtɪzənʃɪp] Staatsbürgerkunde
20 **sustainability** Nachhaltigkeit
21 **provoke sb. into doing sth.** push sb. into doing sth.
23 **preoccupation** main activity
**conduct** [–'–] *(v) here:* do
25 **passionately** ['pæʃənətli] *(adv)* leidenschaftlich
30 **Commissioner for Children** person whose job it is to make children's views known

**⚠ Trouble spot**
**eventually** = schließlich, irgendwann
eventuell = **perhaps**

► LP 28 False Friends (p. 121)

**1 Understanding the issues**

**a** Summarize Kierra Box's key belief.

**b** **Think:** List the issues you think a Commissioner for Children should look at. Give reasons.

**c** **Pair:** Ask your partner what issues he/she has listed and why. Take notes.

**d** **Share:** With another pair, agree on the three most important issues and report to the class.

► SF 4 Taking Notes (p. 134)

## C2 Be the Change DVD 01–03

► SF 21 Viewing a Film (p. 147)

*Here's how the US TV news channel CNN announces its 'Be the change' project on its website. Read about the project and look at the photos. Then watch the DVD and answer the questions below.*

**'We must be the change we wish to see in the world.'**
The participants in this ground-breaking program come from different backgrounds, but hold common values, beliefs and goals. They all want to effect change in our world by helping others.
CNN has equipped a group of volunteers with cameras, laptops and a brand new website. They will blog and post videos of their lives and new jobs as they fan out across three continents for the next twelve months.

**Here are a few of the people involved in just one program:**

*Jennifer Staple, founder of 'Unite for Sight'*

*Dr Aron Rose, US ophthalmologist*

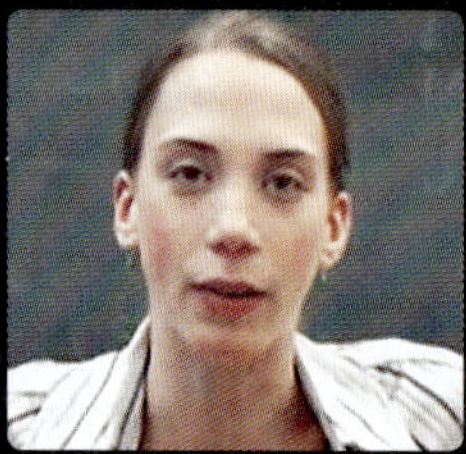

*Sam Diamond, student volunteer with 'Unite for Sight'*

From: http://edition.cnn.com/CNNI/Programs/bethechange

[3] **ground-breaking** totally new
[5] **hold sth.** *here:* have sth.
[7] **effect sth.** *(fml)* make sth. happen
[13] **fan out** sich verbreiten
**ophthalmologist** [ˌɒfθæl'mɒlə-dʒɪst] eye doctor

### 1 Comprehension

a Explain what 'Unite for Sight' does. Who runs it?
b How does Dr Aron Rose describe the materials he had to work with in Ghana? Why do you think he mentions this?
c What were Sam Diamond's reasons for volunteering with 'Unite for Sight'? Did the trip meet her expectations?

### 2 Your reactions

a List qualifications you think are needed for doing volunteer work in the developing world. With your partner, discuss whether you have any of them.
b Would you like to spend a summer working as a volunteer in the developing world? Explain why (not) to your partner.

### 3 Watching a video log

a When you watch a documentary or video log in English, some things help you to understand and some make it more difficult. What made it easy or difficult to follow the video log on the DVD? Use phrases from **Language help** and explain.
b Watch the DVD again. Summarize the report you found most interesting.

### Language help

- When the people talked to the camera, ...
- When you could/couldn't see their faces, it was ...
- When there were pictures of what they were talking about, ...
- When ... was talking, his/her accent made it hard/... to understand.

# Applying for Volunteer Work

*In this chapter task you will produce a personal statement to apply for a place on a summer project, but it will help you when applying for other things as well: a place at an English-speaking university, for example, or a job in a company where English is the working language.*

**1 Understanding a job description: What are they looking for?**
*The first step in writing an application is to find out as much information about the job and the organization as possible. You need to know what sort of person and what qualities they are looking for.*
***Partner B:*** Look at p. 102.

**a** ***Partner A:*** Read the following material from an organization that arranges international volunteer work for students. Make notes on what personal qualities and experience they are looking for. (Some things are said directly; others are implied.)

▸ SF 5 Making Notes (p. 134)

## Overview

Our rural projects in Kenya are located in villages near Lake Nakuru. People there are the poorest in the country, and many villages lack basic facilities and resources.

Our rural projects focus on providing educational facilities, basic sanitation and access to clean water. You may find yourself building a classroom, renovating a school, constructing pit latrines or installing a rainwater harvesting system.

## On the project

You'll be met at the airport and introduced to your fellow volunteers before being taken to the village you'll be calling home for the next five weeks.

You'll be amazed by how quickly you feel at home as you settle into village life, and make new friends on the building site and in the classroom!

On the building site you will work with members of the local community and your team to complete the building before you leave. In the classroom you'll be able to bring your enthusiasm and energy to English, maths, music or sports lessons. Our projects are flexible: you can teach, build, or combine the two.

gapyear.com
great ideas, great deals

**b** Your partner has applied for a place on the Kenyan rural project. Interview him/her to find out if he/she has the qualities needed. Use your notes from **a** to prepare questions, then do the interview.

*Partner A:* Have you ever been to a country in the developing world?
*Partner B:* No, this would be my first time.
*Partner A:* Would you be prepared to get your hands dirty?
*Partner B:* Of course, that's not a problem for me.
*Partner A:* Can you give me an example?
*Partner B:* ...

**c** Now it's your partner's turn to interview you. Answer his/her questions. Be prepared to give examples that show you have the qualities needed.

1 **rural** ['rʊərəl] ländlich
4 **facilities** *(pl) here:* toilets
7 **educational facilities** *(pl) here:* schools
**sanitation** sanitäre Anlagen
10 **pit latrine** [lə'triːn] hole in the ground used as a toilet
11 **rainwater harvesting system** Regenwassernutzungsanlage

## 2 Introducing yourself

*When you introduce yourself – as in a personal statement – you will mostly need to say:*

- *who you are, where you live, what sorts of things interest you (you normally use the simple present for this),*
- *what you are currently doing (you normally use the present progressive for this),*
- *what sorts of things you have experienced and done up to now (you normally use the present perfect for this).*

► LP 2 Simple Present and Present Progressive (p. 106)

**a** Complete the following sentences with the right form of the verbs. Be careful to use the simple present and the present progressive correctly.

1 I (like) animals and (go / ride) twice a week. But I (not just ride); I (take) care of my horse regularly. I (plan / be) a vet.
2 I (currently take) a course at a private language school. I (hope / speak) Italian fluently by the end of the year.
3 Although my parents (support) my decision (do) a gap year, I (try / earn) the money myself.
4 I (enjoy / talk) to old people and (help) them whenever I can.
5 I (currently do) a school project that (involve / test) the water quality of a pond near my house twice weekly.
6 I (think) I (be) good with my hands. I (love / build) things and (now work) on a tree house for children at a local adventure playground.

► LP 5 Present Perfect for 'time up until now' (p. 107)

**b** Complete the following sentences with the right form of the verbs. Be careful to use the simple present and the present perfect correctly.

1 I (always be) interested in other cultures. Today I (be) most interested in Africa.
2 I (take) part in the activities of our local fire brigade's youth organization every weekend and (go) to several week-long events throughout the year.
3 For as long as I (can remember), my parents (encourage) me (explore) my interest in nature.
4 Since the third grade I (want / visit) Africa. My interest in the continent (grow) in the last few years.
5 I (often be told) that I (be) very good with children, and I (think) I (want / be) a teacher.
6 I (never be) interested in the things most kids my age (be) interested in. I (always prefer / read or go / hike).

### Language help

- improve sb.'s life / quality of life
- give one's (free) time
- use one's special skills
- be dedicated to (doing) sth.
- be eager to help sb./sth.
- be reliable / a reliable person
- feel appreciated/needed
- be a learning experience
- be rewarding

**c** Look at the photo and imagine:

- What sort of job is the student volunteer doing?
- Does she work through an organization?
- What is the volunteer's name? What is the woman's name? How did they meet?
- ...

Now write a text of 200–300 words about the student volunteer in the photo. (You can choose any form, e.g. a newspaper article, an interview, a diary entry.) Use as many of the phrases from **Language help** as possible.

## 3 Correcting common mistakes

*When you get back a homework assignment or test that has been corrected, study the corrections carefully. Use them to start a learning log. It will help you to avoid mistakes.*

Rewrite the personal statement below, making the necessary corrections.

► SF 10 Keeping a Learning Log (p. 138)

**Personal statement of Laura Michaelis**

Since I have been a child, I am fascinated by everything African. My room at home is full of African art, and I even take lessons in Swahili at the local night school since the last two years. Seeing the continent myself is a dream of mine as long as I can remember.

But I'm not just curious about the place and the many cultures there. I'm also interested in helping to improve the lives of some of the poor in Africa.

I am currently attending Friedrich Schiller High School, where we are having a group called Young People Helping. As the name of the group says, we aren't just talking about the problems of the world; we try to solve at least a few of them locally.

For example, I am spending my Saturdays to work in a soup kitchen for homeless people. We are meeting at a church hall at 8.30 a.m. to move tables, clean the kitchen and have the food ready by twelve o'clock. It's hard work, but I feel we are making the lives of the poorest people in our community a little bit better. It's difficult, of course, to see young children in this situation, but their smiles when they are leaving the hall every week make it all seem worthwhile.

I am seeing a once-in-a-lifetime chance in the Kenyan rural project to combine my love of Africa with my wish to help. I cannot think of a more satisfying way to spend my last summer before I will start my studies in September.

Laura Michaelis

## 4 Writing a personal statement

**a** Imagine you want to apply for a place on the Kenyan rural project (see **1a** on p. 27). Write your own personal statement. You can use the corrected text above as a model.

- Your statement should be about 200–300 words long.
- It should be easy to read – either printed out from a computer or neatly written.
- It should demonstrate that you have the most important qualities you think the organization is looking for in a volunteer.
- It should be as grammatically correct as possible.

► SF 36 Writing a Personal Statement (p. 156)
► SF 31 The Stages of Writing (p. 152)

**b** Swap personal statements with your partner. Read your partner's statement and make suggestions on how to improve it. Consider what the statement says, the choice of words and grammatical correctness.

**c** Rewrite your statement if you agree with your partner's suggestions. Then put it in your Dossier.

► SF 11 Keeping a Portfolio (p. 138)

Webcode: STAR322305-30

# 2 Our Changing Planet

**'A greener planet will be a more peaceful and prosperous one too.'**

Ban Ki-moon, UN Secretary General, 16 April 2008

**A**

**Natural Numbers** Mike Johnson

*Example: Divide 5000 buffaloes by fifty hunters = almost nothing left.*

1. Divide 200 elephants by seventeen ivory poachers =
2. Divide two rainforests by eight logging companies =
3. Divide one beautiful planet by one greedy species =

**B**

**Give water. Give life. Give £2 a month.**

WaterAid

**C**

**prosperous** rich
**ivory poacher** hunter who kills elephants illegally for their tusks (ivory)
**logging company** company that cuts down trees
**greedy species** ['spi:ʃi:z] gefräßige Art, Gattung

## Language help

- I think what ... says is true, but ...
- ... is so convincing/direct/eye-catching/strange/... that I think ...
- I think pictures always interest people, so I'd vote for ...
- I find ...'s argument very convincing, so ...
- I can/can't imagine that people will pay attention to ...

**1 Different opinions, different aims**

**a Think:** Partner A reads texts A–C, Partner B reads texts D–F. Check that you understand them. Then make notes on the message of each text. What might each text have to do with the chapter title and the picture of the planet Earth?

**b Pair:** Describe your texts to your partner; then compare all six texts. Decide who is most likely to make people think about changing their behaviour: the UN Secretary General (A), the poet (B) or the aid worker (C)? The environmentalists (D), the scientist (E) or the activists (F)? Why? ■ **Language help**

**c Share:** Report to the class. Vote for the most effective text.

D

E

**Why conserve?**

**American scientists have recently estimated that the value [...] of the as yet undiscovered drugs from tropical rainforests is around $150 billion. In other words, the rainforests may be worth more alive, as a source of valuable drugs, than they are dead, when they are used as a source of timber.**

Bath Science 16–19,
*University of Bath, 2001*

F

**plane stupid**
*bringing the aviation industry back down to earth!*

**become extinct** die out
**plane stupid** name of an anti-flying action group (*plane* as in *aeroplane*, but also as in *plain*)
**aviation industry** industry that makes and flies aeroplanes
**down to earth** *(fig)* auf den Boden der Tatsachen (zurück)

**2 How we are changing the planet**

**a** In groups of four, do a placemat activity. In your corner of the placemat, write down all the ways you think people are changing the planet (for good or bad).

**b** Discuss your lists in your group. In the middle of your placemat, write down the two most dangerous and the two best ways we are changing the planet.
▪ **Language help**

**c** Compare your results with those of other groups. Which was easier: listing changes for the better or listing changes for the worse? Why?

**Language help**

- Many things that people do have a positive/negative effect on the planet, e.g. ...
- Through genetic engineering scientists are helping us save threatened species / grow more food / ...
- Eating imported food / Driving / ... is bad for the planet because ...

▸ SF 2 Brainstorming (p. 133)

# People and the Planet

► LP 25 Increase Your Word Power Online (p. 118)

The earliest human beings were hunters: they moved from one place to another, eating whatever they could find. Sustainability was not an issue for them; the food supply was sustainable: new plants grew and animals were born at the same rate that people consumed them.

Today, of course, most people aren't nomadic, and world population and consumption have increased greatly. We settle in places that were once home to different species of animals or plants, and we dispose of our waste there. As we destroy these habitats, species die out. Overpopulation and the resulting destruction of entire ecosystems are the greatest threats to biodiversity.

In recent years, most people in the developed world have become more aware of the damage we are doing to our planet. We try to buy eco-friendly products, i.e. products that will not contribute to the extinction of an endangered species, that don't require too much energy to produce or to transport, and that won't pollute the environment when we throw them away. We prefer things that are made of renewable resources like wood or wool, or at least from materials that can be recycled.

We have become more and more concerned about climate change in the form of global warming. There can be little doubt that the Earth's temperature is increasing, but until recently, there was little agreement on whether the phenomenon was caused by human activity or had some natural cause. Today, no serious scientist would say that climate change is not influenced by what we do.

What can be done about it? It is probably not possible to reverse global warming, but we might be able to slow it down. To do that, we need to reduce emissions of so-called 'greenhouse gases' like carbon dioxide and methane.

To help calculate the impact we have on the Earth's climate, environmentalists have developed the concept of the carbon footprint. The larger our footprint, the more we are contributing to the greenhouse effect and global warming. It is hoped that understanding the carbon footprint will help us to reduce it, e.g. by eating locally grown food or driving less. And if we cannot reduce it, we can try to offset our carbon footprint by planting trees or supporting renewable energy projects.

## Sources of greenhouse gas for a typical family in %

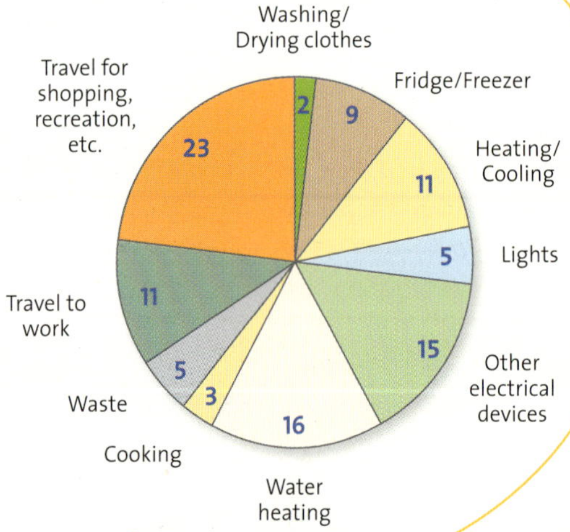


### Language help

- The pie chart clearly shows that ...
- The segment showing ... represents / makes up
  - about/roughly/approximately ... per cent.
  - the biggest/smallest part.
  - more than ... / over half of / three quarters of the whole/total.
- This makes it easier for people to see that ...

► SF 12 Working with Pictures (p. 140)

### 1 Sustainable consumption

Write down different ways in which consumption affects the environment. Compare your ideas with a partner.

### 2 Our carbon footprint

**a** Look at the pie chart. What are the two biggest sources of greenhouse gas for a family? How might a chart like this help people to reduce their carbon footprint? ▪ **Language help**

**b** EXTRA Go to a website where you can calculate your carbon footprint. How does yours compare with that of your classmates / the German average? How could you reduce or offset your footprint?

## 3 Word formation

Complete each sentence with a noun, verb or adjective formed from one of the words on the right. You may need a dictionary to find the right words.

1 People are … oil much faster than the Earth can produce it. Oil is not a sustainable resource.
*The sentence needs a verb related to 'consumption'. The word is …*
2 Thanks to new filtering systems, air … is no longer a problem near modern power stations.
3 Of all the factors that … the existence of life on Earth, climate change is perhaps the biggest problem.
4 It is estimated that three species of plants and animals become … every hour.
5 Unfortunately, some of the biggest polluters haven't agreed to a … of greenhouse gas emissions.
6 The biggest … to greenhouse gases from private households comes from travel.
7 Factories need to be more efficient and … less carbon dioxide.
8 Some scientists are still hoping for a … of the trend towards a warmer climate.

▶ LP 33 Word Formation: Suffixes (p. 124)
▶ SF 8 Using a Dictionary (p. 136)

*▪ consumption ▪ contribute ▪ emission ▪ extinction ▪ pollute ▪ reduce ▪ reverse ▪ threat*

## 4 Interpreting charts and graphs

**a** Which of the following statements best describes what the graph shows?

1 The graph shows how much greenhouse gas five different countries emitted from 1990 to 2005.
2 The graph shows how many tonnes of greenhouse gases each person in one of five different countries emitted each year from 1990 to 2005.
3 The graph shows the price for a tonne of greenhouse gas in five different countries between 1990 and 2005.
4 The graph shows the change in the number of tonnes of greenhouse gases each person in one of five different countries emitted between 1990 and 2005.

### Greenhouse gas emissions in tonnes per capita

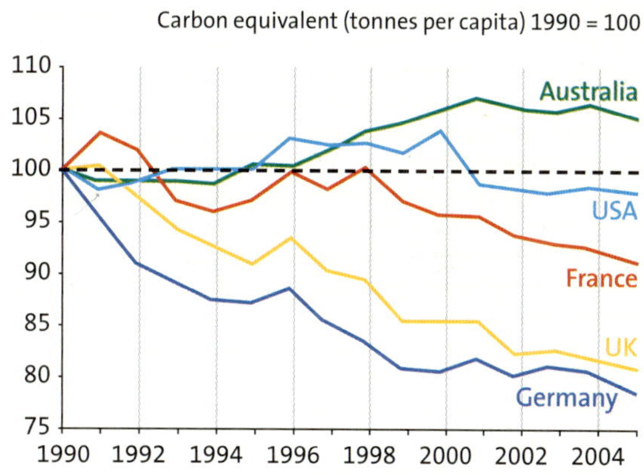


*Source:* UNFCC Greenhouse Gas Inventory

**b** Complete the description of the graph with the words and phrases on the right.

1 Four of the five countries shown, the United States, France, the United Kingdom and Germany, reduced their greenhouse gas emissions in the time period … the graph. Only one country, Australia, had … of greenhouse gas emissions.
2 Australia began with a slight … in levels, but after 1994 the country's greenhouse gas emissions went … upward.
3 Emissions in the USA … slightly at first, but … after 1991 until they … in 1999. There was a … in 2000, and levels went down again slightly in 2001 and 2004.
4 Germany … its emissions between 1990 and 2002, with small … in 1995 and 2000. The UK also made … in this area, … its emissions in every year but 1995 and 2002.

*▪ covered by ▪ decrease ▪ increased levels ▪ reached their highest levels ▪ reducing ▪ rose ▪ sharp decline ▪ significantly lowered ▪ slowly but steadily ▪ upturns ▪ very good progress ▪ went down*

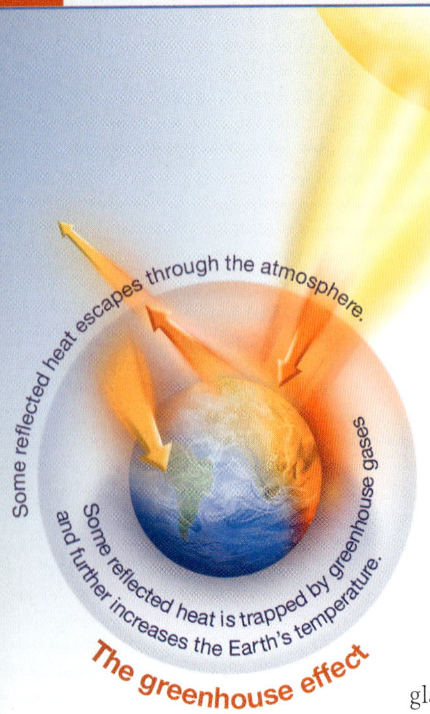


# The Scientist's View

## A1 What Is Global Warming?

*In this section you will read two texts on a scientific topic, but written for different audiences.*

### Is the Earth Getting Hotter? Glenn Murphy

*This text is taken from a book produced by the London Science Museum. It tries to answer young people's questions about the planet we live on.*

**I don't get it.**

Global warming – the planet getting progressively hotter over time – is caused by a process called the 'greenhouse effect'. In simple terms, this happens because the Earth's atmosphere is transparent to sunlight, but not to the heat that comes off the Earth as sunlight heats it up. So the heat is held inside the atmosphere, raising the temperature. This is a bit like the way the glass of a greenhouse lets light in and out but stops heat from escaping, allowing us to grow warm-weather plants in colder countries. Hence the name 'greenhouse effect'. This idea isn't even particularly new. The Irish physicist and mountaineer John Tyndall first described it in 1863 – along with a few other things, like why the sky is blue. He and other scientists also realized that this effect is so important in maintaining global temperatures that there probably wouldn't be life on the planet without it. [...]

**So it's all good, then? What's the problem?**

The problem is that lately this warming effect seems to have been intensifying and speeding up. We think at least part of this might be due to gases spewed out by our cars, planes, factories and power stations, among other things. So most of the arguments about global warming are about whether we should replace or cut down on using these things in order to slow down the pace of the effect. In any case, at the current rate, it looks as if global temperatures will rise by about 2° to 6°C by the year 2100.

**By 2 degrees? That doesn't sound so bad.**

Maybe not, but even this small rise will have a serious effect on countries all over the world. [...]

**Go on, then – what's the worst that could happen?**

Well, everything we've said so far is our best guess of what will happen, based on what we know about how the Earth's atmosphere and oceans interact. But things could get more complicated, and (as we often see with simple weather forecasts) predictions about how the atmosphere and oceans will behave can be wrong. It's possible (although unlikely) that the increased heating of the seas could release enough water vapour into the atmosphere to create a 'runaway greenhouse effect', pushing temperatures up so high that trees and crops across the world would die.

On the other hand, if enough polar ice melted and diluted the oceans, it could affect the way they circulate (through currents) across the world. One result of this might be stopping or reversing the flow of the Gulf Stream – the current that supplies Europe with warm water – plunging Britain and other countries into long, freezing winters similar to those in the Arctic.

From: Glenn Murphy, *Why Is Snot Green?*, 2007

1 **get sth.** *(infml)* understand sth.
8 **hence** *(fml)* for this reason
11 **maintain sth.** keep sth. at a certain level
16 **due to** because of
**spew sth. out** [spjuː] etwas ausstoßen
19 **pace** speed
30 **vapour** *(BE)* Dampf
**runaway** *(adj)* out of control
31 **crop** plant grown for food
32 **dilute sth.** [daɪˈluːt] etwas verdünnen
34 **current** [*BE:* ˈkʌrənt, *AE:* ˈkɜːr-] movement of water in the sea
35 **plunge sth. into sth. else** [plʌndʒ] cause sth. to fall suddenly into sth. else

**Trouble spots**

**raise sth.** = etwas erhöhen
**rise** = (an)steigen

**affect sb./sth.** *(v)* = jdn./etwas beeinflussen
**effect (on sth.)** *(n)* = Wirkung, Auswirkung (auf etwas)

► LP 29 Confusables (p. 122)

## The Science of Climate Change Terence Wood

*This text is taken from a 'discussion paper' published by the Royal Society of New Zealand, the country's independent national academy of sciences.*

### What is the greenhouse effect?

The term 'greenhouse effect' is used to describe the warming of the Earth's surface and lower atmosphere that is caused by the presence of certain gases which let energy from the sun through to the ground but which also absorb energy as it passes from the ground back through the atmosphere into space. [...]

It is important to note that it is not the existence of the greenhouse effect itself that scientists are concerned about. Indeed, the greenhouse effect is a natural phenomenon that has existed since long before human beings began polluting the Earth. And if it weren't for the greenhouse effect, the Earth's climate would be too cold for life as we know it, having an average temperature of –18 °C. What scientists are concerned about is that by increasing the quantities of some of the greenhouse gases in the atmosphere, humans are likely to further increase the temperature of the lower atmosphere and the planet's surface. Some of the gases that play a role in the greenhouse effect are carbon dioxide, methane, nitrous oxide, chlorofluorocarbons, ozone and water vapour. All of these gases except water vapour are currently being emitted into the atmosphere in significant amounts as a result of human activities. The amount that each of the individual greenhouse gases contributes to the overall greenhouse effect varies depending on three things: the extent to which the gas is able to absorb radiation, the amount of the gas existing in the atmosphere, and the period of time that molecules of that gas remain in the atmosphere.

### Human activity and the greenhouse gases

Of the different greenhouse gases being produced in significant amounts by human activities, carbon dioxide is being emitted in by far the greatest quantities and is the largest contributor to anthropogenic climate change. The primary way that humans are increasing the amount of carbon dioxide in the atmosphere is the burning of fossil fuels for energy and transport purposes. In addition to this, deforestation, and in particular deforestation which involves the burning of forested areas, contributes significant amounts of carbon dioxide to the atmosphere.

From: *The Science behind the News, The Gamma Series of the Royal Society of New Zealand,* June 2005

- 3 **presence** ['prezns] *hier:* Vorkommen
- 12 **be likely to do sth.** probably do sth.
- 14 **nitrous oxide** [ˌnaɪtrəs_'ɒksaɪd] Distickstoffmonoxid ($N_2O$), Lachgas
  **chlorofluorocarbon (CFC)** Fluorchlorkohlenwasserstoff (FCKW)
- 15 **emit sth.** [i'mɪt] *(fml)* give sth. off
- 17 **contribute to sth.** zu etwas beitragen
- 19 **radiation** Strahlung
- 20 **remain** stay
- 24 **anthropogenic** [ˌænθrəpə'dʒenɪk] coming from human beings
- 25 **fossil fuel** ['fɒsl ˌfju:əl] fossiler Brennstoff
- 26 **deforestation** cutting down of forests

### 1 Comprehension

In a few sentences, explain the greenhouse effect and why it is a good thing.

### 2 Evaluating the texts

Which text was more useful for finding the answers in 1? Why?

### 3 Looking at structure and style

a Compare the structure and *style of the two texts. Consider headings, sentence length, choice of words and grammatical constructions.
▪ Language help

b Why do you think the texts are different?

**Language help**

- The first/second text uses questions and answers / ... to ...
- The difference between the two headings is that ...
- The sentences in the first/second text are longer / more complicated than ... This has the effect of ...
- The authors' choice of words is quite similar/different. ...

► SF 33 Structuring a Text (p. 153)
► LP 8 Passive (p. 109)
► LP 16 Relative Clauses (p. 113)
► LP 17–18 Participle Constructions (p. 114)

## A2 'There Goes Our Warm Climate' DVD 04–05

*Roland Emmerich's film* The Day After Tomorrow *(2004) tells the story of a climate disaster that takes place, not over a period of many years, but within a few weeks. Most scientists agree that this could not possibly happen at such a speed, and the film was highly criticized as propaganda. Even though many people doubted the scientific basis of the film,* The Day After Tomorrow *was very successful and helped to increase interest in climate issues among non-scientists.*

- *drill (n)*
- *shelf (geological)*
- *ice core* ▪ *evidence*
- *occur* ▪ *trigger sth.*
- *owe sth. to sth.*
- *melt sth.* ▪ *disrupt sth.*
- *Kyoto Accord* ▪ *claim (n)*
- *chunk*

Look at the film poster (below right). It shows the climate disaster that occurs in the film. Identify it and say how and why it might occur.
Before you watch the film clip, make sure you know the meaning and pronunciation of the words and phrases on the left.

▸ SF 21 Viewing a Film (p. 147)

### 1 Comprehension

**a** Watch the film clip. Summarize each of the two scenes in three to five sentences. ▪ **Language help 1**

**b** Explain how the two scenes are related to each other.

**Language help 1**

- The first scene shows a research station in the Antarctic where …
- The second scene takes place in …

### 2 Looking at film techniques

**a** Watch the first scene again. How does the film build up *suspense? ▪ **Language help 2**

**b** Now watch the second scene again. How does the film suggest who viewers should like and who they should dislike?

**Language help 2**

- When we first see the ice breaking up, you suddenly feel …
- The film lets us think …, but then …
- The background music creates tension/suspense / is very dramatic.

### 3 Comparing a written text and a film

The text on p. 34 and the scientist in the film both explain how global warming could lead to an ice age. Read ll. 32–36 of the text and watch scene 2 again. Contrast the two explanations and explain the differences.

### 4 EXTRA Writing

In no more than 200 words, discuss the statement 'Science presented in a film must be accurate'.

# The Artist's View

*On pp. 37–38 you will find four different artistic views of our changing planet. Make notes on the attitude of the poet, the songwriter, the painter and the graphic designer to these changes.*

▸ SF 5 Making Notes (p. 134)

## B1 Countdown for Our Planet

### Earth's Clock Pat Moon

Imagine that the earth was shaped
Twenty-four hours ago,
Then at 6 a.m. rains fell from the skies
To form the seas below.
At 8 a.m. in these soupy seas
The first signs of life appeared.
The dinosaurs called seventy minutes ago
But at twenty to twelve disappeared.
Man arrived just one minute ago,
Then at thirty seconds to midnight,
Raised himself from his stooping stance
And started walking upright.
In the thirty seconds man's walked the earth,
See what he's managed to do.

Earth's clock continues ticking;
The rest is up to you.

[7] **call** come to visit
[11] **stooping stance** way of standing bent over

### River Runs Red Midnight Oil DVD 06

So you cut all the tall trees down
You poisoned the sky and the sea
You've taken what's good from the ground
But you left precious little for me

*Midnight Oil was a popular Australian rock band that sang protest songs – often about the environment. Their lead singer, Peter Garrett, became Australian Minister for the Environment, Heritage and the Arts in 2007.*

**1 Understanding the issues: the poem 'Earth's Clock'**

**a** Summarize the main idea of the *poem in one sentence.
**b** Explain how the poem uses the *metaphor of the clock. ▪ **Language help**

**Language help**
- The 24 hours on the clock stand for ...
- The metaphor makes it easier to see that ...

**2 Understanding the issues: the song 'River Runs Red'**

**a** Look at the poster and speculate on the artists' attitude to the environment.
**b** Watch the video clip. Where is the group singing? Why do you think they chose this location for their concert? Explain.
**c** Summarize the main idea of the song in one sentence.
**d** EXTRA Do you know other bands/singers/stars who speak out on global issues? As a group, collect material on one of these bands/singers/stars and the issues they are addressing. Make a poster for the classroom wall.

**3 Comparing the two**

Compare the poem and the song. Look at the last *line of each and decide who is more optimistic about the future – the poet or the songwriter? Explain why.

▸ LP 23 Comparison of Adjectives (p. 117)

## B2 Climate Change

'Global Warming' painting by Paul Cumes (2001), mixed media, 183 x 137 cm

► SF 12 Working with Pictures (p. 140)

**1 Interpreting a painting**

a Describe the painting – the colours, technique, style. What effects of global warming does it show?

b Write 50–80 words about your reactions to the painting. What message do you think the artist wants to get across? Do you like his painting? Why (not)?

**2 Interpreting a poster**

a Describe the poster.

b Explain how the washing on the line illustrates the title 'Positive proof of global warming'.

**3 Assessing the artists' impact**

Look again at pp. 37–38. Who makes the biggest impression on you: the poet, the songwriter, the painter or the graphic designer? Comment on which of the four artists makes their point most convincingly and how.

**4 Talking about the future**

► LP 7 *Will*-Future (p. 108)
► LP 13 Conditional Sentences: Type I (p. 112)

If you want to talk about environmental problems or other issues that are in the news, you will not only want to talk about what has happened in the past but also about what consequences our actions could have in the future. Here you can practise different ways to do that.

**a** Complete the following sentences using *will*, *may* or *might*.

1 If I'm not careful about my carbon footprint, ...
*... I'll be helping to destroy the planet / there won't be a planet to save / ...*
2 If I don't turn off my computer at night, ...
3 If we don't take better care of the planet now, ...
4 If global warming continues, ...
5 If the ice in the Arctic melts, ...
6 If we don't fly less, ...
7 If we keep buying fruit and vegetables from overseas, ...
8 If we continue to eat so much meat, ...

**b** Discuss your answers with a partner. Agree on the three consequences you find most threatening.

**5 Convincing people**

► LP 37 Persuading People (p. 129)

**a** Here are ten suggestions on how to live a greener life. Choose five of these suggestions and try to convince your partner that they are sensible. Take turns to discuss your explanations.

1 Have a shower, not a bath.
*If you have a shower, you'll use less water than if you have a bath. You'll be saving water and you'll be saving your parents money too.*
2 Walk, don't drive.
3 Don't turn up the heat, put on a jumper.
4 Put an energy-saving light bulb in your desk lamp.
5 Unplug the TV at night.
6 Recycle as much as you can.
7 Find a holiday job in nature conservation.
8 Don't drink bottled water.
9 Reuse shopping bags.
10 Don't use plastic cups.

**b** Choose the three suggestions you think would be most effective and present them, with your arguments, to the class.

**⚠ Trouble spot**
**sensible** ['sensəbl] = vernünftig
sensibel = **sensitive** ['sensətɪv]
► LP 28 False Friends (p. 121)

# Solutions

## C1 The Healthy Climate Pledge

*Many organizations around the world which are concerned about the effects of climate change now offer pledges for people to sign. Here is one issued in the USA for National Public Health Week 2008.*

### Healthy Climate Pledge Statement

This week, I/we begin a life-long commitment to a healthy climate and a healthy future. I/We pledge to:

**Be Prepared**

I/We pledge to prepare for climate-change-related emergencies by becoming informed about the health impacts of climate change and regional climate change issues facing our community.

**Travel Differently**

I/We pledge to leave the car at home, use public transportation, carpool, walk, bike or telecommute.

**Eat Differently**

I/We pledge to eat less meat and buy local produce from our community farmers' market.

**Green Our Work**

I/We pledge to use recycled paper, print less, use energy-saving computer settings and green our office.

**Green Our Home**

I/We pledge to seal and insulate our homes, reduce, reuse, recycle and use water efficiently.

Print name ____________ Date ____________

Signature ____________

From: www.ecdh.org/documents/LivingtheHealthlyClimatePledge.pdf

**pledge** Gelöbnis, Versprechen
1 **commitment to sth.** promise to stick to sth.
5 **health impact** ['ɪmpækt] effect on health
8 **carpool** *(v)* travel to work, etc. in a car with others, instead of alone
9 **telecommute** *(v)* work from home using the phone and Internet
17 **seal and insulate sth.** make sure no heat escapes from sth.

**1 Commitment**

How important do you think pledges are for the future? Explain why you think they can/can't help. ▪ **Language help 1**

**2 Taking the pledge**

**a** Choose one of the points in the pledge and think how it could be relevant to you, your family and/or your school. Make a list of the actions you could take. ▪ **Language help 2**

**b** Find someone who chose the same point and discuss your lists. Decide on at least two actions you could take. Present your choices to the class.

**3 EXTRA Doing research**

**a** How does it help the environment if you eat less meat? Research and write a short report. Present your results to your class with a diagram if possible.

**b** Read your report to a partner and compare your findings.

### Language help 1

- Pledges are important because they force each one of us to ...
- I can't see the point. If we don't all take the pledge ...

### Language help 2

- Green our work: we could print on both sides of the paper; we could ...
- Travel differently: my parents could ...

▸ SF 23 Giving a Presentation (p. 148)

▸ SF 13 Doing Research (p. 141)
▸ SF 33 Structuring a Text (p. 153)

## C2 Buy Local!

*The book* Change the World 9 to 5 *offers some light-hearted but effective tips on reducing your carbon footprint. Here's a suggestion on how to deal with the third point of the pledge on p. 40 – eating differently.*

**Action 051**

### Find out where your lunch has come from

**The average kiwi fruit flown in from New Zealand travels 12,000 miles to be part of your lunch.**

**And, according to the experts, that kiwi fruit creates five times its own weight in greenhouse gases getting there.**

**Which might lead you to imagine that the little fruit spent the entire trip farting. (As quite a lot of people do on planes. And most of them are oblivious to the fact, because they're wearing huge earphones.)**

**But in fact it's just because of the fuel employed in getting the fruit here.**

**Still ... if the image of a farting kiwi fruit makes you think twice about eating stuff flown in out of season, maybe it's a useful one.**

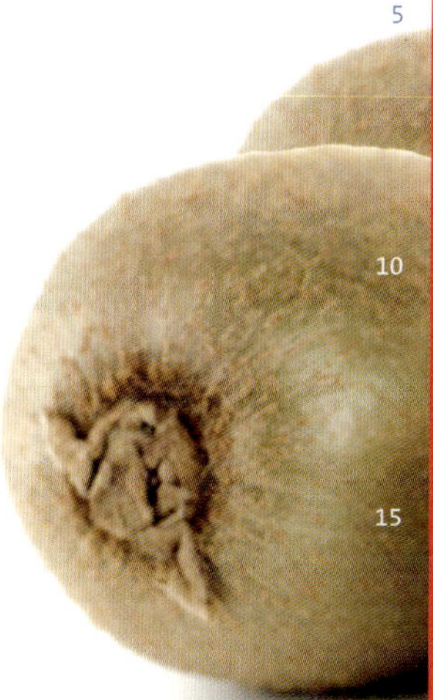

4 **according to experts** experts say
10 **fart** *(taboo, slang)* furzen
12 **be oblivious to sth.** [ə'blɪvɪəs] not know sth.
15 **employ sth.** *(fml) here:* use sth.

From: Steve Henry, *Change the World 9 to 5*, 2006

**1 Comprehension**
How does the kiwi fruit create five times its own weight in greenhouse gases?

**2 Style**

a The text is written in a light-hearted *style. How does the author achieve this? Think of *imagery, *humour and sentence length. Find examples of each in the text.

b Write a short, light-hearted text about the journey of some Chilean apples or other fruit to your local supermarket.

**3 Food footprints**

a More New Zealand kiwi fruit reach us by boat than by plane. Does that change the argument? Why (not)?

b List food and drinks you have at home that come from abroad. With your partner, research how they get to Germany.
Could you replace them with something grown or produced locally?

► SF 13 Doing Research (p. 141)

## C3 Greener Travel

*When it comes to deciding which means of transport to use for long journeys, the book* 50 Ways to Greener Travel *offers this table to help you make the right choices (see the second point of the pledge on p. 40 – travelling differently):*

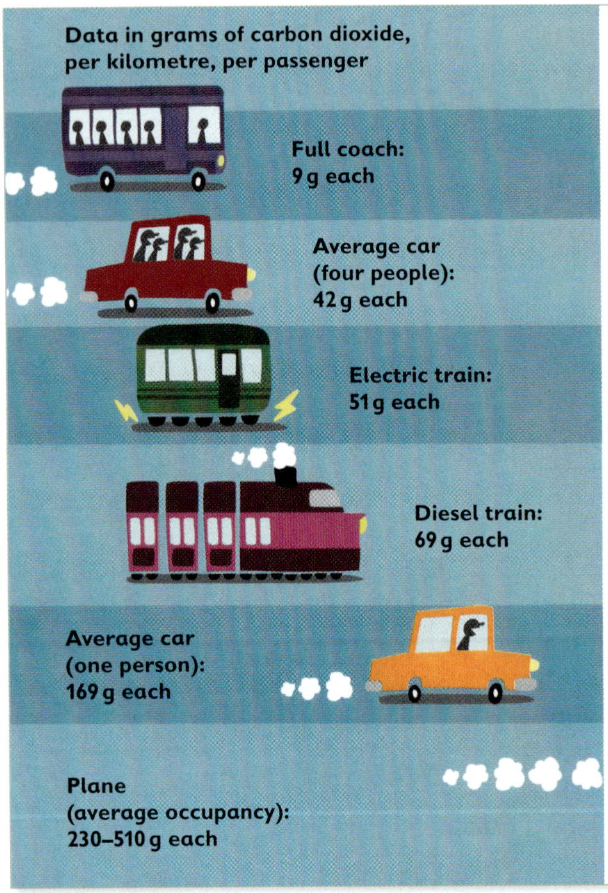


### LONG-DISTANCE TRAVEL

For longer trips, walking and cycling aren't an option, making travelling in greener ways mainly a case of minimizing carbon emissions rather than cutting them out altogether.

An increasing number of long trips in Europe and America are being taken by plane despite the fact that, for trips of less than 500 miles, the train is usually quicker and more convenient.

Even in the UK, where hardly any journeys are more than 500 miles long on our small island, 39% of journeys over 350 miles are now taken by aeroplane. [...]

Luckily, there is lots of scope for increasing our use of more environmentally-friendly modes of transport for long distances, and we can also reduce the impact of car journeys by filling up vehicles more efficiently.

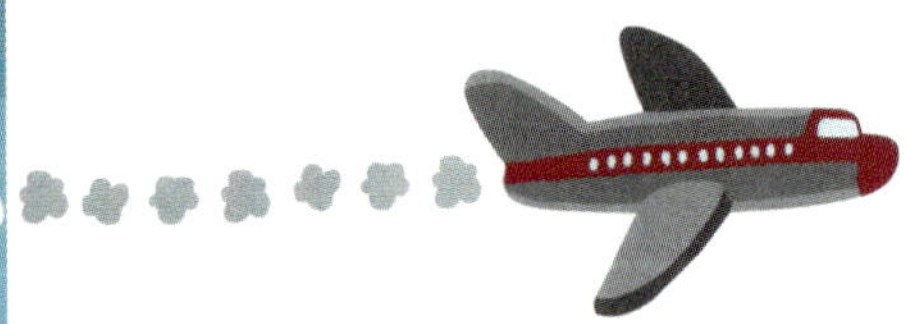

From: Siân Berry, *50 Ways to Greener Travel*, 2008

7 **despite the fact that** although
9 **convenient** [kən'vi:niənt] comfortable, easy
10 **hardly any** almost no
14 **scope** potential

► LP 23 Comparison of Adjectives (p. 117)

**1 Comprehension**

**a** Summarize the information in the above book extract in one sentence.

**b** Explain why the carbon emissions per person when travelling by coach are lower than when travelling by car.

**2 EXTRA Working out the best way to travel**

Work in groups of three. Each group chooses one of these holiday destinations for an imaginary family – mother, father, son of 15 and daughter of 11: Rügen on the Baltic Sea, London, or Torremolinos in southern Spain.

**a** One group member checks out the journey from your hometown by air, one by train and one by car. Think of distances, petrol and ticket prices, time spent travelling, the nearest railway stations and airports, etc.

**b** Present your journey to your group, with arguments in favour of your means of transport (plane, train or car).

**c** Discuss the three journeys and agree on one way to travel. Is it the most environmentally-friendly way? Report back to the class and give reasons for your choice of transport.

# Discussing a Current Affairs Topic

*In this chapter task you will prepare and conduct a group discussion on a topic related to 'Our Changing Planet'. You will find that many of the skills and language aspects of the discussion can be applied to other themes.*

**1 Preparing and conducting a group discussion**
Form groups of five to eight. Each group chooses one of the following topics:

1 No aeroplanes, no problems.
2 Vegetarianism is the answer.
3 Warmer is nicer.
4 Climate change is a myth.

► SF 24 Taking Part in a Classroom Discussion (p. 149)
► SF 13 Doing Research (p. 141)
► SF 5 Making Notes (p. 134)

**Step 1:** Each person collects information on their group's chosen topic. Look through the chapter again, research aspects that interest you in books, on the Internet, in newspapers and magazines, etc. Make notes.

**Step 2:** Organize your notes. Maybe you want to have material ready to show your group during the discussion: facts and figures, graphs and tables, statistics, *cartoons, ...

**Step 3:** Choose a discussion leader. She/He might find the phrases in **Language help** useful.

**Step 4:** Start the discussion. Remember to listen carefully to what other people say. Whenever you can, refer to their points when you speak.

**Step 5:** At the end of the discussion, your discussion leader summarizes the conclusions you have reached. Listen carefully and correct the summary if necessary. ■ **Language help**
Then choose one person to report on the discussion to the class.

### Language help

- The topic that we are going to discuss today is ...
- Let's begin. Who would like to start?
- Please don't interrupt. / Please let ... finish.
- It's ...'s turn next.

- Well, let me summarize: most people in our group think that ... But two people strongly disagree and feel that ...

**2 Reporting what you have read or heard**
*In a discussion, you may want to report something you have read or heard. Or you might want to refer to a point someone else has made. When you do that, you are using indirect speech.*

► LP 11 Indirect Speech: Statements (p. 111)
► LP 30 Verbs of Reporting (p. 122)

**a** Report the following as you would in a classroom discussion. Be careful what tense you use.

1 'Americans use coal to generate 54 % of their electricity, and coal is the single biggest polluter.' (newspaper editorial)
*I read in a newspaper editorial that Americans used coal ..., even though coal was the ...*
2 'Steps are being taken to replace older, dirtier factories with more modern, energy-efficient ones.' (TV news)
*They said on the news on TV last night that ...*
3 'The 1990s were not a good time for the environment here.' (Australian politician)
4 'I have to believe that my party will be able to make a difference on the issue of global warming.' (woman at Green Party meeting)
5 'You Europeans cannot expect developing countries like Ecuador to spend money they don't have on cleaner technologies.' (Ecuadorian environment minister)

**b** Imagine you are having a class discussion. Refer to the following statements made by your classmates earlier in the discussion.

1 'I'm convinced that there's more oil than the oil companies admit.' (Jasper)
*Jasper, you said before that you were convinced there was more …*

2 'The government doesn't care what we think.' (Karin)
*Karin said a while ago that …*

3 'I believed the chancellor when she talked about her climate plans.' (Miriam)

4 'I'll be amazed if anybody can prove this new technology will work.' (Hassan)

5 'I can't believe that global warming will happen as fast as in the film.' (Philip)

**c** EXTRA Look again at the statements in **2a** and **2b**. Which ones do not require a backshift of tenses? (Remember: It is always correct to backshift – but not always necessary or common.)

▸ SF 15 Mediating (p. 144)
▸ SF 7 Paraphrasing (p. 135)

**3 Mediation: Talking about something you have read or heard in German**

*Most of what you read or hear is probably in German, not English. If you want to report ideas from German articles, radio or TV, you will need to summarize and paraphrase.*

**a** Report on these extracts from the Berlin newspaper *Der Tagesspiegel* as you would in a classroom discussion.

**Klimaveränderung ist beispiellos**

Die Klimaveränderungen auf der Erde sind so stark wie seit 5000 Jahren nicht mehr. Das ist das Ergebnis einer am Donnerstag veröffentlichten Studie der Cornell-Universität im US-Bundesstaat New York, die Ökosysteme in der Arktis und im Nordatlantik untersucht hat.

From: 'Klimaveränderung ist beispiellos', *Der Tagesspiegel*, 7 November 2008

**Die nächste Eiszeit steht bevor**

Weite Teile der Nordhalbkugel, darunter auch Deutschland, könnten demnächst wieder von einem Eispanzer bedeckt sein. Das berichten Forscher im Fachmagazin *Nature*. Binnen einer – aus geologischer Perspektive – kurzen Zeit von 10.000 bis 100.000 Jahren wird eine neue Eiszeit anbrechen, zeigen die Berechnungen. […] Möglicherweise könne aber die derzeitige Erderwärmung den Anbruch der Frostperiode noch etwas hinauszögern.

From: 'Die nächste Eiszeit steht bevor', *Der Tagesspiegel*, 13 November 2008

**b** CD I.08 Listen to the radio programme on the CD and take notes. Report on the main points as you would in a classroom discussion.

**4 Species extinction and human activity** CD I.09–10

*The University of Melbourne in Australia broadcasts a regular podcast in which experts from the university talk about their subjects. In this episode host Dr Shane Huntington talks to Prof. Nigel Stork from the university's School of Natural Resources Management.*

- *inhabit* - *on death row* - *preserve* - *recovery* - *progress (v)* - *creation* - *(in)vertebrate* - *lifespan*

**a** Make sure you know the meaning and pronunciation of the words and phrases on the right. Then listen to the podcast.

**b** Read the statements below and make sure you understand everything. Then listen again and say whether the statements are true or false.

1 It's easy for scientists to decide whether a species is extinct.
2 Over the last 300 million years, there have been a number of mass extinctions.
3 Since the last mass extinction, there have been fewer species on the planet.
4 Species such as insects survive much longer than more complex species.
5 Prof. Stork said he didn't believe that vertebrates were becoming extinct.

**c** EXTRA Listen again. Raise your hand for the teacher to pause the CD when you have heard the information you need to correct the false statements above. Say why the statements are wrong. Use indirect speech.
*Statement number 1 is false. Prof. Stork said that there had been examples of species that people had thought were extinct, but that they had turned up again.*

*Threatened with extinction?*

**5 Listening to people's opinions** CD I.11–12

*Discussions are not only about talking. You have to listen carefully too.*

**a** Look at questions 1–3. Then listen to the first part of the classroom discussion on global warming and take notes.

1 Do you think the discussion leader starts the discussion off well? Why (not)?
2 What does Amy say about the greenhouse effect?
3 What does Max add to her point? What does he do to emphasize his points about the effects of global warming?

**b** Compare notes with a partner. If you can't agree on something, listen again to check.

**c** Look at the questions below and listen to the second part of the discussion.

1 What conclusions does the discussion leader draw? Do you agree with her?
2 Which of the following bad discussion habits can you hear? Note down the mistakes and who makes them.
   - Interrupting - Being rude - Talking too much
   - Not listening to what the previous speaker said
   - Not backing up one's statement with facts

**d** Which discussion habit do you think is the worst? Explain why.

Webcode:
STAR322305-46

# 3 The Web of Communication

*What is communication? When, where and how do we communicate? Is it possible not to communicate? Finding our way in the web of communication without getting caught in it is becoming ever more difficult.*

► SF 12 Working with Pictures (p. 140)

**1 Working with pictures**

**a** Work with a partner. Agree on a *caption for each of the eight photos.

**b** Put the photos into groups. Point out which of the photos have something in common. Share your ideas with your partner.

**2 Thinking about a title**

**a** What does the chapter title make you think of? What different meanings can the word *web* have?

**b** Look at the photos again and think of a common title for them.

**c** Collect your ideas in groups of four and choose the best or most original title.

A

► LP 35 Abbreviations in Text Messages (p. 127)

B

**Employers use Facebook when hiring**

Some employers say they use the website to check you out before they hire you. [...] Employers also search websites like MySpace and Friendster, so Career Services warns students to be careful about what they put on the Web. You never know who might be looking.

***Northwestern News Network*, 19 April 2006**

6

C

'Dear Andy: How have you been? Your mother and I are fine. We miss you. Please sign off your computer and come downstairs for something to eat. Love, Dad.'

D

Chris Tarantino goes online to learn about her daughters' school day.

***New York Times*, 4 May 2008**

**soz** *(text message abbr)* sorry
**dd** *(text message abbr)* died
**employer** person or company that gives people jobs
**hire sb.** give sb. a job
**Career Services** Berufsberatung

**3 Working with different texts**

Work in groups of four. Choose one of the above texts each and make notes:

- How did you react when you first read the text?
- What does it reveal about the way people use modern media today?

Exchange your ideas in the group. ▪ **Language help**

**4 Collecting communication terms**

Write an A–Z of different terms to do with communication. Add new words and phrases as you go through this chapter.

*A: advertisement, B: blog, C: chat room, D: ...*

### Language help

- I was surprised that / amused by / shocked that ...
- It made me worry about ...
- The message/cartoon made me think that/about ...
- It reminded me of / made it clear to me that ...
- I think / In my opinion it shows/proves that ...

# You Can't Not Communicate

▶ LP 25 Increase Your Word Power Online (p. 118)

Whenever we transmit information of any kind, we are communicating. Writing and speech are the most obvious means of communication, but we can also communicate our thoughts and feelings through music, dance, poetry, or any other art form. You should choose carefully how you communicate, though, as there are certain conventions to follow. Just as it can be considered rude to send a text message to express your condolences, using your mobile phone in public can be seen as being rude when you speak loudly and annoy others. In conversation with strangers, on the other hand, silence is considered awkward, leading to the necessity of making conversation, or small talk.

**⚠ Trouble spot**
**mobile (phone)** *(BE)*
= **cellphone** *(esp. AE)*
Not: ~~handy~~

▶ LP 28 False Friends (p. 121)

Technological advances have made connecting to like-minded strangers as easy as keeping in touch with friends and family. All we have to do is go on the Internet, read a blog, update our online profile on social networking sites such as Facebook, MySpace or Twitter, chat, send emails or simply use a mobile phone to talk or text. Many social networking sites are growing in popularity. Thus, surfing the Net allows us to contact others with the same interests or the same friends. It brings people together who may never have met otherwise. At the same time, these social networks also allow others to post information about us on the Internet – whether it is good or bad, true or not.

**⚠ Trouble spot**
im Internet = **on the Internet**
im Internet surfen
= **surf the Internet/Net**

Whenever we speak, we not only send a verbal message, but at the same time transmit a non-verbal message through our body language or facial expressions. We send non-verbal messages even when we don't speak, for example when we are simply listening to someone else talk. In short: you can't not communicate. However, communication, or interaction, will only be successful if at least two people with a shared space are involved. In other words, they must have something in common, e.g. belong to the same family, be friends, go to the same school, speak the same language. As a rule, communication is easy and straightforward. Look at the diagram below. A, the sender, speaks to B, the recipient. A wants to communicate something to B: this is A's intended meaning. What B actually understands is the perceived meaning. This may, but must not necessarily, be the same as A's intended meaning.

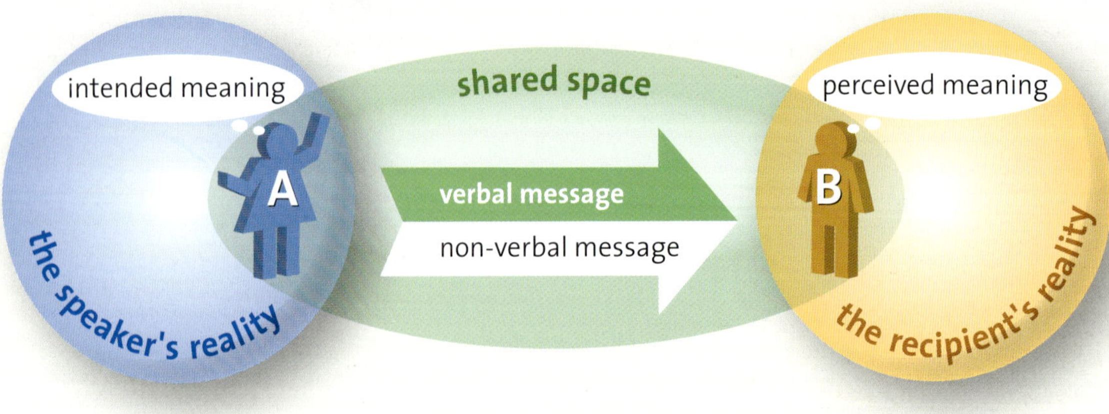


*A communication model*

▶ SF 12 Working with Pictures (p. 140)

## 1 A communication model

Look at the model of what happens during interaction on p. 48 and match these definitions with the terms in the model:

1 the person listening
2 the person speaking
3 what the two people communicating have in common
4 the world a person lives in and the way he or she sees it
5 the words the person speaking uses
6 what the person listening understands
7 body language and facial expressions
8 what the person speaking means

## 2 Matching nouns and verbs

**a** Make collocations with the verbs and nouns below. Use *a/an* or *the* before the nouns if necessary.

▸ LP 26 Collocations (p. 120)

| | |
|---|---|
| ▪ access ▪ change ▪ check out ▪ collect ▪ create ▪ have ▪ make ▪ receive ▪ send ▪ surf ▪ go on ▪ update ▪ use ▪ write | ▪ conversation ▪ information ▪ Internet ▪ mobile phone ▪ profile ▪ small talk ▪ text message |

**b** Choose five of the collocations from **a** and write sentences with them.

## 3 Matching nouns and adjectives

**a** Match each group of adjectives (or adjectivally used nouns) with a noun from the box on the right.

| | |
|---|---|
| ▪ hidden/double/perceived/intended/literal/... | ▪ information |
| ▪ useful/secret/detailed/correct/background/... | ▪ language |
| ▪ important/urgent/phone/text/error/... | ▪ meaning |
| ▪ foreign/first/official/native/body/sign/... | ▪ message |

**b** Choose two collocations from each group and write sentences with them.

## 4 Activating your passive vocabulary

When reading the text on p. 48, you probably understood a lot of English expressions that you may not have seen before. But will you remember them if you need to use them?
Translate the following sentences. Pay special attention to the underlined expressions. Look at the text again if necessary.

1 Das richtige <u>Kommunikationsmittel</u> zu wählen ist ebenso wichtig wie die Botschaft.
2 Um erfolgreich mit jemandem kommunizieren zu können, muss man <u>etwas gemein haben</u>.
3 Dank des Internets ist es heutzutage sehr einfach, <u>mit jemandem in Kontakt zu bleiben</u>.
4 Zu kommunizieren bedeutet <u>Informationen zu übermitteln</u>.
5 Susan <u>aktualisiert</u> täglich ihr <u>Onlineprofil</u>, indem sie neue <u>Informationen</u> über sich <u>ins Internet stellt</u>.

# Connecting through the Internet

## A1 Online Pressure Jan Hoffman

*Have you ever missed lessons without your parents knowing?*
*Have you ever got a bad mark in a test and not told your parents?*
*Discuss how you would like it if your parents had ways of finding out about this.*

**⚠ Trouble spot**
**program** *(BE, AE)*
= Computerprogramm
**programme** *(BE)* / **program** *(AE)*
= Programm, Sendung

**1 Forming your own opinion: Looking at both sides**

With a partner, you will read and work on a newspaper article about online programs called Edline, ParentConnect or PowerSchool which allow parents to check their children's grades and daily progress anytime. Each of you will read different parts of the article before discussing the pros and cons.

***Partner B:*** Look at p. 103.

**a** ***Partner A:*** Read the following extract from the *New York Times* article. Note down arguments in favour of using online programs like Edline.

► SF 29 Reading Non-Fiction (p. 151)

At an age when teenagers increasingly want to manage their own lives, many parents use these programs to tighten the grip. College admission is so devastatingly competitive, parents say, they feel compelled to check online grades frequently. [...]

Paradoxically, many parents who regularly check their children's grades online fondly recall that during their own adolescence, subterfuge was a given. 'I'll admit it,' said Chris Tarantino, Emily's mother. 'I got satisfaction in fooling my parents.'

Programs like Edline do away with that sly pleasure. But Mrs. Tarantino, a PowerSchool fan, said the stakes had changed drastically. Academic pressure a generation ago was not nearly as all-consuming.

It is difficult to demonstrate conclusively what impact these programs have on school performance, because of all the variables. Anecdotally, principals report that the programs have motivated otherwise hard-to-reach parents and students. They have helped some middle-school boys, in particular, become better organized.

**pressure** ['preʃə] Druck
2 **devastatingly** ['devəsteɪtɪŋli] verheerend
6 **fondly** zärtlich
**recall sth.** remember sth.
**adolescence** [ˌædə'lesns] puberty
**subterfuge** ['sʌbtəfjuːdʒ] *(fml)* secret and dishonest behaviour
**be a given** selbstverständlich sein
7 **fool sb.** trick sb. into believing sth. that is not true
8 **do away with sth.** take sth. away
**sly** hinterhältig
10 **all-consuming** taking up all your time or energy
11 **conclusively** endgültig
**impact** ['– –] powerful effect

'Edline opens up communication between parents and teachers,' said Ron Jones, the principal at Huth Middle School, which has a 90-percent minority student population, in Matteson, Ill., a middle-class Chicago suburb. 'It helps keep the children minding their Ps and Qs.'

The software can certainly be a boon to working parents. And divorced parents can log on without having to contact each other. [...]

In Noblesville, Ind., after a survey indicated that parents felt sufficiently informed by PowerSchool and subsequent email exchanges with teachers, the middle-school principal canceled parent-teacher conferences this spring and gave the time back to classes.

From: 'I Know What You Did Last Math Class', *The New York Times*, 4 May 2008

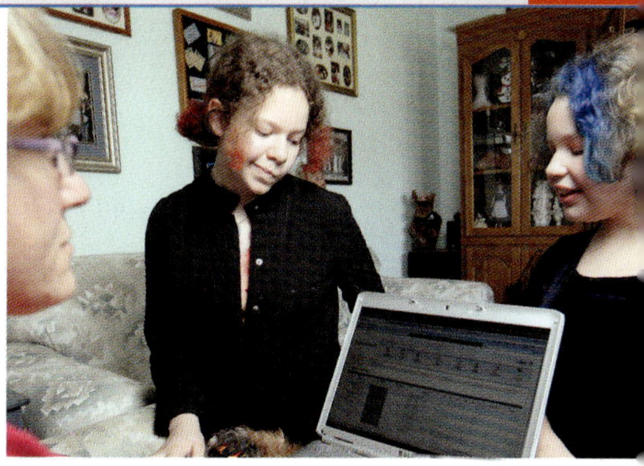

*Daily report card: Chris Tarantino goes online to learn about her daughters' school day*

[19] **boon** blessing
[21] **sufficiently** [sə'fɪʃntli] as much as necessary
[23] **cancel sth.** etwas absagen

**b** With your partner, discuss how software like Edline can be used. Explain how schools use it.

**c** Your partner will read you six words or phrases from your text. Look at the definitions in **A**. Decide which definition each of the words or phrases refers to. Write down the words and phrases and their definitions.

**A**
- put (more) pressure on sb./sth.
- what is at risk
- pressure to get good grades at school
- how students do at school
- describes a situation in which students compete against each other
- be careful about what one says or does (i.e. say 'please' and 'thank you')

Now swap roles and read the words and phrases in **B** to your partner.

**B**
- college admission (p. 103, l. 2)
- feel compelled to do sth. (p. 103, l. 3)
- gifted-and-talented program (p. 103, ll. 12–13)
- monitor one's records (p. 103, l. 15)
- snoop (p. 103, l. 20)
- slip up (p. 103, l. 22)

**d** **Role-play:** You and your child (Partner B) are discussing these programs. Use your notes from **a** to keep the argument going for at least two minutes.

## 2 Looking at adverbs

**a** List the adverbs in the newspaper extract on pp. 50–51. Which word / part of the sentence does the adverb refer to in each sentence? ▪ **Language help**

*At an age when teenagers increasingly want to manage their own lives ...*

**b** Compare the sentences with and without adverbs. Explain why these adverbs are used in each case. Can you formulate a general rule for the effect of the adverbs used here? ▪ **Language help**

## 3 EXTRA Writing

With your partner, write a *letter to the head teacher of a school using Edline and make suggestions on how to use the program wisely. Include arguments from both your texts (on pp. 50–51 and 103).

**Language help**

- Adverbs modify ...
- The adverb ... is used to modify the verb/adjective ...

- This makes ... sound more important/interesting/...
- This highlights the intensity/seriousness/... of the situation.
- In the sentence '...', the adverb makes an otherwise average verb/sentence stronger / clearer / more descriptive / ...

▸ LP 24 Adverbs of Manner (p. 117)

## A2 An Online Hoax Christopher Maag

▸ SF 29 Reading Non-Fiction (p. 151)

*Before reading the following article, think what an online hoax and an online character could be.*

**hoax** [həʊks] act intended to make sb. believe sth. that is not true, esp. sth. unpleasant
12 **insult** ['– –] Beleidigung
16 **sob** *(v)* cry
**closet** ['klɒzɪt] *(esp. AE)* a small room or a space in a wall used for storing things
30 **joined at the hip** *(infml)* inseparable friends
31 **drift apart** lose contact
35 **prescribe sth. for sb.** jdm. etwas verschreiben
38 **minor** ['maɪnə] sb. who is under 18 years old
40 **mess with sb.** sich mit jdm. anlegen
42 **profanity-laden** [prə'fænəti,leɪdn] *(fml)* full of bad language

*Tina Meier with pictures of her daughter Megan*

Megan Meier died believing that somewhere in this world lived a boy named Josh Evans who hated her. He was 16, owned a pet snake, and she thought he was the cutest boyfriend she ever had.

Josh contacted Megan through her page on MySpace.com, the social networking website, said Megan's mother, Tina Meier. They flirted for weeks, but only online – Josh said his family had no phone. On October 15, 2006, Josh suddenly turned mean. He called Megan names, and later they traded insults for an hour.

The next day, in his final message, said Megan's father Ron Meier, Josh wrote, 'The world would be a better place without you.'

Sobbing, Megan ran into her bedroom closet. Her mother found her there, hanging from a belt. She was 13.

Six weeks after Megan's death, her parents learned that Josh Evans never existed. He was an online character created by Lori Drew, then 47, who lived four houses down the street in this rapidly growing community 35 miles northwest of St. Louis.

In seventh grade, Megan Meier had tried desperately to join the popular crowd at Fort Zumwalt West Middle School, only to be teased about her weight, her mother said. At the beginning of eighth grade last year, she transferred to Immaculate Conception, a nearby Catholic school. Within three months, Ms. Meier said, her daughter had a new group of friends, lost 20 pounds and joined the volleyball team.

At one time, Lori Drew's daughter and Megan had been 'joined at the hip', said Megan's great-aunt Vicki Dunn. But the two drifted apart, and when Megan changed schools, she told the other girl that she no longer wanted to be friends, Ms. Meier said. [...]

*Lori Drew (right) and her daughter*

Because Ms. Drew had taken Megan on family vacations, she knew the girl had been prescribed antidepression medication, Ms. Meier said. She also knew that Megan had a MySpace page.

Ms. Drew had told a girl across the street about the hoax, said the girl's mother, who requested anonymity to protect her daughter, a minor.

'Lori laughed about it,' the mother said, adding that Ms. Drew and Ms. Drew's daughter 'said they were going to mess with Megan.' [...]

Other youngsters who had linked to Josh's MySpace profile joined the increasingly bitter exchange and began sending profanity-laden messages to Megan, who retreated to her bedroom. No more than 15 minutes had passed, Ms. Meier recalled, when she suddenly felt something was terribly wrong. She rushed to the bedroom and found her daughter's body hanging in the closet.

From: 'A Hoax Turned Fatal Draws Anger but No Charges', *The New York Times*, 28 November 2007

**1 Your reactions**
Make notes on how you felt as you read the text. Share your feelings with a partner. ▪ **Language help**

**Language help**
- The text made me angry/sad/upset/... because ...
- I found it interesting/surprising/shocking/...
- I was speechless because ...
- I couldn't believe it when ...
- I felt sorry for ... when ...

**2 Comprehension**
a Write down the chronology of events leading up to Megan's death.
b Explain why Ms Drew wanted to 'mess with' Megan (l. 40).

**3 Language check**
a Look at the examples of indirect speech below. Explain why the past tense forms *was*, *had* and *wanted* are used. What tense would have been used in direct speech?
- She thought he was the cutest boyfriend. (ll. 4–5)
- Josh said his family had no phone. (ll. 9–10)
- She told the other girl that she no longer wanted to be friends. (l. 32)

b Translate the three sentences into German and comment on the differences between indirect speech in English and German.

▸ LP 11 Indirect Speech: Statements (p. 111)

## A3 Risky Behaviour CD I.13

*The interview you are going to listen to presents research carried out by Dr Megan Moreno from the University of Wisconsin on references to sex, drugs and violence in MySpace profiles.*

**1 Comprehension**
a Make sure you know the meaning and pronunciation of the words and expressions on the right. Then listen to the interview.
b Point out the aim of the research.
c Describe the behaviour the research focused on.
d Explain what was done to change this behaviour and to what extent it was successful.

▪ *substance abuse* ▪ *savvy* ▪ *disclose sth.* ▪ *mortality* ▪ *homicide* ▪ *suicide* ▪ *boast (v)* ▪ *cyberbully* ▪ *foster sth.* ▪ *cautionary message* ▪ *influence sth.*

**2 Positive and negative aspects of social networking sites**
a In groups of four, do a placemat activity. In your corner of the placemat, write down positive and negative aspects of social networking sites such as Facebook or MySpace.
b Discuss your lists with your group. Write the two most positive and the two most dangerous aspects in the middle of your placemat.
c Compare your results with those of other groups. Would you change your four central ideas now?

▸ SF 2 Brainstorming (p. 133)

**3 EXTRA Working with posters**
Write an email or make a poster or flyer warning your peers of the risks of sharing information about themselves on social networking sites like MySpace.

▸ SF 12 Working with Pictures (p. 140)

# To Talk or Not to Talk?

## B1 Meeting the Stepmother David Mitchell

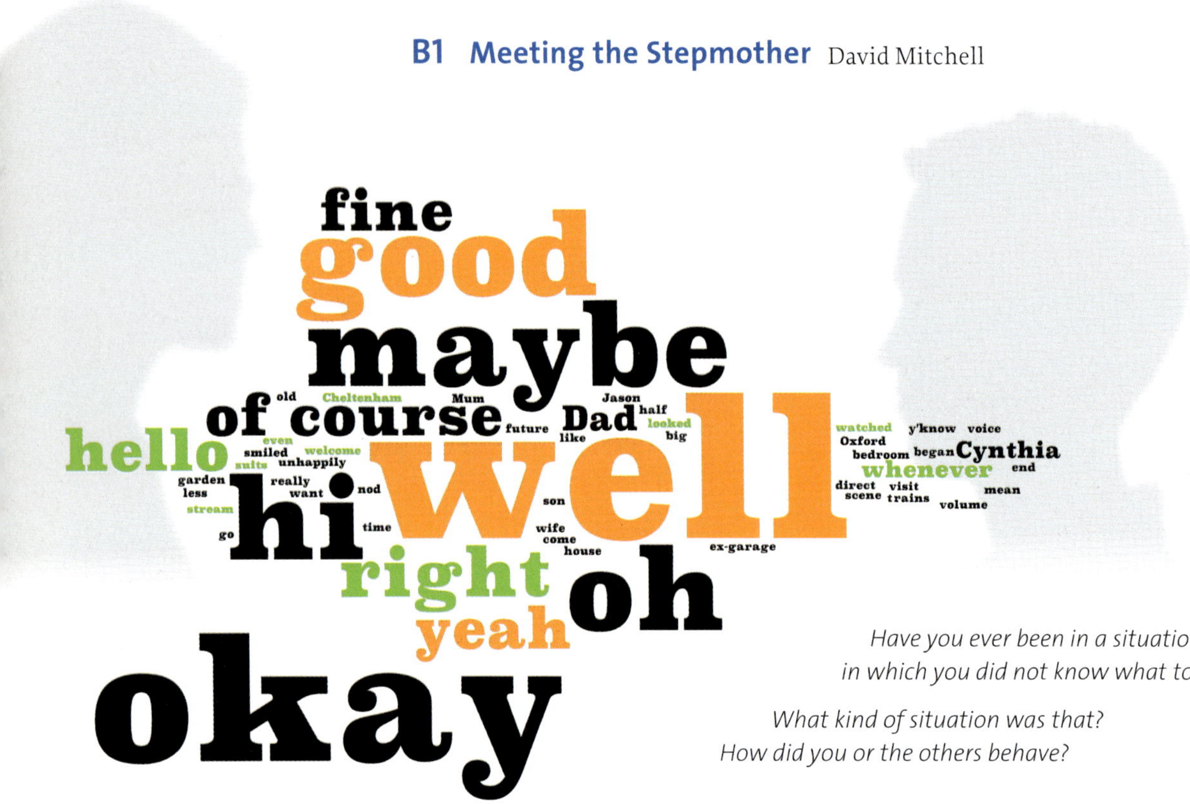


*Have you ever been in a situation in which you did not know what to say?*

*What kind of situation was that? How did you or the others behave?*

*The father of Julia and Jason Taylor has left the family for another woman, Cynthia. Read this extract about the first meeting between father and son after the separation.*

'Hi, Dad.'

'Oh!' Dad's expression was a mountaineer's, the moment his rope snaps. 'Jason. I didn't expect you to –' Dad'd been going to say 'to be at home' but he changed his sentence. 'I didn't hear you.'

'I heard the car.' Obviously. 'Mum's at work.' Dad knew that.

'She left some things for me. I've just come to pick them up.'

'Yeah. She said.'

A moon-grey cat strolled into the garage and settled down on a cushion of potatoes.

'So ...' Dad said. 'How's Julia?'

Dad meant *Does Julia hate me?* But not even Julia could answer that. 'She's ... fine.'

'Good. Good. Say hi from me.'

'Okay.' *Tell her yourself, why don't you?* 'How was Christmas?'

'Oh ... fine. Quiet.' Dad looked at the pyramid of bin-bags. 'Horrendous. For obvious reasons. Yours?'

'Mine was horrendous too. Are you growing a beard, Dad?'

'No, I just haven't ... maybe I will. I don't know. Are the Richmond relatives all well?'

'Aunt Alice's as you'd expect, all clucky 'cause of ... y'know.'

'Of course.'

2 **mountaineer** sb. who climbs mountains as a sport
**snap** *(v)* break
14 **horrendous** [hɒ'rendəs] terrible
19 **clucky** *(infml)* gluckenhaft

'Alex just played on his BBC computer. Hugo's smarmy as ever. Nigel's doing quadratic equations for fun. Uncle Brian ...' Finishing the sentence about Uncle Brian was hard work.

'... got drunk as a lord and prattled on about me?'

'Dad, is Uncle Brian an idiot?'

'He can *act* like one.' Something's unknotted in Dad. He looks hollow and unhappy but he's definitely more peaceful. 'But how someone acts isn't what they are. Not necessarily. Best not to be too judgemental. Maybe there's stuff going on you don't know about. You know?'

I do know.

The horriblest part was, being friendly to Dad makes me feel disloyal to Mum. However much they *say* 'We both still love you', you *do* have to choose. Words like 'maintenance' and 'best interests' don't leave you alone. A figure sat in the sky-blue Jetta. 'Is ...' I didn't know what to call *her*.

'Cynthia drove me over, yes. She'd like to say hello, if ...' (a mad organist thumped my panic chords) '... if you'd like to.' A pleading note bent Dad's voice. 'Would you?'

'Okay.' I didn't want to. 'Okay.'

Outside the cave of the garage, rain fell so lightly it wasn't even falling. Before I'd got to the Jetta, Cynthia'd got out. She's not a big-boobed bimbo *or* an evil-eyed witch.

She's frumpier than Mum, *any* day, and mousier. Brown hair in a bob, brown eyes. She doesn't look a *thing* like a stepmother. Which is what she'll be, by and by.

'Hello, Jason.' The woman Dad'd rather spend the rest of his life with than Mum looked at me like I had a gun pointed at her. 'I'm Cynthia.'

'Hi. I'm Jason.' This was very, very, *very* weird. Neither of us tried to shake hands. In the back of her car was a BABY ON BOARD sticker. 'You've got a baby?'

'Well, Milly's more of a toddler now.' If you just heard her voice next to Mum's, you'd say Mum's posher. 'Camilla. Milly. Milly's father – my ex-husband – we're already ... I mean, he's not on the scene. As they say.'

'Right.'

Dad watched his future wife and his only son from his ex-garage.

'Well.' Cynthia smiled unhappily. 'Come and visit whenever you want, Jason. Trains go to Oxford from Cheltenham, direct.' Cynthia's voice is less than half the volume of Mum's. 'Your dad would like you to. He *really* would. So would I. It's a big old house we're in. There's a stream at the end of the garden. You could even have your –' (she was about to say 'your own bedroom'.) 'Well, you're welcome, any time.'

All I could do was nod.

'Whenever it suits.' Cynthia looked at Dad.

'So how –' I began, suddenly scared of having nothing to say.

'If you –' she began in the same second.

'After you –'

'No, after you. Really. You go ahead.'

'How long' (no grown-up's ever made me go first) 'have you known Dad?' I'd meant the question to sound breezy but it came out all Gestapo.

'Since we were growing up,' Cynthia was working hard to iron out any extra meanings, 'in Derbyshire.'

Longer than Mum, then. If Dad'd married this Cynthia in the first place, instead of Mum, and if they'd had a son, would it have been me? Or a totally different kid? Or a kid who's half me?

From: David Mitchell, *Black Swan Green*, 2006

**⚠ Trouble spot**
**look unhappy** *(adj)*
**smile unhappily** *(adv)*

► LP 9 Emphasis: Stress, *do/does/did*, Word Order (p. 110)

21 **smarmy** *(infml)* too polite in a way that is not sincere
24 **prattle on about sth./sb.** talk a lot about unimportant things
28 **judgemental** [dʒʌdʒ'mentl] judging people and criticizing them too quickly
33 **maintenance** ['meɪntənəns] Unterhalt
34 **Jetta** type of car ('Volkswagen')
36 **pleading** begging
39 **big-boobed** *(slang)* with big breasts
**bimbo** *(infml, disapproving)* usu. a young woman who is sexually attractive but not very intelligent
41 **frumpy** altmodisch
47 **toddler** child who has just learned to walk
48 **posh** *(BE, infml)* *here:* belonging to a high social class
65 **breezy** cheerful and relaxed
66 **iron sth. out** ['aɪən] get rid of sth.

**⚠ Trouble spot**
**How long have you known Dad?**
Not: ~~How long do you know Dad?~~

► LP 5 Present Perfect for 'time up until now' (p. 107)

▸ LP 3 Simple Present to Talk about Texts (p. 106)

## 1 Comprehension

a Summarize the situation briefly in your own words.

b How does Jason feel about his father? How does the father feel about Jason? What makes the communication between father and son so difficult?

**Language help**

- The atmosphere is grim/gloomy/dismal/strained/hostile/icy/...
- Everyone feels awkward / is tense / ...

▸ LP 13–15 Conditional Sentences (pp. 112–113)

## 2 *Stylistic devices and *point of view

a Describe the *atmosphere. Analyse the stylistic devices the author uses to create it (*metaphors, *similes). ■ **Language help**

b Collect all the information in the text on Cynthia. Who provides this information? What effect does it have on you, the reader?

## 3 Language check

In ll. 47–48 and 68–69, Jason uses conditional sentences. State the type of conditional sentence and what it expresses.

## 4 Applying a communication model

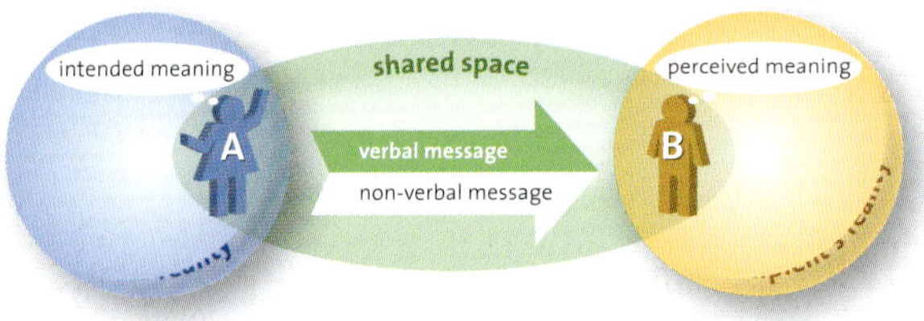


Relate the situations in ll. 10–13 or ll. 43–45 to the communication model (p. 48): In these situations, is the intended meaning the same as the perceived meaning? Do sender and recipient have a shared space? What connection, if any, is there between a shared space and the success of communication?

## 5 EXTRA Writing

Choose one of the following tasks – **a** or **b**:

a ***Partner A*** (Jason): Write a *letter to your father in which you tell him everything that remained unsaid during your conversation. Will you be angry or understanding? Will you want to keep in touch?
***Partner B*** (Jason's father): Write a letter to your son in which you tell him everything that remained unsaid during your conversation. Will you just feel sorry for your son? Will you try to explain openly why you left the family for another woman?
When you have finished writing your letters, swap them and write a reply to your partner's letter.

b Imagine Cynthia had described the meeting from her point of view. Rewrite ll. 43–70.

## B2 A New Kind of Connectedness?

CD I.14

*In the interview you're going to hear in this section, the Canadian sociologist Barry Wellman presents results of his survey on the effect of modern media on family togetherness.*

*Family togetherness, ca. 1900*

### 1 Speculating

Do mobile phones and the Internet promote family life, or do they lead to isolation? Discuss this with a partner.

### 2 Comprehension

**a** Make sure you know the meaning and pronunciation of the words and expressions on the right. Then listen to the interview.

*▪ evaluate ▪ variety ▪ data ▪ dispel sth. ▪ myth ▪ assembly line ▪ notion ▪ respondent ▪ reliance ▪ fear-mongering ▪ spin on sth. (n) ▪ ratio ▪ substitute ▪ complement (n) ▪ blur sth. ▪ distinction*

▸ SF 18 Answering Multiple-Choice Questions (p. 145)

**b** Choose the best answer or answers.

1 Traditional nuclear families make most use of ...
A mobile phones. B texting. C emails.

2 Using modern technology leads to ...
A social isolation. B a more intense form of connectedness.
C less authentic communication.

3 The fear that people no longer communicate much with each other ...
A was proven in the survey. B was evaluated in the survey.
C was not investigated in the survey.

4 What is the advantage of modern technology?
A People use it where they hadn't been able to communicate before.
B It acts as a substitute for family life.
C It can help in planning and arranging appointments.

5 How do most people feel about relying on digital technology?
A Women think men look at their computer more than at them.
B The two surveys mentioned showed different results, so there is no reliable data on this.
C More than 80 % consider modern technology to be useful for their family life.

6 What does Jon Gordon say about the effect modern technology has on working life?
A Employers can reach staff more easily. B People tend to work more.
C There is no clear distinction between work and home anymore.

*The Simpsons: family togetherness, ca. 2000*

### 3 Making a choice

**a** What is your experience regarding the research findings – do you use the media mentioned to connect or to distance yourself? Give examples.

**b** EXTRA The report mentions that people on assembly lines use mobile phones to communicate during work. What other general changes in business communication have been caused by modern media? Think of some examples.

### 4 EXTRA Writing

In no more than 200 words, write about the importance, advantages and disadvantages of modern media. You can use your A–Z from p. 47 for ideas.

# Rhythm Is It

## C1 Expressing Yourself through Music DVD 07–09

*To some, music is a means of expressing their feelings. For others, one could say that they need it 'like the air they breathe' (Sir Simon Rattle). Do you express yourself through music? If so, when?*
Rhythm Is It! *is a documentary about the Berlin Philharmonic's first educational project, in which 250 Berlin pupils worked together with the Berlin Philharmonic Orchestra to perform Igor Stravinsky's ballet 'Le sacre du printemps'. Most of these pupils had never danced before in their lives and all rehearsed for three months to perform this 30-minute ballet.*

**1 Before viewing**

a With a partner, discuss:
- what music means to you,
- what kind of music you listen to in different situations,
- whether or not you could live without music.

b Make a mind map with 'rhythm' as the topic word to answer the following questions:
- Where do you encounter rhythm?
- What does the title *Rhythm Is It!* make you think of?

c Make sure you know the meaning and pronunciation of the words on the left. They all come up in the film clips you are going to watch.

▸ SF 1 Mind Mapping (p. 132)

▪ *pre-civilized* ▪ *descend from* ▪ *lizard* ▪ *primal origin* ▪ *physically* ▪ *emotionally* ▪ *mentally* ▪ *catch up with sb.* ▪ *indicator* ▪ *society*

*Choreographer Royston Maldoom*

*Rehearsing for the big day (from the film* Rhythm Is It!*)*

*Conductor Sir Simon Rattle*

## 2 Watching scene 1: Looking at rhythm

**a** Watch scene 1 of the film *Rhythm Is It!*. Point out what the conductor Sir Simon Rattle says about rhythm and why he thinks 'rhythm is it'.

**b** Rattle tells us how his love of music began. Have you had a similar experience? Share your experience with a partner.

**c** Describe what you see and hear besides the speaker's narrative. Watch the scene again. Use a viewing log to take notes on colour, movement, sounds, camerawork, etc. ▪ **Language help**

**d** Talk to a partner. Why do you think this part of the film has been edited the way it has? What effect does it have on you?

### Language help

- There is a voice-over when the orchestra is playing.
- The music gets louder / gets softer / fades out when ...
- There is a close-up of the speaker/...
- The ...'s movements are very smooth/sudden/... when ...
- The shot cuts from ... to ...
- The camera sweeps / moves quickly/slowly from ... to ...
- The colours are very dark/dull/bright/serious/...

► SF 21 Viewing a Film (p. 147)

## 3 Watching scene 2: Looking at body language

**a** Watch scene 2. Describe what the dancing class learns about communication through body language.

**b** Explain how you can tell whether or not the class has understood this particular lesson.

**c** With a partner, discuss the British choreographer Royston Maldoom's statement that the body and the mind have a strong influence on each other.

**d** Tell your partner which of Maldoom's statements impressed you most and why.

## 4 What would you do?

Would you like to take part in a project like the one in the film? Why (not)? Make notes and report to the class.

► SF 5 Making Notes (p. 134)

## 5 Mediation: Helping pupils understand their teacher

In the film, German teenagers are taught to dance by a British choreographer. Watch scene 3 and take notes. Summarize in German what Maldoom says.

► SF 15 Mediating (p. 144)
► SF 7 Paraphrasing (p. 135)

## C2 Expressing Yourself through Poetry

*In this section, you will experience how writing *poetry can be a means of expressing your thoughts and feelings.*

**1** Poems for everyone

What do you expect when you read the title of the *poem below?
What *metaphor does the poem make use of?
Perhaps its message can help you when writing your own poem.

**napkin** serviette – **core** hard central part of the fruit that contains the seeds – **stem** *hier:* Stiel
**rind** [raɪnd] thick skin of some fruits – **pit** *(AE)* stone-like, large seed of some fruit

**2** Writing a poem

Look at the following three poems. Choose one as a model to write a poem about yourself. If you don't want to write about yourself, choose another person or topic. Then have a partner guess who or what the poem is about (or keep it to yourself).

1 A **poem skeleton** offers you the basic structure of a poem and leaves it up to you to fill it out. The title and last *line are the same.

*Charlotte the shy*
I am the colour of *winter.*
If I was a sound, *I would be a whisper.*
Many people think *I'm not even there,* but *I am.*
If I was a garden, *I would be overgrown and wild, a secret hiding place.*
I taste of *winter.*
I dream of *freedom* and one day *I will fly.*
My friends say I*'m a closed book.*
My mother doesn't want me to *become an astronaut,* yet I *still dream on.*
If I was a book, *my cover wouldn't give away much.*
I hope that one day *I will be able to do anything I want.*
*Charlotte the shy*

⚠ **Trouble spot**
She doesn't want me to ...
Not: ~~She doesn't want that I ...~~

2 In a **biography poem**, what is said in each line is fixed, but fewer words are given, leaving a bit more room for creativity than the poem skeleton.

| | |
|---|---|
| *Barack* | (first name) |
| *Charismatic, determined, powerful* | (three descriptive adjectives) |
| **Who loves** *his country* | **Who loves ...** |
| **Who wants** *change to come* | **Who wants ...** |
| **Always** *working*, **never** *giving up* | **Always ..., never ...** |
| *Obama* | (last name) |

3 Of the three types of poem, the **rondo** is the most open form. It consists of eight lines. Lines 1, 4 and 7 are the same, as are lines 2 and 8. Because of the repetition, these five lines are the most important.

*Life wasn't easy*
*When I was a young boy*
*I had to leave my home country*
*Life wasn't easy*
*Before I took a chance*
*And music and dance changed my life*
*Life wasn't easy*
*When I was a young boy*

**Trouble spot**
Life wasn't easy.
Not: ~~The life wasn't easy~~.

## 3 Writing is ... CD I.15

**a** Make sure you know the meaning and pronunciation of the words on the right. Then listen to four Native American teenagers present their own poem for the 11th International Youth Poetry Slam Festival in Washington, D.C.

**b** What effect does this poem have on you? ▪ **Language help**

**c** What is the poem about?

**d** What do you like about it? What would you do differently when presenting your poem/ project/video/...? Consider tempo, articulation, etc.

▪ *convey sth.* ▪ *emotion* ▪ *innocent* ▪ *antidote* ▪ *absolution* ▪ *boundary* ▪ *continuous* ▪ *knowledge* ▪ *claw at sth. (v)*

**Language help**

- The poem has no / little / a great / a powerful effect (on me).
- It's powerful/moving/ bizarre/...
- When they all speak together, I ... / it's ...
- It made me thoughtful/...
- It made me think that ...

# Presenting Yourself Creatively

*In this chapter task, you will learn how to 'sell yourself' to people your age in an informal situation, such as trying to get a flat share.*

## 1 Getting it right

Hi there,
I'm Linda. I don't like pizza, like everybody else does. I'm 16 years old. I have a sister, Pam – she's a real pain, I can tell you!! Don't get me wrong, I like her, but most of the time she's just a pain. My dad lives in London with his second wife, Anna. Anna is 26. When my dad said he was leaving us for a woman 15 years younger than him, I thought that was gross, but Anna is cool, and so is London. I love going clubbing there. To be honest I'm not really into studying, but I do love Maths, although most of my friends say Maths sucks. I had a dog once, but it died – like they sometimes do. I don't really know what else to write, so I'll sign off now.
If you want to get back to me, send me an email to

**a** Comment on Linda's text above. Consider
- how she expresses herself,
- whether or not she has structured her text well,
- who she might have written it for,
- what kind of impression she gives of herself.

**b** Linda uses a lot of very informal language. Find the informal words or expressions she uses to mean the following:

▪ not really interested in sth. ▪ contact sb.
▪ end a letter, radio programme, etc.; say goodbye ▪ misunderstand sb.
▪ very unpleasant ▪ fashionable, attractive, nice, interesting
▪ be very bad or uninteresting ▪ an unpleasant or annoying person

**c** Now note down some information about yourself that you could use to present yourself to somebody your own age that you have not yet met. Structure your notes as well as you can. You will need them in **3a** (on p. 63).

## 2 Being creative DVD 10

*In the film* Legally Blonde, *Elle's boyfriend breaks up with her because, as a Law student at Harvard, the oldest and perhaps most famous US university, he feels he needs a more serious girlfriend. Elle wants to show him how serious she can be. So she also applies for admission to Harvard.*

*▪ lawyer ▪ sorority*
*▪ command attention*
*▪ maintenance ▪ generic*
*▪ chafe ▪ fashion major*
*▪ diversity*
*▪ extra-curricular activity*
*▪ faux-fur panties*
*▪ philanthropist*

**a** Make sure you know the meaning and pronunciation of the words and phrases on the left. Then watch the video in which Elle presents herself to the admissions team. Look again at the communication model on p. 48. What mistakes, if any, does Elle make? Discuss:
- Elle's reality and that of the admissions team,
- their shared space,
- her verbal and non-verbal message(s),
- what makes her application funny.

**b** List situations in which Elle's application would be more suitable.

**c** Explain why the admissions team accepts Elle even though her application seems inappropriate to Harvard. ▪ **Language help**

**d** Formulate three rules for applications based on your answers to **a** and **c**. Discuss whether you need different rules for formal and informal situations.

### Language help

- Elle is accepted because she shows determination / goes against the norm / ...
- Her application shows initiative/creativity/...
- It is funny/unconventional/original/unexpected/...

**3 Putting together an application**

**a** Imagine one of the following situations and how you would present yourself. Collect some ideas. Use the notes you made in **1c** (on p. 62).

- A TV station wants to produce a musical with teenage amateurs (like *Rhythm Is It*) and you want to apply for an audition. You don't have to be a professional singer, dancer or actor, but you have to be able to express yourself creatively.
- You plan to go abroad for some work experience or to spend a term at a university and have found a shared flat. Your potential flatmates ask you to send them information about yourself so they can see whether or not you would fit in.

**b** Share your ideas with your partner and give each other feedback: What is good? What could be improved? What could be added?

► SF 14 Doing a Project (p. 143)

**c** Choose a medium, then prepare your application. Bear in mind that the medium you choose also says something about you. Here are some suggestions:

1 **A dossier** (folder or computer-assisted presentation) including e.g.

- a text in which you introduce yourself and photos showing you doing what you are good at or something that characterizes you,
- other texts you have written (about yourself), e.g. some poems, a rap or anything else you made up yourself,
- descriptions or photos of creative projects or performances you have taken part in.

► SF 11 Keeping a Portfolio (p. 138)

2 **A video**

- How long should the video be? It has to be long enough to say something about you, but shouldn't bore your audience. Was Elle's video in **2** a good length?
- Should there be other people in it apart from you?
- Should you do all the talking? Should friends/teachers/family say something about you? Should there be a '*narrator'?
- Do you need a script or music?

**d** In class, decide how you can best organize a presentation of the different applications.

► SF 23 Giving a Presentation (p. 148)

Webcode:
STAR322305-64

# 4 Migrants and Minorities

*For some time now, the migration of people from one country to another and all the consequences this has – from positive effects on the economy to racial conflict – has been making the news.*

**migrant** ['maɪgrənt] person who goes to live in another area or country, especially in order to find work
**migration** the movement of large numbers of people

### Language help

- The most popular country among immigrants from ... is ...
- They must leave/flee their homeland(s) because ...
- There may be war/famine/poverty/... in their home country.
- They choose a host country that ...
- They travel by bus/car/train/plane/ ...

▸ LP 1 Modal Verbs (p. 105)

**1 Thinking about migration**

**a Think:** What do you know about
- people who immigrate to / emigrate from Europe,
- the countries they come from / go to,
- how they travel?

**b Pair:** Exchange your ideas with a partner and make notes.

**c Share:** Discuss your views in class. ▪ **Language help**

**2 Looking at headlines**

Look at the six * headlines on p. 65. Choose two that you find interesting or surprising and tell a partner what stories they make you expect.

## Immigration intake 'good for business'

*The Age*, 27 October 2008

## Europe expects a flood of climate refugees

*Guardian Weekly*, 14–20 March 2008

## Emigration to Australia has doubled in the past decade

*The Independent*, 5 March 2008

## One in ten people in the UK now foreign-born

*Daily Mail*, 25 June 2007

## Dramatic increase in employers prosecuted for hiring illegal immigrants

*Mail on Sunday*, 5 May 2008

## IMMIGRANT USED FAKE ID TO STAY HERE

*Express and Echo*, Exeter, 3 May 2008

**intake** the number of people who are allowed to enter a place
**increase in** ['– –] Anstieg von
**prosecute sb.** ['prɒsɪkjuːt] jdn. verklagen
**hire sb.** give sb. a job
**fake** false
**ID (identification)** Ausweis

**3 The new slave trade?** CD I.16

**a** Make sure you know the meaning and pronunciation of the words and phrases on the right. Then listen to the interview with Jean-Philippe Chauzy from the International Organization for Migration (IOM) in Geneva and answer the following questions:

- Which definition of the term 'migrant' is given?
- What are 'push factors' and 'pull factors'? Give examples of both.
- According to Mr Chauzy, what is the worst form migration can take?

**b** With a partner, discuss whether or not 'slave trade' is an appropriate term for networks that smuggle illegal immigrants.

▪ *policy* ▪ *clandestine* ▪ *enforced labour* ▪ *exploitation* ▪ *country of transit* ▪ *destination* ▪ *estimate (n)* ▪ *hover* ▪ *staggering* ▪ *prospect* ▪ *civil strife* ▪ *diaspora* ▪ *facilitate sth.* ▪ *trafficking*

# On the Move

▸ LP 25 Increase Your Word Power Online (p. 118)

Although migration is a term used more and more often today, it is not a recent phenomenon, but dates back to the earliest times in history. People have always been on the move in search of better living conditions – at certain times in the past many countries have even relied on migrant workers.

After World War II, Britain welcomed the influx of immigrants when it opened its doors to people from former British colonies who were granted the right to settle and work there. The majority of these immigrants, who are often now in their second and third generations, came from the Indian subcontinent and Afro-Caribbean countries.

At the beginning of the 21st century, the enlargement of the European Union and the UK and Ireland's booming economies tempted Eastern Europeans to make a temporary move across the water. Earning their living in the UK and Ireland, they returned home at the end of the work season. Many immigrants have come to stay, which isn't always looked upon favourably by the native population, who sometimes fear that the immigrants will take away their jobs.

Africans and especially Nigerians have also been known to seek refuge on the shores of the British Isles. Many are seasonal migrants hoping to earn some money, while others are political refugees, fleeing from war or political or religious persecution. Most of them apply for asylum when they arrive. If asylum seekers' applications are rejected, however, they must leave the country or risk being deported.

**⚠ Trouble spot**
**persecute sb.** = jdn. (politisch, religiös) verfolgen
**prosecute sb.** = jdn. verklagen

▸ LP 29 Confusables (p. 122)

Some prefer taking that risk to taking the risk of going to prison or worse in their home country. They stay in the host country as illegal immigrants, with severe consequences for the whole family: no home, no job, no schooling. The odd job they do take on is badly paid (if at all) and often dangerous, and they live in constant fear of being deported.

*Rotimi Adebari, Mayor of Portlaoise*

Even legal immigrants do not always find the life that they had imagined, because with the existence of ethnic minorities comes racial conflict – a problem that Britain has been no stranger to in recent years. Nevertheless, the UK and Ireland have been quite successful in accommodating and integrating minority groups into society. If granted residency, the new citizens of foreign origin can vote in elections and even be elected Members of Parliament. In one notable case, an immigrant from Nigeria, Rotimi Adebari, was elected Mayor of Portlaoise.

**Portlaoise** [ˌpɔːtˈliːʃə] Irish town

## 1 Word families

**a** Add the missing words to a copy of the chart below. Some of the words you need are in the text on p. 66; you can find the others in a dictionary.

► LP 33 Word Formation: Suffixes (p. 124)
► LP 34 Word Stress (p. 126)
► SF 8 Using a Dictionary (p. 136)

| Abstract noun | Noun: person | Verb / Verbal phrase | Adjective |
|---|---|---|---|
| *immigration* | ... | ... | ——— |
| *emigration* | ... | ... | ——— |
| ... | ... | *deport* | ——— |
| *asylum* | ... | ... | ——— |
| ... | ... | *persecute* | ——— |
| ... | *racist* | ——— | ... |
| *residency* | ... | ... | ... |
| ... | ... | *seek refuge* | *fugitive* |

**b** Make sentences with five of the words or phrases you have added to the chart, but leave a gap for the words/phrases. Swap papers with a partner. Can he/she complete your sentences with the correct words?

**c** Look up the nouns *migration*, *emigration* and *immigration* in a dictionary and make sure you understand the difference between them. Use each of the nouns (or the corresponding verbs) in a sentence that clearly shows each word's meaning.

## 2 Word power

► LP 26 Collocations (p. 120)
► SF 1 Mind Mapping (p. 132)

Collect the words and phrases highlighted in the text on p. 66 in a table or a mind map, using the following categories:
*person, action, problems, pull factors, push factors* and *general migration terms*.
Add more words you already know from other sources. Remember to add new words and phrases as you go through this chapter.

## 3 Activating your passive vocabulary

When reading the text on p. 66, you probably understood most of the English expressions that you may not have seen before. But will you remember them if you need to use them?
Translate the following sentences, paying special attention to the underlined expressions. Look at the text again if necessary.

1 Auf der Suche nach besseren Lebensbedingungen wanderten die Flüchtlinge von einem europäischen Land zum nächsten.
2 Weil sie immer in Bewegung waren, dachten sie nie daran, sich irgendwo niederzulassen.
3 Als sie ihr Ziel erreicht hatten, beantragten die Einwanderer Asyl.
4 Die jungen Leute afrikanischer Herkunft hoffen, in Europa ihren Lebensunterhalt verdienen zu können.
5 Der saisonbedingte Zustrom von Wanderarbeitern nimmt jeden Sommer zu.

## 4 Analysing a photo

► SF 12 Working with Pictures (p. 140)

**a** In 50–80 words, describe and analyse the photo of Rotimi Adebari. Give it a *caption that reflects your analysis.

**b** Compare your description and analysis with those of a partner. Discuss the differences and decide whether both of your captions are equally good.

# Westward Bound?

## A1 Warsaw on the Thames William Underhill

*Make a list of the English names of the Eastern European member states of the EU. Make sure you know how to pronounce them. The map at the front of the book will help you to locate them.*

▸ SF 29 Reading Non-Fiction (p. 151)

Work in groups of three. Read the text below, each concentrating on one of the following aspects:
- reasons for Polish immigration to the British Isles
- success of Poles in the UK
- changes in everyday life in Britain caused by Polish immigration

▸ SF 4 Taking Notes (p. 134)

Take notes.

For a footloose generation of Poles, home increasingly means Britain or Ireland. In the three years since Poland joined the EU, millions of Poles have joined a westward exodus, with these two countries as clear favorites. By some reckonings, Ireland now plays host to 200,000 Polish expats – equivalent to 5 percent of the population – while Britain accommodates at least 700,000. By contrast, Spain (population: 40 million), another leading magnet for Poles, has pulled in a mere 150,000. France has been issuing barely 10,000 work permits to Polish citizens. While the mass influx of Eastern Europeans has stirred controversy across Western Europe, it is largely a move of Poles to the British Isles, where they are reshaping culture from politics to schools, media to pub life.

Behind this new Polish connection: Britain and Ireland's warm invitation. When Poland and nine other countries joined the EU in 2004, current members were given the right to delay opening their labor markets to job seekers from the East. Big countries like France and Germany kept their doors shut. But Britain and Ireland threw them wide open, perhaps not quite realizing what they had done. Government experts predicted just 13,000 migrants would come in annually from the new member states.

Some from every country took the bait. Others stayed put. Slovenia's economy was strong. Hungarians have little tradition of emigration. Czechs and Slovaks tended to look for jobs closer to home. But tens of thousands of Latvians and Lithuanians moved across the continent. And Poles responded in record numbers, creating the largest in-migrations in recent British history.

With a population of 39 million, Poland is by far the largest of the new EU members, and it also has a tradition of migration. Facing double-digit unemployment back home, Poles were drawn to Britain and Ireland by strong job prospects in two of Europe's top-performing economies, by the chance to learn English and by budget airlines that slashed the cost of travel. British forecasters were wrong again when they predicted that most newcomers would stay only long enough to make some money. A survey this summer found that roughly half the new Polish migrants had no intention of leaving.

Now Britain is pondering its new life with a permanent Polish minority. Unlike other migrant groups, the Poles spread out across Britain, often ignoring the allure and

1 **footloose** prepared to move regularly
3 **exodus** *(biblical)* situation in which many people leave a place at the same time
**reckoning** Schätzung
4 **play host to sb.** jdn. zu Gast haben
**expat** *(infml)* person who lives outside his/her home country
**equivalent to sth.** [ɪ'kwɪvələnt] of the same value as sth.
6 **a mere** only
7 **issue sth.** give out sth.
8 **stir controversy about sth.** ['kɒntrəvɜːsi] make people argue about sth.
12 **current** aktuell
18 **take the bait** anbeißen; den Köder (= *bait*) schlucken
**stay put** *(infml)* stay where you are
25 **face sth.** be confronted with sth.
**double-digit** ['dɪdʒɪt] zweistellig
27 **prospect** ['prɒspekt] Aussicht
29 **slash sth.** etwas drastisch reduzieren
34 **ponder sth.** think about sth. carefully
36 **allure** [ə'lʊə] Verlockung

expense of the big cities. Polish can be heard in the shipyards of north-eastern England, the raspberry fields of Scotland and the meatpacking plants of western Wales. Some areas of Britain now display road signs in English and Polish. At least one police force gives officers prompt cards with Polish translations of vital phrases. In Ireland, Polish priests have restocked the ranks of the Roman Catholic clergy, and Polish barmen staff the pubs in rural areas. The smartest are already climbing the employment ladder. 'At first people were just grabbing any job they could get,' says Bartek Wasiewski, a London shipping agent who arrived in 2004. Now some who had started out on construction sites have moved into financial jobs or set up their own companies.

With greater affluence comes attention. The largest British supermarket chain, Tesco, now stocks a range of Polish food. The giant Borders bookshop chain offers more than 100 titles in Polish. British pubs sell Polish lager on tap. The Polish-language media include a daily, four weekly magazines and five radio stations. This month a Polish university plans to open a London branch.

From: 'Warsaw on the Thames', *Newsweek*, 8 October 2007

38 **raspberry** [*BE:* 'rɑːzbəri; *AE:* 'ræzberi] Himbeere
**plant** *here:* factory
40 **prompt cards** cards with key words
**vital** ['vaɪtl] very important
41 **restock the ranks of the Roman Catholic clergy** ['klɜːdʒi] fill the posts of Catholic priests
47 **range** Auswahl
48 **lager** ['lɑːgə] type of beer
**on tap** vom Fass
49 **daily** *(n)* daily newspaper

## 1 Comprehension

In your group, exchange the information you concentrated on while reading the text. Take notes while the others are speaking.

## 2 Word power

In your group, re-read one third of the text each (ll. 1–17; ll. 18–33; ll. 34–50). Identify and write down new words and expressions to do with migration. Make sure you include collocations and not just individual words. Look up any item whose meaning you are unsure of and note down the definition. Exchange lists and add the items to your table/list from p. 67, **2**.

▸ SF 8 Using a Dictionary (p. 136)

## 3 Giving an oral summary

**a** Compare your notes from **1** and **2**. In your group, write down the key facts. Make sure you cover the aspects mentioned in the introduction at the top of p. 68 as well as the following questions:

- When did Polish immigration to the British Isles start?
- Where do Polish immigrants work?

(Scan the text again for the answers if necessary.)

▸ SF 32 Writing an Outline (p. 153)
▸ SF 27 Scanning (p. 150)

**b** Choose one person to give an oral summary to the rest of the class on the basis of your outline of the key facts, using as much of your thematic vocabulary as possible. The rest of the class should listen carefully and comment on how well you covered all of the questions.

## 4 EXTRA Doing research

Research the migrant situation in a European country of your choice.

▸ SF 13 Doing Research (p. 141)
▸ SF 14 Doing a Project (p. 143)

## A2 From Kiev to Kent Marina Lewycka

► SF 2 Brainstorming (p. 133)

*Have you ever been away from home for more than three weeks, or considered going abroad as an exchange student? Imagine the situation, and brainstorm with a partner what kind of feelings you and your parents would have about your leaving and your reception abroad. Then read this *novel extract about a Ukrainian girl leaving home to go strawberry-picking in England.*

'Irina, my baby, you can still change your mind! You don't have to go!'
Mother was wailing and dabbing at her pinky eyes with a tissue, causing an embarrassing scene at Kiev bus station.

'Mother, please! I'm not a baby!'

You expect your mother to cry at a moment like this. But when my craggy old Pappa turned up too, his shirt all crumpled and his silver hair sticking up like an old-age porcupine, OK, I admit it rattled me. I hadn't expected him to come to see me off.

'Irina, little one, take care.'

'*Shcho ti*, Pappa. What's all this about? Do you think I'm not coming back?'

'Just take care, my little one.' Sniffle. Sigh.

'I'm not little, Pappa. I'm nineteen. Do you think I can't look after myself?'

'Ah, my little pigeon.' Sigh. Sniffle. Then Mother started up again. Then – I couldn't help myself – I started up too, sighing and sniffling and dabbing my eyes, until the coach driver told us to get a move on, and Mother shoved a bag of bread and salami and a poppy-seed cake into my hands, and we were off. From Kiev to Kent in forty-two hours.

OK, I admit, forty-two hours on a coach is not amusing. By the time we reached Lviv, the bread and salami were all gone. In Poland, I noticed that my ankles were starting to swell. When we stopped for fuel somewhere in Germany I stuffed the last crumbs of the poppy-seed cake into my mouth and washed it down with nasty metallic-tasting water from a tap that was marked not for drinking. In Belgium my period started, but I didn't notice until the dark stain of blood seeped through my jeans into the seat. In France I lost all sensation in my feet. On the ferry to Dover I found a toilet and cleaned myself up. Looking into the cloudy mirror above the washbasin I hardly recognized the wan dark-eyed face that stared back at me – was that me, that scruffy straggle-haired girl with bags under her eyes? I walked about to restore the circulation in my legs, and standing on the deck at dawn I watched the white cliffs of England materialize in the pale watery light, beautiful, mysterious, the land of my dreams.

**⚠ Trouble spot**
**expect sb. to do sth.** = erwarten, dass jemand etwas tut

2 **wail** cry loudly
**dab at sth.** etwas (ab)tupfen
5 **craggy** rough
7 **porcupine** ['pɔːkjupaɪn] Stachelschwein
**rattle sb.** *(infml)* make sb. nervous
12 **pigeon** ['pɪdʒɪn] Taube
14 **shove sth.** [ʃʌv] push sth.
18 **ankle** joint ('Gelenk') connecting foot and leg
21 **tap** Wasserhahn
25 **wan** [*BE:* wɒn; *AE:* wɑːn] pale
26 **scruffy** dirty, untidy
**straggle-haired** with hair that has not been combed or brushed
27 **dawn** first light of day

At Dover I was met off the boat by Vulk, waving a bit of card with my name on it – Irina Blazkho. Typical – he'd got the spelling wrong. He was the type Mother would describe as a person of minimum culture, wearing a horrible black fake-leather jacket, like a comic-strip gangster – what a *koshmar!* – it creaked as he walked. All he needed was a gun.

He greeted me with a grunt. 'Hrr. You heff passport? Peppers?'

His voice was deep and sludgy, with a nasty whiff of cigarette smoke and tooth decay.

This gangster-type should brush his teeth. I fumbled in my bag, and before I could say anything he grabbed my passport and Seasonal Agricultural Worker papers and stowed them in the breast pocket of his *koshmar* jacket.

'I keep for you. Is many bed people in England. Can stealing from you.'

He patted the pocket, and winked. I could see straightaway that there was no point in arguing with a person of this type, so I hoisted my bag onto my shoulder and followed him across the car park to a huge shiny black vehicle that looked like a cross between a tank and a ZIL, with darkened windows and gleaming chrome bars at the front – a typical mafia-machine. [...]

33 **koshmar** *(Ukrainian)* Albtraum
**creak** knarzen
36 **sludgy** muddy
**tooth decay** [dɪ'keɪ] Karies
39 **Seasonal Agricultural Worker** person working on a farm for a season
43 **hoist sth.** lift sth. heavy
45 **tank** Panzer
**ZIL** Russian make of car
**gleam** *(v)* shine

**Trouble spot**
**wink** = zwinkern, blinzeln
winken = **wave**

► LP 28 False Friends (p. 121)

I didn't take in the scenery that flashed past through the black-tinted glass – I was too tired – but my body registered every twist in the lane, and the sudden jerks and jolts when he braked and turned. This gangster-type needs some driving lessons.

He had some potato chips wrapped in a paper bundle on the passenger seat beside him, and every now and then he would plunge his left fist in, grab a handful of chips and cram them into his mouth. Grab. Cram. Chomp.

Grab. Cram. Chomp. Not very refined. The chips smelt fantastic, though. The smell of the cigar, the lurching motion as he steered with one hand and stuffed his mouth with the other, the low dragging pain from my period – it was all making me feel queasy and hungry at the same time. In the end, hunger won out. I wondered what language this gangster-type would talk. Byelorussian? He looked too dark for a Belarus. Ukrainian? He didn't look Ukrainian. Maybe from somewhere out east? Chechnya? Georgia? What do Georgians look like? The Balkans? Taking a guess, I asked in Russian, 'Please, Mister Vulk, may I have something to eat?'

He looked up. Our eyes met in the rear-view mirror. He had real gangster-type eyes – poisonous black berries in eyebrows as straggly as an overgrown hedge. He studied me in that offensive way, sliding his eyes all over me.

'Little flovver vants eating?' He spoke in English, though he must have understood my Russian. Probably he came from one of those newly independent nations of the former Soviet Union where everyone can speak Russian but nobody does. OK, so he wanted to talk English? I'd show him.

**Trouble spot**
**potato chips** *(BE)*
= **French fries** *(AE)*
= Pommes frites
**potato crisps** *(BE)*
= **potato chips** *(AE)*
= Kartoffelchips

► LP 28 False Friends (p. 121)

56 **queasy** sick
57 **Byelorussian** [bi,eləʊ'rʌʃən] *(also:* **Belo-**) the language of Belarus ('Weißrussland')
59 **Chechnya** ['tʃetʃniə] republic in southern Russia
**Georgia** ['dʒɔ:dʒə] former Soviet republic, now independent
62 **hedge** Hecke

► LP 6 Simple Past, Past Progressive and Past Perfect (p. 108)

68 **oblige sb.** [ə'blaɪdʒ] *(fml)* do sb. a favour
**inconvenience sb.** [ˌɪnkən'viːniəns] cause trouble for sb.
69 **appreciate sth.** [ə'priːʃieɪt] *here:* be happy to get sth.
78 **seam** Naht
79 **dandruff** (Haar-)Schuppen
84 **appalling** [ə'pɔːlɪŋ] awful
86 **crook** *(infml)* criminal

'Yes indeed, Mister Vulk. If you could oblige me, if it does not inconvenience you, I would appreciate something to eat.'

'No problema, little flovver!'

He helped himself to one more mouthful of chips – grab, cram, chomp – then scrunched up the remnants in the oily paper and passed them over the back of the seat. [...]

'Thank you,' I said politely, for rudeness is a sign of minimum culture.

'No problema. No problema.' He waved his fist about as if to show how generous he was. 'Food for eat in transit. All vill be add to your living expense.'

Living expense? I didn't need any more nasty surprises. I studied his back, the creaky stretched-at-the-seams jacket, the ragged ponytail, the thick yellowish neck, the flecks of dandruff on the fake-leather collar. I was starting to feel queasy again.

'What is this, expense?'

'Expense. Expense. Foods. Transports. Accommodations.' He took both hands off the steering wheel and waved them in the air. 'Life in vest is too much expensive, little flovver. Who you think vill be pay for all such luxury?'

Although his English was appalling, those words came rolling out like a prepared speech. 'You think this vill be providing all for free?'

So Mother had been right. 'Anybody can see this agency is run by crooks. Anybody but you, Irina.'

From: Marina Lewycka, *Two Caravans*, 2007

### 1 Comprehension

**a** What feelings does Irina show in the account of her journey from Kiev to Kent? Write them down chronologically and compare them with the feelings you brainstormed before reading. Which of Irina's feelings surprised you most?

**b** What is Vulk's job? Explain.

**c** 'Translate' what Vulk says into correct English. It might help to read aloud what he says and to consider the context.
*l. 35: 'You heff passport? Peppers?' – Do you have a passport? Papers?*

### 2 Looking at the *characters

▸ SF 8 Using a Dictionary (p. 136)

▸ SF 38 Writing a Characterization (p. 156)

▸ SF 31 The Stages of Writing (p. 152)

▸ LP 14 Conditional Sentences: Type II (p. 112)

**a** Using a bilingual dictionary, write down as many adjectives as possible to describe Vulk's appearance and behaviour. Compare your list with that of a partner, and agree on the five to seven most suitable adjectives.

**b** On the basis of your 'translation' (**1c**) and your list of adjectives (**2a**), write a *characterization of Vulk.

**c** Look at Irina's use of English in ll. 68 ff. Explain what she wants to say, how she says it (*register), and why she does it this way.

**d** **EXTRA** Discuss the topic 'Irina: a naive dreamer or a brave young adult?' in 250–300 words.

### 3 What would you do?

**a** Can you imagine going abroad to earn money? Which country would you go to? What kind of work could you imagine doing?

**b** Apart from financially, how else could you profit from this experience? Discuss in class.

### 4 Creative writing

Imagine you are Irina and have just arrived in England. Write a *letter to your mother, telling her of your experiences and your feelings.

## A3 The Pendulum Effect

Gareth Jones and Kuba Jaworowski

*Modern-day migration can turn out to be quite short-lived. Before reading this article from a British newspaper, list reasons why some migrants might want to return home.*

Four years after Polish graphic designer Chris Rychter headed to Britain to find work, he and his wife have returned home to Warsaw. Part of a swelling tide of migration back east, they are having a house built in a suburb of the Polish capital.

'It took me just three days to find a job back in Warsaw,' Mr Rychter, 27, said. 'We never saw Britain as home. We went for the adventure and to get some professional experience.'

Their return highlights strong economic growth in the new European Union member states and an accelerating slowdown in Britain – and also how quickly a pragmatic, younger European generation has adapted to working in the 21st-century globalized economy.

Mr Rychter's wife, Sabina, has taken her job with a British credit insurance company back to Poland with her.

'You could say I am telecommuting,' she said. 'In today's world, with computers and mobile phones, my presence in head office is not required as before. I can sit here in Warsaw and have the flexibility to do my job.'

Helped by cheap travel as flights between Warsaw and London grew almost tenfold after Poland joined the EU in 2004, the Rychters show how Europe has shrunk and that, contrary to the popular view, migrant flows are not all one-way.

Economists now talk of a turnstile, or pendulum, effect, with people moving between countries after quite short stints in search of better conditions.

About half the one million people from eastern Europe who moved to Britain after EU enlargement in 2004 have already returned home, according to the Institute for Public Policy Research. And work applications from those eight new states were down 13 per cent in the first quarter of this year, compared with 2007.

For many eastern European migrants, recent currency trends favour a return, and Poland's government wants people back to help plug labour gaps.

From: 'Migration Tide Turns as East Europeans Head Back Home', *The Scotsman*, 17 June 2008

**pendulum** ['pendjələm] Pendel
2 **swelling tide** increasing number
8 **accelerate** [ək'seləreɪt] get quicker
9 **pragmatic** thinking of the practical consequences

**⚠ Trouble spot**
**adapt to doing**
Not: ~~adapt to do~~

► LP 20 Gerund after Prepositions (p. 115)

11 **credit insurance** [ɪn'ʃʊərəns] Kreditversicherung
17 **shrink, shrunk, shrunk** become smaller
19 **turnstile** Drehkreuz
20 **stint** *here:* period of time spent working somewhere
26 **plug sth.** fill a hole with sth.
**gap** space or hole in sth.

► SF 29 Reading Non-Fiction (p. 151)

### 1 Comprehension

**a** Why are a lot of Polish workers going back home? Look at the list of reasons you made before reading and compare it with the reasons given in the article.

**b** Collect the information given about the Rychters. Then write a paragraph explaining why they could be called typical modern migrants.

### 2 Talking about *imagery

**a** The title contains the image of a pendulum. Describe what this makes you think of and explain what it means in the context of modern migration.

**b** The writer makes use of more images, e.g. 'a swelling tide of migration' (l. 2), 'Europe has shrunk' (l. 17), 'migrant flows' (l. 18), 'plug labour gaps' (l. 26). Choose one of these images and write down what you think it illustrates in this context.

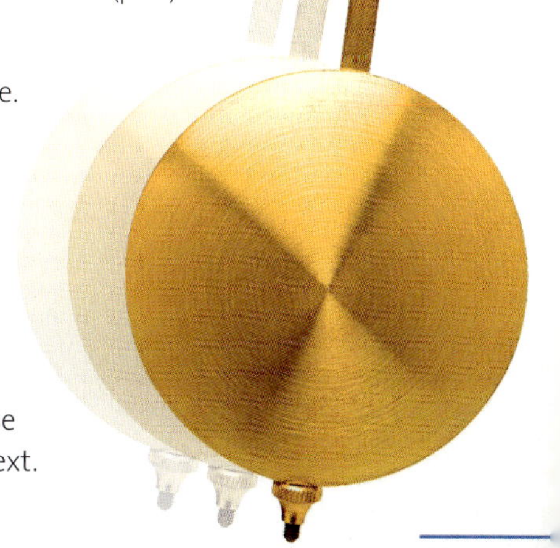

# Migrants as Minority Groups

## B1 'It's Not All Take, Take, Take' CD I.17–18

- *an issue fraught with tension*
- *place strain on sth.*
- *community cohesion*
- *offset sth.*
- *turnover*
- *application*
- *NHS*
- *feeding allowance*
- *PhD*

*You are going to hear a radio report in which three different views on immigration are presented: that of Andrew Green from Migration Watch, a non-political organization concerned about the scale of migration to the UK; that of Prof. Caroline Whitehead from the London School of Economics; and that of Stella Njaka from Brent Women's Advisory Centre, an institution which works with migrants. Before you listen to the report, make sure you know the meaning and pronunciation of the words and phrases on the left.*

▸ SF 19 Listening for Gist (p. 146)
▸ SF 20 Listening for Detail (p. 146)

**1 Looking at both sides**

a Listen to the first part of the report. What immigration issues are mentioned?

b Listen again with a partner and take notes. One of you focuses on Andrew Green and listens out for problems regarding the scale of immigration in the UK. The other focuses on Caroline Whitehead and listens out for the types of migrants and migration mentioned.

c Share your information with your partner. What is the general attitude of these two experts towards immigration? ▪ **Language help**

d **Role-play:** Discuss the pros and cons of immigration as if you were Caroline Whitehead and Andrew Green. Use the arguments brought up by the two experts in the interview as well as additional arguments of your own. Prepare the discussion by adding to your notes.

### Language help

- … has a positive/negative view of immigration.
- … is in favour of / welcomes / recognizes the benefits of immigration.
- … is clearly against …
- … warns of the problems/dangers immigration can bring.
- … has no opinion on / is indifferent to the immigration situation.

**2 The immigrants' perspective**

a Listen to the second part of the report. What do the two immigrant women, Stella Njaka and her client Fatima, say about the problems immigrants face? Exchange ideas with your partner.

b At the end of the report, Stella Njaka is asked about a possible solution. Whose job does she think it is to solve the problems of illegal immigration?

▸ LP 39 Making Comparisons (p. 131)

**3 Comparing the two parts of the interview**

Compare the issues mentioned in each part of the report and explain the difference in effect between the two parts.

**4 Classroom discussion: Can people be illegal?**

Who or what is legal or illegal? Although there is much talk of 'illegal immigrants', can a person really be considered 'illegal'? Discuss this in class. Start by looking at the *cartoon: Explain who the people are and where and when the scene is taking place.

► SF 24 Taking Part in a Classroom Discussion (p. 149)

**5 Talking about sensitive issues**

**a** Have you ever been in a situation in which you found it difficult or impossible to react properly because the topic being discussed was so sensitive? Describe the situation to your partner and try to remember what was said. Discuss whether your reaction was right and helpful. Then try to think of other, similar situations.

**b** Imagine the following situations:

1 A friend's father has lost his job.
2 The residence permit of your friend's parents isn't going to be renewed.
3 A classmate's mother has died.
4 A classmate is too poor to go to the cinema, but makes excuses.

With a partner, write down possible reactions for both sides. Try to be as polite and diplomatic as possible. ▪ **Language help**

**c** In class, discuss the difficulties you had reacting to these situations and compare different solutions. Make changes to your notes if necessary.

**d** **Role-play:** With your partner, act out one of the four situations. Make sure both of you join in the conversation.

**⚠ Trouble spot**

**sensitive** ['sensətɪv] = heikel; sensibel
**sensible** ['sensəbl] = vernünftig

► LP 28 False Friends (p. 121)

**Language help**

- I'm so/very sorry to hear that.
- Can I ask what happened?
- Do you want to talk about it?
- That's a shame / too bad.
- How are you / is your family coping with that / the news?
- It's nice of you to ask.
- If you really want to help, ...
- Could you do sth. for me / do me a favour?
- It's an awkward situation for me.
- It's a bit embarrassing for me to talk / go into detail about ...

## B2 The Changing Face of Ireland DVD 11–12

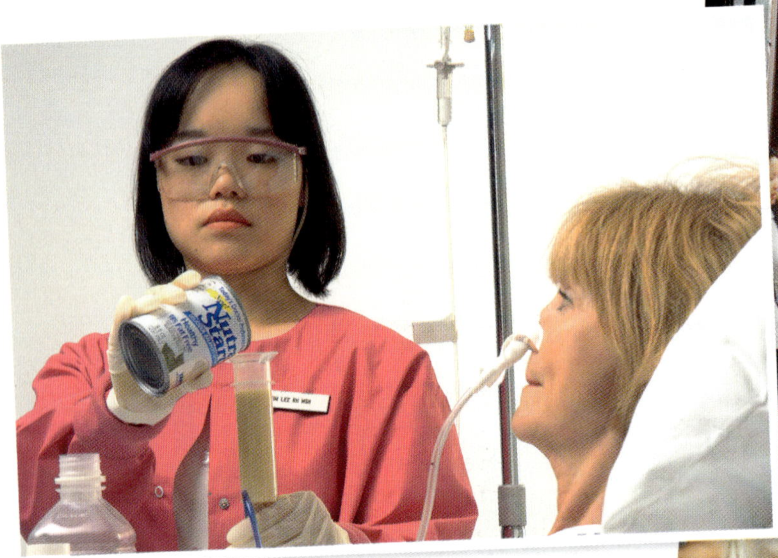

Due to a lack of nurses in Ireland, many Irish hospitals are now recruiting staff from abroad

Moore Street in central Dublin

▸ SF 21 Viewing a Film (p. 147)

*You are going to watch a report which deals with various aspects of immigration and the challenges Ireland faces. Before you watch, make sure you know the meaning and pronunciation of the words and phrases on the left.*

- *embarkation*
- *in short supply* ▪ *recruit*
- *tiger economy*
- *emerge* ▪ *approach sb.*
- *come to terms with sth.*
- *awareness*
- *benefit (n)* ▪ *diversity*
- *work permit*

### 1 Comprehension and analysis (part 1)

**a** Watch the first part of the report. Explain what the main focus is.

**b** Work with a partner. Take turns telling each other what images you remember.

**c** Prepare a viewing log with who?, what?, and how? (for the film techniques used such as camera angles, images, voice-over and sound). Watch the report again and fill in the viewing log for the person presenting the ballad, the reporter, the nurse and the politician. Discuss your findings with a partner.

**d** Explain what is referred to as a 'new issue' and what the politician thinks might turn up as a side effect.

### 2 Comprehension (part 2)

**a** Watch the second part of the report. Describe what schools are doing to 'broaden minds'.

**b** Describe how the female student might be feeling in the mock interview and explain your answer. ▪ **Language help**

**c** State what long-term goals these initiatives to 'broaden minds' are aiming at.

#### Language help

- She might feel uncomfortable/insecure/awkward/... because ...
- Maybe she feels self-confident/ courageous/... because ...

### 3 Evaluating a report

**a** The report uses different film techniques. With a partner, discuss why the producers may have used the same music at the beginning and at the end of the report, and what emotions they might want to create with the images of the sea.

**b** What do you think: Can schools help to promote integration? In class, discuss the approach shown in the film.

▸ SF 24 Taking Part in a Classroom Discussion (p. 149)

# The Downside of Migration

► The door shuts. I wait for the screams ...

► They've no case, says Ms Nigeria.

► You have no right to speak like that, she says.

► That's the project ... It's about stereotyping.

► I'm wearing a hoodie. I must be guilty.

► We were doing a project, I say.

## C1 Black Hoodie Roddy Doyle

*In the *short story 'Black Hoodie', set in modern-day Dublin, three students do a school project on stereotypes. As part of their experiment, the *narrator himself, 'Ms Nigeria' (a girl from Nigeria), and 'not-Superman's brother' (who is in a wheelchair) steal goods from shops, but give them back again so that shop managers will know how best to protect themselves against shoplifters. Only once do the students keep some stolen sweets. They are arrested shortly after.*

**hoodie** *(BE, infml)* **1.** hooded sweatshirt ('Kapuzenjacke'); **2.** (esp. criminal) young person wearing a hoodie

### 1 Doing a text jigsaw

**a** Work in pairs. Your teacher will give each pair one of six different text snippets from the story. Make a table with columns for the five W's (who?, what?, when?, where?, why?). Read your snippet and fill in the table. Then compare notes with your partner and write down questions that might be answered in the other snippets.

**b** Form groups of six so that each text snippet is represented. Tell each other the most important information in your snippet, and ask your questions.

**c** Together, work out the chronology of the snippets, based on your understanding of what happens. ▪ **Language help**

**d** What do you think happens next in the story? What makes such an ending likely? Exchange ideas and report to the class. ▪ **Language help**

**Language help**

- My part comes before/after your part because ...
- But the next part says ...
- Shouldn't we learn something about ... before ...?
- It makes sense / doesn't make sense to describe ... before ...

- ... is probably going to ...
- There will be ...
- There isn't likely to be ... / ... isn't likely to ...
- I'm sure that ...
- In the next few moments ...
- I believe that ... because ...
- I don't agree because if ..., then ...

### 2 Talking about the *characters

**a** Look again at your text snippet and mark those passages that show you the narrator's feelings either directly (from what you're told) or indirectly (through his behaviour).

**b** Compare your findings in your group. Which of the adjectives on the right best describe the narrator? Use a dictionary where necessary.

**c** Now decide which adjectives best describe Ms Nigeria and the police detectives involved. Using different colours, mark the relevant passages in your group's snippets. Discuss your decisions in your group.

*▪ angry ▪ anxious ▪ arrogant ▪ brave ▪ calm ▪ cowardly ▪ disciplined ▪ impolite ▪ innocent ▪ insecure ▪ naive ▪ protective ▪ proud ▪ racist ▪ rude ▪ self-assured ▪ self-conscious ▪ sensible ▪ silly ▪ strong*

► SF 8 Using a Dictionary (p. 136)

## 3 Understanding and discussing the project

**a** In his interview with the police detective, the narrator explains the school project and how it works. Make sure you understand this by summing up the different steps of the project in class.

**b** Discuss the project with a partner. What stereotypes are the young people trying to uncover and change?

**c** With your partner, focus on the character of Ms Nigeria and discuss why such 'obvious' immigrants are so often the target of prejudice.

**stereotype** /'steriətaɪp/ *noun*
a fixed idea or image that many people have of a particular type of person or thing, but which is often not true in reality: ***cultural / gender / racial stereotypes*** ◊ *He doesn't conform to the usual stereotype of the businessman with a dark suit and briefcase.*
**prejudice** /'predʒudɪs/ *noun*
an unreasonable dislike of or preference for a person, group, custom, etc., especially when it is based on their race, religion, sex, etc.: *a victim of* ***racial prejudice*** ◊ *Their decision was based on ignorance and prejudice.* ◊ *There is little prejudice against workers from other EU states.* ◊ *I must admit to a prejudice in favour of British universities.*

From: *Oxford Advanced Learner's Dictionary*, 2005

## 4 Language and *style

**a** The story is written as if the first-person narrator was talking to us, the readers. In groups of three, rewrite lines 1–5 in a more neutral way without changing the basic communication pattern. Begin like this:
*Have you ever seen a person in a wheelchair wearing handcuffs behind his back? They could have just locked him ...*

**b** Which expressions did you find most necessary to change?

**c** Discuss the effect of the *register change in class.

## 5 EXTRA Writing for a newspaper

You are a reporter for the local paper and want to write a short article on the arrest of the young people in the story. Base your article on the information given in the extract, pretending you have interviewed the narrator. Speculate on how the story ends. Use mainly indirect speech in your article, but do not report everything that was said.
Your report could start like this:

*There was an unusual situation at the local police station yesterday when four youngsters, one of them in a wheelchair, were arrested for shoplifting in a local department store. The security people were obviously convinced that an African girl in the company of a teenager wearing a hooded sweatshirt had to be guilty of the crime. The young 'hoodie' claims that the plain-clothes detective who interviewed him ordered him to ...*

► LP 11–12 Indirect Speech (p. 111)
► LP 30 Verbs of reporting (p. 122)

## C2 It's a Free World DVD 13–14

▸ SF 21 Viewing a Film (p. 147)

*The film* It's a Free World *is about Angie, a woman in her thirties, who sets up a job placement agency that gives migrant workers temporary jobs.*

**1 Viewing two scenes of a film**

**a** Prepare a viewing log with the five W's. Watch scene 1: what happens in the scene? Fill in the viewing log and sum up the action in two sentences.

**b** In class, collect and discuss what you learned about the situation in which the migrants find themselves in the scene. Refer to the entries in your viewing log and analyse how the film shows the feelings of the people involved.

**c** Watch scene 2. One half of the class concentrates on details of the Iranian family's situation. The other half concentrates on Angie's behaviour and her conflict with Rose. Continue your viewing logs.

**d** Watch the scene again and pay attention to the camerawork, lighting, facial expressions and tone of voice. How do they influence the interpretation of the scene? Complete your viewing log and exchange your findings with a partner.

**2 Thinking about the two scenes**

**a** In class, collect and describe the different types of conflict shown in the extracts.

**b** Individually, write a paragraph about one image or series of images in the two scenes that moved and impressed you most, and explain why.

**3 Mediation: Writing subtitles**

Watch scene 2 again and concentrate on the last part, in which Rose and Angie argue about helping the Iranian family. Read the script your teacher will give you and write (short) German subtitles for this dialogue.

▸ SF 15 Mediating (p. 144)

**4 EXTRA Comparing texts**

In the course of this chapter, you have come across migrants in different situations. Choose one of the texts you have dealt with and compare the situation of the migrants in this text with the information given in the film extracts.

*Angie's new job, deciding who will get work for the day, isn't easy*

# Writing an Essay

► SF 39 Writing an Essay (p. 157)
► SF 33 Structuring a Text (p. 153)
► SF 34 Linking Ideas (p. 154)

*In this chapter task, you will write an argumentative essay. Writing argumentative essays means looking at different sides of an issue in a fair manner before coming to a conclusion: your personal opinion. Balancing arguments before forming your own opinion is an essential skill in communication – which is why essay-writing is part of most English exam papers.*

► SF 31 The Stages of Writing (p. 152)

## 1 Preparing your essay

**a** Choose one of the topics below as a basis for your essay and brainstorm the topic you have chosen; do some research if necessary. Make one list with the arguments in favour of your topic and one with the arguments against it.
1 'German should be the only language spoken at school'
2 'You can learn a lot from minority groups'
3 'Multiculturalism is the aim'
4 'An annual limit on immigration numbers is necessary'

**b** Based on the information and arguments you have collected, form your own opinion.

► SF 32 Writing an Outline (p. 153)

## 2 Writing a first draft

**a** Write an outline. Organize your ideas and decide whether you want to discuss all arguments in favour first, then all arguments against, or whether you want to discuss just one argument in favour followed directly by one against, and so on. End with the most convincing argument, making sure it supports your opinion.

**b** Write a first draft. Don't worry about grammar or spelling. Just make sure you include the most important arguments from your outline.

### Language help

- I would like to discuss ...
- I intend to show that / present arguments for and against ...
- In the following I will look at the question of whether ...

- On the one hand, ... On the other hand, ...
- For example/instance ...
- In addition / Furthermore, ...
- For this reason ...

- In summary, ...
- In conclusion, ...
- To sum up, ...
- To conclude, ...

## 3 Preparing a final draft

**a** Before rewriting your first draft, consider the following points:
- Make sure that your first sentence states your intention in a way that catches the reader's attention.
- Support your arguments with examples. Use suitable connectors and participle constructions to link ideas.
- Sum up your opinion and arguments in a concluding sentence.
- **Language help**

**b** Go through the essay on p. 81. With a partner, discuss whether the different elements mentioned in **a** are used effectively.

► LP 17–18 Participle Constructions (p. 114)

## 4 Using participle constructions to link sentences

**a** Go back to Text A1 on p. 68 and look at the *-ing* constructions in lines 15, 21, 25 and 36. With a partner, rewrite each of the sentences without the present participle.

**b** Use *-ing* forms in place of the underlined verb forms in the essay on p. 81 to link sentences and make them more readable.

► SF 11 Keeping a Portfolio (p. 138)

## 5 Writing the final draft

Consider all of the above tips on contents and form again. Then rewrite your essay. Check your text for grammar, spelling and vocabulary. Put the essay in your portfolio.

**Immigration isn't the problem – integration is**

In the following, I would like to discuss the importance of integration for the immigration process.

We are often informed by the press of the problems that immigration causes in the host society. Some people argue, however, that immigration itself does not lie at the root of the problem. They claim that the next step after immigration, i.e. integration (or rather, non-integration), is the real source of difficulty.

On the one hand, the success of any integration depends on the immigrants' willingness to integrate into society. If we take the Turkish community in Germany as an example, we get a better understanding of the difficulties associated with non-integration. Although almost half of the Turkish migrants living in Germany were born there, only 32 per cent own a German passport. Having German citizenship seems to have a great effect on successful integration, though: almost twice as many Turkish people with a German passport leave school with a qualification as those with a Turkish passport. This proves that there is a close relationship between the willingness to integrate into society and successful integration. However, there are also many (seldom-heard) success stories of integration. This suggests that it isn't always a problem. Many immigrants from other countries in the EU, for example, have made a home for themselves in Germany. They have integrated so well into society that 61 per cent of all married immigrants are married to German citizens. Indeed, more immigrants from these countries than native Germans themselves go on to sit their A levels.

On the other hand, integration depends just as much on the local community's attitude towards immigration as it does on the immigrants' willingness to integrate. Many people welcome the diversity of immigration, while others are strictly against it. They fear, for instance, that too many foreigners might mean fewer job prospects for themselves or their children. This often leads to racial violence, which, in turn, can upset the integration process.

To sum up, there is much evidence to support the fact that integration is the key to successful immigration. And that successful integration is of extreme importance for the functioning of any society is as obvious as the negative side effects of unsuccessful integration.

Webcode: STAR322305-82

# 5 A Good Read

*This chapter introduces you to different novels and helps you to judge whether or not you would like to read them.*

## 1 Speculating

**a** Look at the covers and titles of the seven *novels for young-adult readers. Which book do you find most interesting? Why? Take a vote in class.

**b** Based on the book covers and titles, speculate on what each book might be about. Discuss your ideas with a partner.

## 2 What makes for a good read?

**a** Write down four or five features which make for a good read. ▪ **Language help**

**b** Share your ideas with a partner. Agree on the four most important features, then name a book that, for you, fulfils these requirements.

### Language help

- A good book has to be exciting / romantic / scary / realistic / full of suspense / informative / believable / ...
- It has to challenge me / grab my attention / make me laugh/cry/...

3

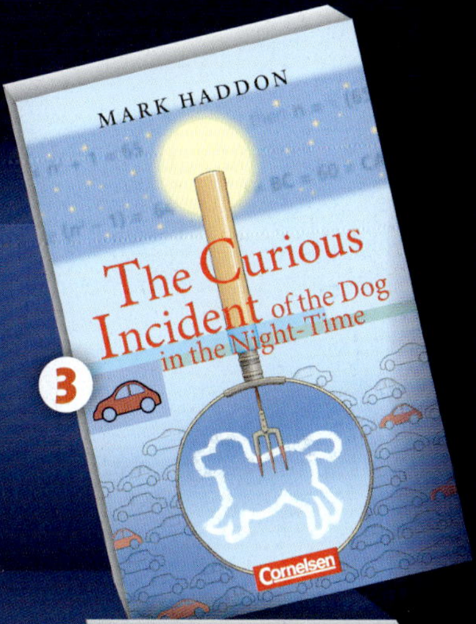


7

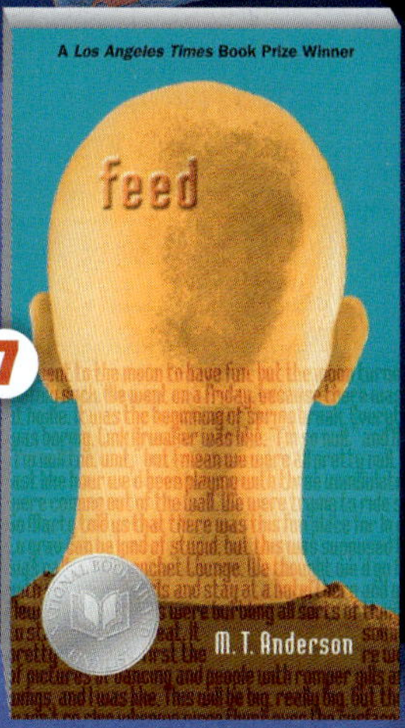


**A**

Reasons to read my book:
- You can learn all sorts of secrets about me
- You can have lots of laughs
- You might even cry a bit, too
- PLUS, you get to find out a lot more about BOYS!

**B**

Will is thirty-six but acts like a teenager. He meets Marcus, the oldest twelve-year-old in the world. Perhaps if Will can teach Marcus how to be a kid, Marcus can help Will grow up.

**C**

'We went to the moon to have fun, but the moon turned out to completely suck.'
So says Titus, a teenager whose ability to read, write, and even think for himself has been almost completely obliterated by his 'feed', a transmitter implanted directly into his brain.

**D**

Fifteen-year-old Christopher has a photographic memory. He understands maths. He understands science. What he can't understand are other human beings. When he finds his neighbour's dog lying dead on the lawn, he decides to write a murder mystery about it.

**E**

Jenna Abbott separates her life into two categories. Before the wreck, she was leading a normal life with her mom in suburban New York. After ...

**F**

Junior is picked on by everyone but his best friend. Determined to get a good education, Junior leaves the rez to attend an all-white school in the neighboring farm town where the only other Indian is the school mascot.

**sth. sucks** *(slang)* sth. is very bad
**obliterate sth.** remove sth., destroy sth.
**lawn** area of short grass in a garden
**pick on sb.** tease sb., bully sb.
**determined to do sth.** [dɪˈtɜːmɪnd] entschlossen, etwas zu tun
**rez (reservation)** *here:* area of land in the USA kept for Native Americans to live in
**mascot** [ˈmæskɒt] Maskottchen

## 3 Reading blurbs

▸ LP 22 Articles (p. 116)

**a** Read the six extracts from the blurbs (i.e. the short descriptions) on the backs of the books and match the texts to the covers. There is one more cover than you need.

**b** EXTRA Speculate what the novel without a blurb could be about. Write a short blurb that would make your classmates want to read the book.

**c** Look at **1a** again. Do you still find the same book the most interesting, or have you changed your mind after reading the blurbs? Why (not)?

# The World of Books

The worldwide success story of the book began in 1439 with the invention of the printing press by Johannes Gutenberg, which made books available to a larger audience. Our problem today, though, is how to keep up an interest in reading. In 1997, a survey on the reading habits of young adults revealed that in Great Britain 35 % of 16- to 25- year-olds read regularly in their free time. By 2001 the figures had risen to almost 40 %. Many parents, teachers, librarians and booksellers like to think that it was the arrival of the teenage wizard Harry Potter that really inspired kids to read for pleasure.

Reading habits change with age, and those teenagers who are not put off by the set books at school quickly move on from children's literature to young-adult fiction (YA for short) and adult fiction. But regardless of age, it is often the same genres that appeal to readers, namely science fiction, horror, love stories, murder mysteries, biographies, and of course fantasy novels like *Harry Potter*.

When the final volume of the *Harry Potter* series was published in 2007, booksellers wondered whether another book could achieve sales similar to these bestsellers. But they needn't have worried: Stephenie Meyer's *Twilight* saga about the love between a girl and a vampire has kept a large readership in suspense despite its dreary setting – Forks, Washington, is the rainiest place in the USA. And the film adaptation of *Twilight* (released in 2008) was not only an immediate success, but in turn raised the sales of the book.

At the Frankfurt Book Fair in 2008, ebooks were one of the main talking points due to their many (and partly future) advantages: they will make it easier for unknown authors to get published, they are searchable and better for the environment as no transport costs arise, and the pollution connected, for example, with printing and transporting books is avoided. Moreover, ebook readers can easily contain a small library. Some day they may even be cheaper than printed books because of the paper saved. Still some people fear that ebooks will stop readers from buying printed books. The question remains open – but will avid readers really enjoy looking at a screen for hours as much as they previously enjoyed reading a book and turning its pages?

⚠ **Trouble spot**
reader = 1. Leser/in
2. Lesebuch
3. Lesegerät

### 1 Word power

Collect the words and phrases highlighted in the text above in a table or a mind map, starting with 'The World of Books' as your topic phrase and the categories *books*, *readers*, *the book trade* as branches. Add more words you already know from other sources. Remember to add new words and phrases as you go through this chapter. Make sure you include collocations.

▸ SF 1 Mind Mapping (p. 132)

▸ LP 26 Collocations (p. 120)

### 2 Activating your vocabulary

Complete the sentences below using (not only the highlighted) words and expressions from the text above.

1 As a child, he read under the bedcovers, kept ... by murder mysteries and fantasy ... alike.
2 Don't let yourselves be ... by the length of the book – the *plot and the *characters will make up for it.
3 Victoria is not an ... reader – the only thing she reads are fashion magazines.
4 Books can be studied, analysed and interpreted, but they can also be read for ...
5 I only read bestsellers; if a book is not an ... success, I won't touch it.

### 3 Evaluating a chart

**a** In 2008, the National Year of Reading was launched by British Prime Minister Gordon Brown with the aim of encouraging reading. A survey was done on teenage reading habits and a report published on 27 March 2008. Read the following list of top ten likes and dislikes.

| Read up | Ranking | Fed up | Ranking |
|---|---|---|---|
| Heat magazine | 1 | Homework | 1 |
| Bliss magazine | 2 | Shakespeare | 2 |
| Song lyrics online | | Books over 100 pages | 3 |
| Computer-game cheats online | 3 | Reading about skinny celebrities in magazines | 4 |
| My own online blog or fan fiction | 4 | The books I am made to read by school / my teachers | 5 |
| The Harry Potter series | 5 | Encyclopedias and dictionaries | 6 |
| Anne Frank's Diary | 6 | The Beano | 7 |
| Film scripts | 7 | The Harry Potter series | 8 |
| Books by Anthony Horowitz | 8 | Maps/Directions | |
| The Lion, the Witch and the Wardrobe | 9 | Facebook | 9 |
| BBC Online | 10 | Financial Times | 10 |
| Books by Louise Rennison | | Anything in another language | |

From: 2008 National Year of Reading, www.literacytrust.org.uk/readingconnects/RUFUreport.pdf

**read up on sth.** read a lot about sth.
**be fed up with sb./sth.** jdn./etwas satthaben
***Heat*** British celebrity gossip and news magazine
***Bliss*** British teenage girls' magazine
**cheat** *(n) here:* a program by which you can go to the next level of a computer game
**Anthony Horowitz** British screenwriter and author of mystery and adventure stories
***The Lion, the Witch and the Wardrobe*** fantasy novel by C.S. Lewis
**Louise Rennison** British author of a series for teenage girls
***The Beano*** British children's comic
***Financial Times*** britische Wirtschaftszeitung

**b** In groups of four, analyse the ranking in the above list: Organize the reading material according to category (e.g. comics). Some may go in more than one category. Which category was most popular in 'Read up', which in 'Fed up'? Which categories surprised you most? Explain.

**c** Discuss what the German equivalents of the reading materials in the list could be. How would you rank them? Create your own top five list and present your results in class.

**d** Sum up what you can say about the reading habits of British teenagers based on the two lists and your discussion.

### 4 Teenage reading habits CD II.02–03

**a** Make a table. *Across:* the names of the five teenagers interviewed (Andrew, Lorna, Caroline, Merlene, Daniel). *Down:* the questions they answer (what they read; why they read this literature; when and where they read). Then listen to the interview and fill in the table.

**b** Answer the questions for yourself. With a partner, compare the teenagers' answers to your own.

► LP 4 Present Perfect and Simple Past (p. 107)

### 5 EXTRA What is reading?

**a** With a partner, describe 'reading' – what it is, what it means to you, what it implies ('Reading is …' or 'Reading means …').

**b** Think of 'READING' as an acronym and find a suitable word for each letter. Discuss the different solutions in class. Agree on the best two.

### 6 EXTRA Classroom discussion: The future of books

Will ebooks change reading habits? Will printed books still exist in a hundred years' time? Discuss this in class. Use as many of the words and phrases from the text on p. 84 as possible.

► SF 24 Taking Part in a Classroom Discussion (p. 149)
► LP 7 *Will*-Future (p. 108)

# For Starters: Opening Lines

*Sometimes the opening lines of a *novel immediately make you want to read on, sometimes you have to force yourself to read on, and sometimes you stop reading altogether.*
*Read the opening passages of* The Curious Incident of the Dog in the Night-Time *and* The Absolutely True Diary of a Part-Time Indian *and give each a grade from* ***A–D****:*

## A1 The Curious Incident of the Dog in the Night-Time Mark Haddon

[13] **wound** [wuːnd] injury
[16] **cancer** Krebs(erkrankung)

**2**

It was 7 minutes after midnight. The dog was lying on the grass in the middle of the lawn in front of Mrs Shears' house. Its eyes were closed. It looked as if it was running on its side, the way dogs run when they think they are chasing a cat in a dream. But the dog was not running or asleep. The dog was dead. There was a garden fork sticking out of the dog. The points of the fork must have gone all the way through the dog and into the ground because the fork had not fallen over. I decided that the dog was probably killed with the fork because I could not see any other wounds in the dog and I do not think you would stick a garden fork into a dog after it had died for some other reason, like cancer for example, or a road accident.

But I could not be certain about this.

From: Mark Haddon, *The Curious Incident of the Dog in the Night-Time*, 2008
(first published in 2003)

### Language help

The narrator ...
- writes in very short/long sentences.
- joins many main clauses using conjunctions such as ...
- uses very simple/complicated words.
- repeats nouns within the same sentence instead of using ...
- writes the way he thinks.
- uses (humorous) imagery / stylistic devices to ...
- has a very direct/witty/straightforward/matter-of-fact style of writing.

### 1 Speculating

**a** From what you have read, speculate on the *narrator. Consider the following questions and give reasons for your answers.
- Is the narrator male or female?
- Is he or she popular at school?
- Is he or she intelligent?
- Does he or she have a sense of humour?

**b** Look at the book title. Speculate on what the book might be about. What genre could it be?

### 2 Looking at style

Describe the language and *style of the extract. Consider words, syntax, etc.
- **Language help**

*A: I have to read this book!*
*B: This book sounds interesting. I would have to read more to know if I would like it.*
*C: I'm not sure whether I would like this book. Perhaps I'll read it in a year or so.*
*D: I will definitely not read this book.*

## A2 The Absolutely True Diary of a Part-Time Indian Sherman Alexie

### The Black-Eye-of-the-Month Club

*

I was born with water on the brain.

Okay, so that's not exactly true. I was actually born with too much cerebral spinal fluid inside my skull. But cerebral spinal fluid is just the doctors' fancy way of saying brain grease. And brain grease works inside the lobes like car grease works inside an engine. It keeps things running smooth and fast. But weirdo me, I was born with too much grease inside my skull, and it got all thick and muddy and disgusting, and it only mucked up the works. My thinking and breathing and living engine slowed down and flooded.

My brain was drowning in grease.

But that makes the whole thing sound weirdo and funny, like my brain was a giant French fry, so it seems more serious and poetic and accurate to say, 'I was born with water on the brain.'

From: Sherman Alexie, *The Absolutely True Diary of a Part-Time Indian*, 2009 (first published in 2007)

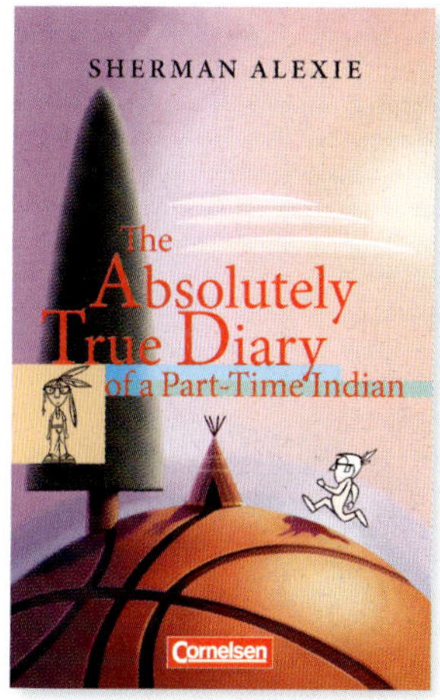


**have a black eye** ein blaues Auge haben
3 **cerebral spinal fluid** [ˌserəbrəl ˌspaɪnəl ˈfluːɪd] Hirn- und Rückenmarksflüssigkeit
4 **skull** Schädel
5 **fancy** *(adj)* complicated so it sounds good; intended to impress
**brain grease** Hirnschmalz
6 **lobes** *(pl)* *hier:* Hirnlappen
8 **weirdo** *(infml)* strange
10 **muck up the works** *(infml)* prevent sth. from working properly

**⚠ Trouble spot**
**French fries** *(AE)*
= **(potato) chips** *(BE)*
= Pommes frites
**(potato) chips** *(AE)*
= **(potato) crisps** *(BE)*
= Kartoffelchips

### 1 Speculating

**a** From what you have read, speculate on the *narrator. Consider the following questions and give reasons for your answers.
- Is the narrator male or female?
- Is he or she popular at school? Consider the chapter title again.
- Is he or she intelligent?
- Does he or she have a sense of humour?

### 2 Looking at style

Describe the language and *style of the extract. Consider words, syntax, etc. Then compare this extract to the one on p. 86. ▪ **Language help** (p. 86)

# Who Is Telling the Story?

## B1 The Curious Incident ... Mark Haddon

*15-year-old Christopher Boone is talking to his teacher Siobhan about the book he is writing.*

**⚠ Trouble spot**
**murder** = Mord
**murderer** = Mörder/in

▶ LP 28 False Friends (p. 121)

This is a murder mystery novel.

Siobhan said that I should write something I would want to read myself. Mostly I read books about science and maths. I do not like proper novels. In proper novels people say things like, 'I am veined with iron, with silver and with streaks of common mud. I cannot contract into the firm fist which those clench who do not depend on stimulus.' What does this mean? I do not know. Nor does Father. Nor do Siobhan or Mr Jeavons. I have asked them.

Siobhan has long blonde hair and wears glasses which are made of green plastic. And Mr Jeavons smells of soap and wears brown shoes that have approximately 60 tiny circular holes in each of them.

But I do like murder mystery novels. So I am writing a murder mystery novel.

In a murder mystery novel someone has to work out who the murderer is and then catch them. It is a puzzle. If it is a good puzzle you can sometimes work out the answer before the end of the book.

Siobhan said that the book should begin with something to grab people's attention. That is why I started with the dog. I also started with the dog because it happened to me and I find it hard to imagine things which did not happen to me.

Siobhan read the first page and said that it was different. She put this word into inverted commas by making the wiggly quotation sign with her first and second fingers. She said that it was usually people who were killed in murder mystery novels. I said that two dogs were killed in The Hound of the Baskervilles, the hound itself and James Mortimer's spaniel, but Siobhan said that they weren't the victims of the murder, Sir Charles Baskerville was. She said that this was because readers cared more about people than dogs, so if a person was killed in the book readers would want to carry on reading.

I said that I wanted to write about something real and I knew people who had died but I did not know any people who had been killed, except Edward's father from school, Mr Paulson, and that was a gliding accident, not murder, and I didn't really know him.

I also said that I cared about dogs because they were faithful and honest, and some dogs were cleverer and more interesting than some people.

From: Mark Haddon, *The Curious Incident of the Dog in the Night-Time*, 2008

▶ LP 9 Emphasis: Stress, *do/does/did*, Word Order (p. 110)

**Siobhan** [ʃə'vɔːn] female Irish first name
11 **approximately** [ə'prɒksɪmətli] about
18 **attention** Aufmerksamkeit
22 **make the wiggly quotation sign** *here:* use the index and middle fingers of both hands to show you are not being serious
24 ***The Hound of the Baskervilles*** a Sherlock Holmes detective story
25 **hound** dog that is used for hunting

## 1 Comprehension

a State what the extract on p. 88 is about.
b Name Christopher's reading habits (ll. 3–8 and 12–16).
c List what Siobhan says Christopher should consider when writing his book.

## 2 Reading between the lines

a List characteristics of the types of books mentioned (**1b**) and state what Christopher's (not) liking these types of books tells us about him.
b With a partner, analyse the text for additional information about Christopher: How does Christopher behave? What is he like? Read between the lines. Would you use the adjectives on the right to describe Christopher? Give examples from the extract to support your statement.

▪ *obedient* ▪ *stubborn* ▪ *eloquent* ▪ *naive* ▪ *mysterious* ▪ *simple*

*Mark Haddon*

## 3 The *narrator CD II.04

a Make sure you know the meaning of the words and phrases on the right. Then listen to the first part of the interview with Mark Haddon, the author of *The Curious Incident of the Dog in the Night-Time*.
b Sum up Christopher's problem. What medical terms are used? Assess the meaning of this diagnosis for Christopher as a narrator.
c Why doesn't Haddon mention the diagnosis in the *novel? Comment on this decision.
d Describe 'the biggest paradox' concerning Christopher as a narrator.

▪ *cognitive* ▪ *empathize with sb.* ▪ **literal* ▪ *label sb.* ▪ *have a disability* ▪ *be obsessed with sth.* ▪ *keep sth. at bay* ▪ *incomprehensible* ▪ *circumscribed* ▪ *wreck sth.* ▪ *diverse*

## 4 The narrator's voice CD II.05

a Make sure you know the words and phrases on the right. Then listen to the second part of the interview. Explain why Haddon finds Christopher's voice attractive for a narrator.
b EXTRA Haddon describes his narrator as having a 'flat, emotionless' voice. State whether, in your eyes, Haddon has succeeded in achieving this tone of voice. Comment on (the effect of) the extract he reads in the interview.

▪ *impale sb./sth. on sth.* ▪ *forensics* ▪ *loopy* ▪ *intuitive* ▪ *size sb./sth. up* ▪ *clue* ▪ *approach sth.* ▪ *weep*

## 5 Talking about what you've read

Tell a partner about something you have read recently. State how you heard about it, where you read it (e.g. on the bus, lying in bed), and what you liked / didn't like about it. Say whether its beginning 'grabbed your attention' (p. 88, ll. 17–18) or not. ▪ **Language help**

### Language help

- What I liked (a lot) / didn't like (at all) was ...
- I read a book / something in a magazine / on the Internet / ... about ...
- I couldn't put it down.
- It was a real page-turner.
- It was extremely boring/interesting/fascinating/...

## B2 Looking for Alaska John Green

*16-year-old Miles Halter is transferring to boarding school. His mother can't believe her son was not popular at his old school and insists on throwing him a going-away party.*

**1 *Point of view: Getting to know the *narrator**

***Partner B:*** Look at p. 104.

**a** ***Partner A:*** Read the following extract describing the going-away party.

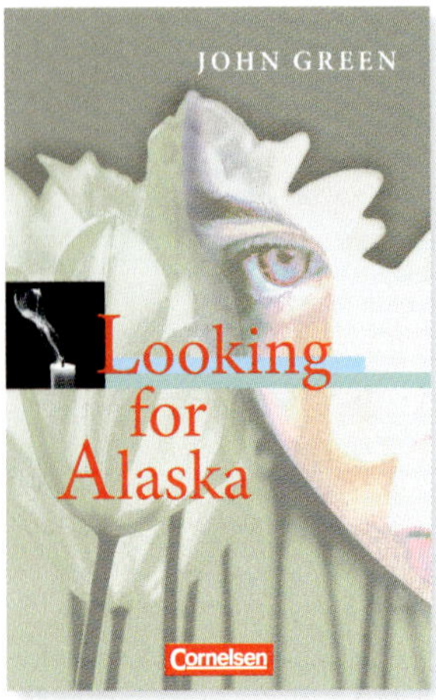


And when that final Friday came, when my packing was mostly done, she sat with my dad and me on the living-room couch at 4:56 P.M. and patiently awaited the arrival of the Good-bye to Miles Cavalry. Said cavalry consisted of exactly two people: Marie Lawson, a tiny blonde with rectangular glasses, and her chunky (to put it charitably) boyfriend, Will.

'Hey, Miles,' Marie said as she sat down.

'Hey,' I said.

'How was your summer?' Will asked.

'Okay. Yours?'

'Good. We did Jesus Christ Superstar. I helped with the sets. Marie did lights,' said Will.

'That's cool.' I nodded knowingly, and that about exhausted our conversational topics. I might have asked a question about Jesus Christ Superstar, except that *1.* I didn't know what it was, and 2. I didn't care to learn, and 3. I never really excelled at small talk. My mom, however, can talk small for hours, and so she extended the awkwardness by asking them about their rehearsal schedule, and how the show had gone, and whether it was a success.

'I guess it was,' Marie said. 'A lot of people came, I guess.' Marie was the sort of person to guess a lot.

Finally, Will said, 'Well, we just dropped by to say good-bye. I've got to get Marie home by six. Have fun at boarding school, Miles.'

'Thanks,' I answered, relieved. The only thing worse than having a party that no one attends is having a party attended only by two vastly, deeply uninteresting people.

They left, and so I sat with my parents and stared at the blank TV and wanted to turn it on but knew I shouldn't. I could feel them both looking at me, waiting for me to burst into tears or something, as if I hadn't known all along that it would go precisely like this. But I had known. I could feel their pity as they scooped artichoke dip with chips intended for my imaginary friends, but they needed pity more than I did: I wasn't disappointed. My expectations had been met.

From: John Green, *Looking for Alaska*, 2009 (first published in 2005)

3 **cavalry** ['kævlri] part of an army that fights on horses
5 **chunky** heavily built
**charitably** ['tʃærətəbli] kindly
11 **set** Bühnenbild
13 **exhaust sth.** [ɪɡ'zɔːst] etwas erschöpfen, aufbrauchen
16 **excel at sth.** [ɪk'sel] be very good at sth.
17 **extend sth.** make sth. longer
**awkwardness** ['ɔːkwədnɪs] Peinlichkeit
25 **vastly** extremely
31 **pity** feeling of sympathy and sadness

**⚠ Trouble spot**
**blank** = *hier:* leer, schwarz
blank *(German)* = **shiny**

► LP 28 False Friends (p. 121)

**b** 1 Who comes to the party?
2 Describe the *atmosphere. ▪ **Language help**
3 Read ll. 13–16 again and state what they tell us about Miles and his attitude towards his classmates and the party.

**c** Speculate on what happened after the party. Tell your partner. Then ask your partner to tell you what actually happened.

**d** Swap roles: Listen to your partner's speculations on how the party went. Then tell your partner how it actually went, using the information from your answers to the above questions.

**e** **Role-play:** Imagine you are Miles's mother. You and your partner (Miles's father) are discussing your son's decision to go to boarding school. First, make notes on possible arguments Miles's mother might bring up against boarding school. Then act out the scene. Try to keep the discussion going for at least two minutes.

> **Language help**
> - The atmosphere is grim/gloomy/dismal/strained/hostile/icy/...
> - Everyone feels awkward / is tense / ...

## 2 Reading between the lines

**a** With your partner, discuss the 'Great Perhaps' mentioned in extract B, p. 104.

**b** Based on the information you gathered in **1**, discuss what kind of person Miles is.

**c** Now write a brief *characterization of Miles. ▪ **Language help**

> **Language help**
> - When Miles describes / talks about / discusses / ..., he reveals that he is ...
> - Miles's comments on ... give us the impression that he is ...
> - The language Miles uses (e.g. ...) shows that ...
>
> ▸ SF 38 Writing a Characterization (p. 156)

## 3 EXTRA Creative writing

You are an editor of the student magazine at Miles's present school in Florida. Interview Miles to find out why he is leaving, then write your article. Here are some questions you might ask:

- What do you dislike about your present school?
- What are you hoping to find?
- What would you like to tell your ex-classmates?

## 4 Changing perspective

Christopher and Miles tell their *stories from their own limited perspective as first-person narrators.

**a** Write 150 words about the party as Miles's mother might describe it:
- How does she feel about her son leaving?
- What are her motives for throwing a party despite Miles's reluctance to have one?

**b** Look up the terms 'limited point of view' and 'unlimited point of view' in the Glossary (p. 160). Note down the differences. When would you choose a limited point of view? When is an unlimited view more suitable?

## 5 EXTRA Comparing the narrators

> ▸ LP 23 Comparison of Adjectives (p. 117)
> ▸ LP 39 Making Comparisons (p. 131)

**a** Work with a partner. Make two lists: one with what the narrators Christopher and Miles have in common, and one with the differences between them. List as many items as possible, then report to another pair.

**b** Tell each other
- which of the two narrators you can identify with more easily and why,
- which of the two narrators you like better as a person and why,
- which of the two narrators you think is more interesting.

# Presenting the Characters

## C1 Junior and Penelope Sherman Alexie

*Arnold Spirit, called 'Junior', is a 14-year-old Native American living on the Spokane reservation in Washington State. From one day to the next, he decides to go to Reardan, a white school outside 'the rez'.*

*■ impetus ■ ostracize sb. (fml) ■ nerdy (infml) ■ panel ■ dork (infml) ■ maiden name ■ venture (n)*

*Sherman Alexie*

**1 'A very autobiographical novel'** DVD 15

*Before watching the DVD, speculate on reasons why Alexie, like the hero in his novel, left the reservation school he had gone to.*

**a** Make sure you know the meaning and pronunciation of the words on the left. Then watch the panel discussion with Alexie.

**b** State the reason Alexie mentions for why he left the reservation school. Explain why this incident had such an impact. Does knowing that the *novel is autobiographical change your interest in it?

**c** Comment on how writing helps Alexie deal with his painful past.

**d** Were you surprised about Alexie's reaction to receiving handwritten *letters? Have you ever wanted to write to an author? Make a list of questions you would like to ask Alexie.

**2 Penelope's dreams**

*Junior is now at Reardan, where one day he hears someone being sick in the girls' bathroom. It turns out to be his popular classmate Penelope, who confesses to having bulimia. They become friends although Penelope's racist father Earl doesn't like this. Read the extract.*

So I say to Penelope what I always say to Dad when he's drunk and depressed and ready to give up on the world.

'Hey, Penelope,' I say. 'Don't give up.'

Okay, so it's not the wisest advice in the world. It's actually kind of obvious and corny.

But Penelope starts crying, talking about how lonely she is, and how everybody thinks her life is perfect because she's pretty and smart and popular, but that she's scared all the time, but nobody will let her be scared because she's pretty and smart and popular.

You notice that she mentioned her beauty, intelligence, and popularity twice in one sentence?

The girl has an ego.

But that's sexy, too. […]

Everybody is absolutely shocked that Penelope chose me to be her new friend. I'm not some ugly, mutated beast. But I am an absolute stranger at the school.

And I am an Indian. […]

Okay, so Penelope and I became the hot topic because we were defying the great and powerful Earl.

And, yeah, you're probably thinking that Penelope was dating me ONLY because I was the worst possible choice for her.

She was probably dating me ONLY because I was an Indian boy.

And, okay, so she was only semi-dating me. We held hands once in a while and we kissed once or twice, but that was it.

I don't know what I meant to her.

**bulimia** [bu'lɪmiə] Ess-Brech-Sucht
[1] **Penelope** [pə'neləpi]
[5] **obvious** ['ɒbviəs] clear
**corny** *(infml)* not original
[18] **defy sb.** refuse to obey sb.

I think she was bored of being the prettiest, smartest, and most popular girl in the world. She wanted to get a little crazy, you know? She wanted to get a little smudged.

And I was the smudge.

But, hey, I was kind of using her, too.

After all, I suddenly became popular.

Because Penelope had publicly declared that I was cute enough to ALMOST date, all of the other girls in school decided that I was cute, too.

Because I got to hold hands with Penelope, and kiss her good-bye when she jumped on the school bus to go home, all of the other boys in school decided that I was a major stud.

Even the teachers started paying more attention to me.

I was mysterious.

How did I, the dorky Indian guy, win a tiny piece of Penelope's heart?

What was my secret?

I looked and talked and dreamed and walked differently than everybody else.

I was new.

If you want to get all biological, then you'd have to say that I was an exciting addition to the Reardan gene pool.

So, okay, those are all the obvious reasons why Penelope and I were friends. All the shallow reasons. But what about the bigger and better reasons?

'Arnold,' she said one day after school, 'I hate this little town. It's so small, too small. Everything about it is small. The people here have small ideas. Small dreams. They all want to marry each other and live here forever.'

'What do you want to do?' I asked.

'I want to leave as soon as I can. I think I was born with a suitcase.'

Yeah, she talked like that. All big and goofy and dramatic. I wanted to make fun of her, but she was so earnest.

'Where do you want to go?' I asked.

'Everywhere. I want to walk on the Great Wall of China. I want to walk to the top of pyramids in Egypt. I want to swim in every ocean. I want to climb Mount Everest. I want to go on an African safari. I want to ride a dogsled in Antarctica. I want all of it. Every single piece of everything.'

28 **smudge sb./sth.** make sb./sth. dirty
37 **stud** *(infml)* sexually attractive man
40 **dorky** *(infml)* clumsy, stupid, boring
46 **gene pool** [dʒiːn] all the genes of one species
48 **shallow** oberflächlich
56 **goofy** ['guːfi] *(infml)* silly, stupid

From: Sherman Alexie, *The Absolutely True Diary of a Part-Time Indian*, 2009

© Ellen Forney

## 3 Looking at the *characters

a List the reasons Junior names for Penelope dating him. List the effects of their relationship on Junior's status at Reardan.

► SF 3 Marking Up a Text (p. 133)

b Note down the information given about Penelope. Then mark your notes with different colours to show what the *narrator tells us (direct *characterization) and what he shows us (indirect characterization).

c Comment on your results. Consider how your view of Penelope might have been influenced by Junior's feelings for her. Make a statement on first-person narration based on your observations.

## 4 Changing perspective

a Work with a partner. Partner A rewrites the extract on pp. 92–93 from Penelope's *point of view, Partner B from an omniscient third-person narrator's point of view (i.e. an unlimited point of view). Be creative: you can, but don't have to, include direct speech, you can summarize the given information and you needn't stick to every given detail.

b Contrast the effect of first- and third-person narration on the basis of the original and your own texts. ■ **Language help**

**Language help**

- As a first-person narrator, Penelope is limited to what she sees ...
- Therefore she can win the reader over / can get the reader to see (only) her perspective / ...
- An omniscient third-person narrator is limited only by ...
- He/She can give a balanced view of things / can describe characters objectively / ...

## 5 EXTRA Doing research

► SF 13 Doing Research (p. 141)
► SF 14 Doing a Project (p. 143)

Both in the book extract and in the panel discussion (p. 92, 1), Alexie mentions the problem of alcohol. Do some research on Native American reservations in the USA. Besides historical facts, consider quality of life and laws.
Explain why alcohol and gambling are such a big problem on reservations.
Make suggestions on how to change the current situation.

© Ellen Forney

## 6 EXTRA Creative writing

Write a diary entry for Penelope in which she describes Junior and her relationship with him.

## C2 Miles and Alaska John Green CD II.06

*One evening Miles meets his fellow student Alaska on a swing on the school campus. Alaska quotes from a historical *novel about Simón Bolívar, a South American independence fighter. On his death bed Bolívar is believed to have said, 'Damn it. How will I ever get out of this labyrinth!'*

**1 Pre-listening**

**a** Do you sometimes listen to audiobooks?
- If so, which ones have you listened to?
- Did you enjoy the experience or not?

List (dis)advantages of audiobooks compared to printed books.

**b** Make sure you know the meaning and pronunciation of the words on the right (mostly parts of the body). Then speculate on the context in which they appear in the novel extract you are going to listen to.

*▪ emerald ▪ hot (infml) ▪ tank top ▪ flip-flops ▪ calf ▪ hip ▪ arc ▪ waist ▪ arch ▪ butt (n, infml)*

**2 Listening to novels**

**a** Listen to the extract from the audiobook of *Looking for Alaska*. Exchange your first impressions of Alaska with a partner.

**b** Were you right about the context of the words (**1b**)? Listen again. One of you notes down what Alaska talks about, the other how Miles describes Alaska. Compare your results.

**c** Did you enjoy listening to the extract, or would it have been better to read it? Why?

**3 *Showing or *Telling?**

Put your findings together and write a *characterization of Alaska. Say whether you are influenced more by what you are shown or by what Miles tells us about her.

▸ SF 38 Writing a Characterization (p. 156)

**4 EXTRA Comparing the three novels**

**a** How important are telling and showing in order to make the *characters in the novels come alive? ▪ **Language help**

**b** From what you have read, which of the three characters – Christopher, Junior or Miles – seems most like a 'real person'? ▪ **Language help**

**c** Explain your findings to a partner and discuss them with him/her. Agree on the most convincing character.

**Language help**
- Telling/Showing is important for ...
- When the narrator tells/shows us something, the characters come alive / remain 'flat' / ...
- ... reminds me of ..., so I think he's very realistic.

# Turning a Book into a Film

## D1 EXTRA About a Boy Nick Hornby DVD 16

*Think of film adaptations of *novels you have read and note down two arguments in favour of making changes and two against. Discuss them with a partner.*

### 1 Reading the book

*36-year-old Will is single and doesn't have to work for a living. He invents a 2-year-old son, Ned, in order to meet single mothers. At a picnic for single parents, Will meets 12-year-old Marcus, who has come with his mother's friend, Suzie, to give his mother, Fiona, a break. Some time later, Marcus rings Will up.*

In groups of three, read the following two passages. One of you deals with Will, one with Marcus, and one with Fiona. Find out what you can about your *character. Discuss your findings and your impression of the character.

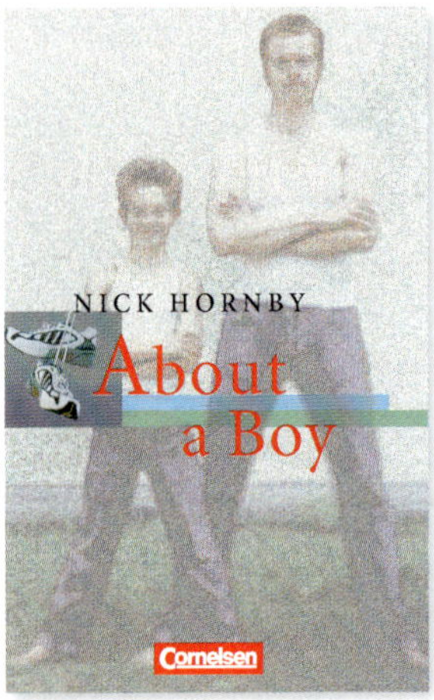


'Hi, Will, it's Marcus.'

'Hi. Funnily enough. I was just wondering –'

'Suzie said you want to take me out for the day somewhere.'

'Yeah, well, that's just –'

'I'll come if my mum can come.'

'I'm sorry?'

'I'll come if you can take my mum too. And she hasn't got any money, so either we'll have to go somewhere cheap or you'll have to treat us.'

'Right. Hey, say what you mean, Marcus. Don't beat around the bush.'

'I don't know how else to say it. We're broke. You're not. You pay.'

'It's OK. I was joking.'

'Oh. I didn't get it.'

'No. Listen, I'm quite safe, you know. I thought it might be better just you and me.'

'Why?'

'Give your mum a break?'

'Yeah, well.'

Suddenly, belatedly, he got it. Giving Marcus's mum a break was what they had been doing last weekend; she had spent the leisure time tipping a bottle of pills down her throat and having her stomach pumped.

'I'm sorry, Marcus. I was being dim.'

'Yeah.'

'Of course your mum can come. That would be great.'

'We haven't got a car either. You'll have to bring yours.'

'Fine.'

'You can bring your little boy if you like.'

He laughed. 'Thanks.'

'That's OK,' Marcus said generously. 'It's only fair.' Sarcasm, Will was beginning to see, was a language that Marcus found peculiarly baffling, which as far as Will was concerned meant it was absolutely irresistible.

'He'll be with his mum again on Saturday.'

'Fine. Come round about half past twelve or something. You remember where we live? Flat 2, 31 Craysfield Road, Islington, London N1 2SF.'

'England, the world, the universe.'

'Yeah,' Marcus said blankly – simple confirmation for a simpleton.

'Right. See you then.'

8 **treat sb.** pay for sb.
9 **beat around the bush** not say sth. directly
10 **be broke** *(infml)* have no money
13 **safe** *here:* not dangerous
16 **give sb. a break** give sb. a period of rest
18 **belatedly** *(adv)* happening a little too late
21 **dim** *(infml)* stupid
29 **baffling** hard to understand
35 **blankly** *(adv)* not showing any reaction
**simpleton** *(old-fashioned)* sb. with little intelligence

*Will takes Marcus and Fiona to a restaurant called Twenty-Eight.*

'I'll have the swordfish steak,' said Will. 'No vegetables, just a side salad.'

Fiona was having difficulty deciding.

'Why don't you have the swordfish steak?' said Marcus.

'Ummm ...'

He tried to get his mother's attention across the table without Will noticing. He nodded hard, once, and then he coughed.

'Are you all right, sweetie?'

He just felt it would help if his mum ordered the same food as Will. He didn't know why. It wasn't like you could talk for ages about swordfish steak or anything, but maybe it would show them that they had something in common, that sometimes they thought the same way about things. Even if they didn't.

'We're vegetarian,' said Marcus. 'But we eat fish.'

'So we're not really vegetarian.'

'We don't eat fish very often though. Fish and chips sometimes. We never cook fish at home, do we?'

'Not often, no.'

'Never.'

'Oh, don't show me up.'

He didn't know how saying she never cooked fish was showing her up – did men like women who cooked fish? Why? – but that was the last thing he wanted to do.

'All right,' he said. 'Not never. Sometimes.'

'Shall I come back in a couple of minutes?' said the waiter. Marcus had forgotten he was still there.

'Ummm ...'

'Have the swordfish,' said Marcus.

'I'll have the penne pesto,' said his mother. 'With a mixed salad.'

Will ordered a beer, and his mum ordered a glass of white wine. Nobody said anything again.

Marcus didn't have a girlfriend, nor had he ever come close to having one, unless you counted Holly Garrett, which he didn't. But he knew this: if a girl and a boy met, and they didn't have a boyfriend or a girlfriend, and they both looked all right, and they didn't mind each other, then they might as well go out together. What was the point in not? Will didn't have a girlfriend, unless you counted Suzie, which he didn't, and his mum didn't have a boyfriend, so ... It would be good for all of them. The more he thought about it, the more obvious it seemed.

[20] **show sb. up** *(infml)* jdn. bloßstellen

From: Nick Hornby, *About a Boy*, 2002 (first published in 1998)

▶ SF 21 Viewing a Film (p. 147)
▶ SF 4 Taking Notes (p. 134)

**Language help**

- I can tell from ...'s thoughts that ...
- We know that ... is nervous/ happy/content/relaxed / feels awkward because ...
- Fiona lets out a hysterical laugh / stares out of the window when ... This shows that ...
- ...'s quietness suggests that ...
- When ..., the camera turns to / cuts to / zooms in on ...

**2 Viewing for gist**

Work in the same groups of three. Watch the film clip. Take notes on any obvious differences between the film and the novel. Discuss your observations.

**3 Viewing for detail: Will, Marcus and Fiona**

a In your groups of three, watch the extract again. Concentrate on either Will, Marcus, or Fiona and note down
- what they are thinking,
- what their behaviour, facial expressions and gestures reveal about them,
- how the camera is used to underline their thoughts and behaviour.

b Tell each other what you have found out. ▪ **Language help**

**4 Comparing the novel and the film**

a Compare the presentation of your character in the novel to that in the film. State whether the impression you got from the novel has changed and if so, how.

b Go back to the arguments you noted down on p. 96 about making changes to a novel. Decide which is more effective: the novel or the film version of *About a Boy*. Tell your classmates why.

## D2 Twilight Stephenie Meyer

**1 What makes for a good film?**

Write down four features which make for a good film. With a partner, agree on the two most important features, then name a film that, in your opinion, fulfils these requirements.

**2 Mediation: Writing an article for a student magazine**

a Four American e-pals have emailed you their impressions of the film adaptation of Stephenie Meyer's *novel *Twilight*. Summarize the reviews in German, then write a short article for your German school magazine based on your summary.

**Angel:** I loved the books but the movie is just pissing me off. If you ask me the director completely killed everything! They've removed my favorite parts, added a bunch of crap and overall gotten everything wrong.

**Ben:** My girlfriend loves this but it was rather disappointing for me. Special effects? WHAT EFFECTS? Voice-over? Unnecessarily annoying. My girlfriend has been happy to pay to see it five times now; I'd prefer she paid more attention to me than badly acted emo-vampires ...

**Dana:** Was a fairly decent film if not compared to the book. If you have read the book, then you should notice that Bella is in actual fact the most annoying heroine in fiction. She is constantly whining, and it gets no better in the books to come. So keeping that fact in mind, I think Kristen Stewart did a great job.

**Kay:** I'm a fan of the book, but I can totally understand what went wrong. They totally changed the plot, and left out some of the really sweet important bits. As a teenager, I should be rating this higher, especially with all those boys, but somehow the movie messed up the book. The book was way better!

b Look at the reviews again. Make a table: In one column, list those things the teenagers didn't like about the film adaptation. In a second column, note down how you might answer this criticism.
*'removed favourite parts' → A film can't be an exact copy of a book's contents.*

▶ SF 15 Mediating (p. 144)

**bunch of crap** *(slang)* sth. of bad quality
**voice-over** ['– – –] comments in a film by a person not seen on screen
**emo-** ['i:məʊ] emotional
**decent** ['di:snt] *(adj)* of fair standard or quality
**whine** complain in an annoying voice.
**mess sth. up** *(infml)* etwas verhunzen

# Keeping a Reading Journal

*In this chapter task you will learn how to keep a reading journal to make your reading experience more rewarding – and not only for study purposes.*
*A reading journal*
- *can help you to gain insight into the story, its topic(s), its *characters and its narrative *style by making you think about what you've read,*
- *can help you to remember the *plot and the characters.*

► SF 30 Keeping a Reading Journal (p. 151)

## 1 Read and Recap

► SF 28 Reading Fiction (p. 151)

**a** Just 'go with the flow' – don't worry about understanding every word. Only look up words which confuse you or which interrupt the flow. However, make sure you can follow what is happening.
► *Read the following extract.*

> ***Keeping your journal: the six R's***
> ***R**ead and **R**ecap*
> ***R**eflect and **R**eact*
> ***R**eview and **R**eport*

*Junior is talking about books to his classmate Gordy, whom he calls the 'Genius White Boy'.*

'You have to read a book three times before you know it. The first time you read it for the story. The plot. The movement from scene to scene that gives the book its momentum, its rhythm. It's like riding a raft down a river. You're just paying attention to the currents. Do you understand that?'

'Not at all,' I said.

'Yes, you do,' he said.

'Okay, I do.' I said. I really didn't, but Gordy believed in me. He wouldn't let me give up.

'The second time you read a book, you read it for its history. For its knowledge of history. You think about the meaning of each word, and where that word came from. I mean, you read a novel that has the word "spam" in it, and you know where that word comes from, right?'

'Spam is junk e-mail,' I said.

'Yes, that's what it is, but who invented the word, who first used it, and how has the meaning of the word changed since it was first used?'

'I don't know,' I said.

'Well, you have to look all that up. If you don't treat each word that seriously then you're not treating the novel seriously.'

I thought about my sister in Montana. Maybe romance novels were absolutely serious business. My sister certainly thought they were. I suddenly understood that if every moment of a book should be taken seriously, then every moment of a life should be taken seriously as well.

'I draw cartoons,' I said.

'What's your point?' Gordy asked.

'I take them seriously. I use them to understand the world. I use them to make fun of the world. To make fun of people. And sometimes I draw people because they're my friends and family. And I want to honor them.'

'So you take your cartoons as seriously as you take books?'

'Yeah, I do,' I said. 'That's kind of pathetic, isn't it?'

'No, not at all,' Gordy said. 'If you're good at it, and you love it, and it helps you navigate the river of the world, then it can't be wrong.'

Wow, this dude was a poet. My cartoons weren't just good for giggles; they were also good for poetry. Funny poetry, but poetry nonetheless. It was seriously funny stuff.

From: Sherman Alexie, *The Absolutely True Diary of a Part-Time Indian*, 2009

> ⚠ **Trouble spot**
> **its** rhythm *(possessive form)*
> **it's** = it is

3 **momentum** movement and speed of sth.
**raft** Floß
4 **current** [*AE:* 'kɜːrənt] Strömung
12 **spam** *ursprünglich:* Dosen- oder Frühstücksfleisch

> ⚠ **Trouble spot**
> **take sth. seriously**
> Not: ~~take sth. serious~~

27 **honor sb.** *(AE)* show respect to sb.
30 **pathetic** [pə'θetɪk] weak, useless
33 **dude** *(AE, infml)* guy
**giggle** *(n)* Kichern

▶ SF 37 Writing a Summary (p. 156)
▶ LP 3 Simple Present to Talk about Texts (p. 106)

**b** At the end of a reading session, think about what you have read. It might be useful to write short summaries at certain points (e.g. after every other chapter, after a third of the book) as a memory aid.

▶ *For practice, write a summary of the extract on p. 99. It shouldn't have more than 80 words. You can start like this:*
*Gordy explains that you have to read a book more than once ...*

▶ SF 8 Using a Dictionary• (p. 136)

**c** Sometimes words come up again that you didn't look up. Or you're curious to see whether you guessed them correctly. Note down any vocabulary items you think you should remember or which might be useful.

▶ *Choose five words from the extract that you think would be good to remember. Using a dictionary, write down each word with its context and an English explanation or German translation. Compare your list with that of a partner.*

## 2 Reflect and React

**a** Note down any ideas, opinions, reactions, thoughts, questions or interpretations that come up during your reading. This will help you to make the most of your reading.

▶ *Write down your reactions to the extract on p. 99.* ▪ **Language help**
*Do Native Americans really still live on reservations created by Whites? What is it like on a reservation? Is it really that bad? Why don't they just leave? ...*

### Language help

- My favourite character is ... because ...
- I found this part fascinating/funny/moving/boring/depressing/scary/exciting/... because ...
- I felt angry/sad/shocked/surprised/... when ...
- I didn't understand why ... / the part where ...
- I thought the style of writing was ...
- I think the setting is important because ...
- This part is very (un)realistic because ...
- I think the relationship between ... and ... is interesting because ...
- This reminded me of a similar experience I had / of something else I read. ...

**b** Brainstorm whatever ideas you come up with, with your reading as the starting point. Then answer some of the following questions – you don't have to answer all of them each time.

- Why is the *narrator telling this story?
- What do you like about the characters? What don't you like?
- What do you think of the way they act in the *novel?
- Does what you have read remind you of personal experiences or of other novels? Does it have a relevance to you or your life?
- How might the story continue?

▶ *Choose two of the above questions and answer them for the extract you read.*

**c** You can also react to a novel creatively, e.g. by doing one of the following tasks to help you focus on one of the novel's topics or characters.

- Write a *letter to one of the characters.
- Interview one of the characters.
- Write a newspaper article about an event in the novel.
- Retell a passage from another character's point of view.
- Add a passage which explains events that are not explained in the text itself.
- Write a blurb about a book you have read.
- Write a diary entry for one of the characters.

▶ *Read the beginning of Gordy's diary entry below and finish it based on the extract.*
*Talked to Junior about books today. He pretends to be a bit dim, but I know he's not. So I explained my little theory of how to read a book to him. He told me he draws cartoons and ...*

## 3 Review and Report

**a** After you have finished a book, you can write a review. This can help you to focus your ideas on the book and decide whether you want to recommend it to others.

- The first part of a review is a (short) summary of the whole book. Thinking of the five W's (who?, what? when?, where?, why?) may help you.
- The second part of a review is a (short) analysis. Part of the analysis in a book review can be to evaluate whether or not the book lived up to your expectations.
- An important part of a review is stating your own opinion and making a recommendation.
- ▸ *When you've finished the novel, look again at its cover (see p. 82) and the blurb (see p. 83) and say whether you think they give an accurate impression of the novel.*

**b** If you read an interesting book and want to share it with your class, you can give a book report on it:

▸ SF 22 Giving a Book Report (p. 148)

- Illustrate the contents of your book briefly and in a structured manner. Choose the most suitable format (e.g. an outline, a text, a diagram, a sketch).
- Introduce the most important characters.
- Present the narrator and the narrative structure (e.g. the time that passes in the book, chapter headings).
- Read a short extract that illustrates an important topic or feature of the book (or bring the audiobook).
- Say something about the time/society that the story takes place in. Choose the most suitable medium (e.g. a poster, a presentation) and visual aids (e.g. film clips, photos, *cartoons).
- Say something about the author, his or her biography and the book's reception, e.g. in (online) reviews.
- To sum up, say why you liked or didn't like the book.

▸ SF 5 Making Notes (p. 134)

**1 Understanding a job description: What are they looking for?**

**a** Read this excerpt from an article by a student who has just returned from a volunteer job in Kenya. Make notes on the qualities you think are necessary for doing a job like the one described. (Some things are said directly; others are implied.)

We took our first five-minute walk to the school, where we were introduced to the head teacher – clearly a very caring and enthusiastic guy – and given a tour. Our duties were explained, which included assisting in and teaching lessons in maths, English and science, and helping to build a new library.

A small point on practicalities: you have to be careful about the water you drink in this part of the world, including ice cubes. Unfortunately, I didn't know this beforehand and spent my second afternoon in Kenya running between my mattress and the loo.

On a typical morning we got up at about seven o'clock. This might sound ridiculously early but it was no problem with early nights and morning sun. Showers were cold and usually delayed until the smell got unbearable.

At about nine o'clock we would head over to the school and meet with the builders who we worked with most days and quickly befriended. It was physically demanding work especially in the first two or three weeks when the foundations had to be dug and rock had to be moved.

I also gave lessons with another volunteer, which eased the pressure a bit. The pupils sat through every lesson without making a sound and never let their attention slip. Without wanting to sound too dramatic, it makes you realize how lucky we are in the UK when it comes to education.

From: 'African Adventure', *Times Online*, 30 October 2007

**b** You have applied for a place on a rural project in Kenya. Your partner is interviewing you. Answer his/her questions. Be prepared to give examples that show you have the qualities needed.

*Partner A:* Have you ever been to a country in the developing world?
*Partner B:* No, this would be my first time.
*Partner A:* Would you be prepared to get your hands dirty?
*Partner B:* Of course, that's not a problem for me.
*Partner A:* Can you give me an example?
*Partner B:* Well, I've never done anything like this project, but I've often gone camping. There I'm usually the one who sets up the tent, digs the hole for the fire, ...

**c** Now interview your partner. Use your notes from **a** to prepare questions to find out if he/she has got the qualities needed, then do the interview.

## 1 Forming your own opinion: Looking at both sides

**a** Read the following extract from the *New York Times* article and note down arguments against using online programs like Edline.

► SF 29 Reading Non-Fiction (p. 134)

At an age when teenagers increasingly want to manage their own lives, many parents use these programs to tighten the grip. College admission is so devastatingly competitive, parents say, they feel compelled to check online grades frequently. [...]

Kathleen DeBuys, a mother of four in Roswell, Ga., used to check her email first thing in the morning: the ParentConnect alerts would fly in by 6 a.m. The subject line might read, 'Claire has received a failing grade. ...'

'And I'd freak out,' said Mrs. DeBuys, speaking of her oldest child, then a high school freshman. 'I'd be waking her up, shouting: "Claire! What did you fail? What is wrong with you?" She'd pull the pillow over her head and say, "Leave me alone!"'

Usually the explanation was benign: there was an inputting error, or Claire had missed the class because she had been sick or pulled out for a gifted-and-talented program. But the family's morning was already flayed.

'It was horrible,' Mrs. DeBuys said.

Many students, in fact, like the programs, which let them monitor their records. Their biggest complaint is their parents' unfettered access. 'I don't think kids have privacy,' said Emily Tarantino, 13, a middle-school student from Farmingdale, N.Y. 'It's not like anyone asked our opinion before they gave parents the passwords.'

In thousands of Facebook postings about the programs, teenagers bitterly denounce parental access as snooping. Emily Cochran, 18, a Pittsburgh senior, writes on Facebook about Edline, 'It's like having our parents or guardians stand over us and watch us all day at school, waiting for us to slip up.' [...]

Many districts do not educate parents about how to use the programs in a measured, judicious fashion with their children. That lapse is implicit in the angry, humorous and poignant Facebook postings. [...] 'Before, the screaming and disappointment only had to be endured four times a year. Now it can happen every night.'

From: 'I Know What You Did Last Math Class', *The New York Times*, 4 May 2008

2 **devastatingly** ['devəsteɪtɪŋli] verheerend
6 **alert** [-'-] warning of danger or a problem
**subject line** Betreffzeile
7 **fail** be unsuccessful
8 **freak out** *(infml)* react very strongly, *here:* angrily
11 **benign** [bɪ'naɪn] *(fml)* harmless
**inputting error** Eingabefehler
13 **flayed** *here:* ruined
16 **unfettered** unlimited
20 **denounce sb./sth** [dɪ'naʊns] strongly criticize sb./sth. that you think is wrong
**access** ['ækses] Zugang
**senior** *(US)* student in grade 12 / the last high-school year
21 **guardian** ['gɑːdiən] Erziehungsberechtigte(r)
24 **lapse** mistake
25 **poignant** ['pɔɪnjənt] moving

**b** With your partner, discuss how software like Edline can be used. Explain how kindergartens and schools use it.

**c** Look at **A** and read the six words and phrases from your partner's text. Ask him/her for the right definitions. Then swap roles.
Your partner will read you six words or phrases from *your* text. Look at the definitions in **B**. Decide which definition each of the words or phrases refers to. Write down the words and phrases and their definitions.

**A**
- tighten the grip (p. 50, l. 2)
- competitive (p. 50, l. 3)
- the stakes (p. 50, l. 9)
- academic pressure (p. 50, l. 9)
- school performance (p. 50, l. 12)
- mind one's Ps and Qs (p. 51, l. 18)

**B**
- classes for students who are naturally good at sth.
- gaining a place at a university
- spy on sb. behind their back
- do sth. wrong
- follow how one is doing at school
- feel it is necessary to do sth.

**d** **Role-play:** You and your mother/father (Partner A) are discussing these programs. Use your notes from **a** to keep the argument going for at least two minutes.

## 1 *Point of view: Getting to know the *narrator

**a** Read the following extract about the talk Miles and his parents have after the party.

2 **mull sth. over** think about sth. carefully
10 **on campus** *here:* at college
**simultaneously** [*BE:* ˌsɪml'teɪniəsli; *AE:* ˌsaɪml'teɪniəsli] *(adv)* at the same time
**raise hell** *(infml)* behave wildly
**ace sth.** *(v)* get top grades for sth.
24 **the likes of** *(infml)* people like

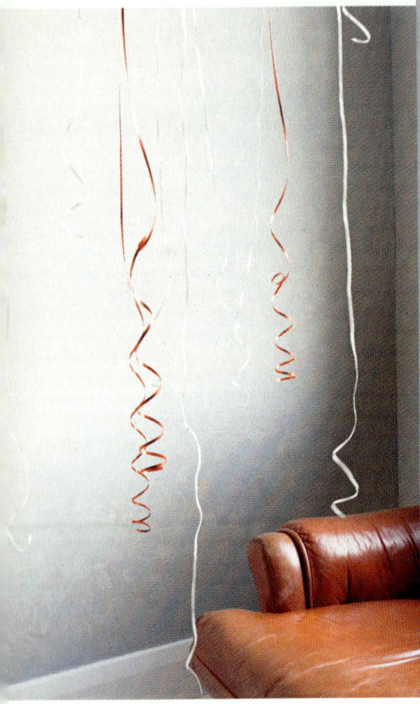

'Is this why you want to leave, Miles?' Mom asked.

I mulled it over for a moment, careful not to look at her. 'Uh, no,' I said.

'Well, why then?' she asked. This was not the first time she had posed the question. Mom was not particularly keen on letting me go to boarding school and had made no secret of it.

'Because of me?' my dad asked. He had attended Culver Creek, the same boarding school to which I was headed, as had both of his brothers and all of their kids. I think he liked the idea of me following in his footsteps. My uncles had told me stories about how famous my dad had been on campus for having simultaneously raised hell and aced all his classes. That sounded like a better life than the one I had in Florida. But no, it wasn't because of Dad. Not exactly.

'Hold on,' I said. I went into Dad's study and found his biography of François Rabelais. I liked reading biographies of writers, even if (as was the case with Monsieur Rabelais) I'd never read any of their actual writing. I flipped to the back and found the highlighted quote ('NEVER USE A HIGHLIGHTER IN MY BOOKS,' my dad had told me a thousand times. But how else are you supposed to find what you're looking for?).

'So this guy,' I said, standing in the doorway of the living room, 'François Rabelais. He was this poet. And his last words were, 'I go to seek a Great Perhaps.' That's why I'm going. So I don't have to wait until I die to start seeking a Great Perhaps.'

And that quieted them. I was after a Great Perhaps, and they knew as well as I did that I wasn't going to find it with the likes of Will and Marie. I sat back down on the couch, between my mom and my dad, and my dad put his arm around me and we stayed there like that, quiet on the couch together, for a long time, until it seemed okay to turn on the TV, and then we ate artichoke dip for dinner and watched the History Channel, and as going-away parties go, it certainly could have been worse.

From: John Green, *Looking for Alaska*, 2009 (first published in 2005)

**b** 1 List the kind of books Miles likes to read.
2 In your own words, say what you think the 'Great Perhaps' might stand for.
3 Compare the *atmosphere at the beginning of the extract to that at the end.
▪ **Language help**

**Language help**
- The atmosphere is grim/gloomy/dismal/strained/hostile/icy/relaxed/pleasant/informal/...
- Everyone feels awkward / is tense/calm/relieved/quiet/...

**c** Speculate on what happened at the party. Then have your partner tell you what really happened.

**d** Swap roles: listen to your partner speculate on what happened afterwards. Then summarize the extract above for your partner based on the information from your answers to the questions.

**e** **Role-play:** Imagine you are Miles's father. You and your partner (Miles's mother) are discussing your son's decision to go to boarding school. First make notes on what you know about Miles's father and what arguments for boarding school he might bring up. Then act out the scene. Try to keep the discussion going for at least two minutes.

## Overview

### Grammar

1 Modal Verbs . . . 105
2 Simple Present and Present Progressive . . . 106
3 Simple Present to Talk about Texts . . . 106
4 Present Perfect and Simple Past . . . 107
5 Present Perfect for 'time up until now' . . . 107
6 Simple Past, Past Progressive and Past Perfect . . . 108
7 *Will*-Future . . . 108
8 Passive . . . 109
9 Emphasis: Stress, *do/does/did*, Word Order . . . 110
10 Emphasis: Inversion . . . 110
11 Indirect Speech: Statements . . . 111
12 Indirect Speech: Questions and Instructions . . . 111
13 Conditional Sentences: Type I . . . 112
14 Conditional Sentences: Type II . . . 112
15 Conditional Sentences: Type III . . . 113
16 Relative Clauses . . . 113
17 Participle Constructions in Place of Relative Clauses 114
18 Participle Constructions in Place of Adverbial Clauses . . . 114
19 *To*-Infinitive and Gerund after Verbs . . . 115
20 Gerund after Prepositions . . . 115
21 Uncountable Nouns . . . 116
22 Articles . . . 116
23 Comparison of Adjectives . . . 117
24 Adverbs of Manner . . . 117

### Vocabulary

25 Increase Your Word Power Online . . . 118
26 Collocations . . . 120
27 One German Word, Two English Translations . . . 121
28 False Friends . . . 121
29 Confusables . . . 122
30 Verbs of Reporting . . . 122
31 Phrasal Verbs . . . 123
32 Word Formation: Prefixes . . . 124
33 Word Formation: Suffixes . . . 124
34 Word Stress . . . 126
35 Abbreviations in Text Messages . . . 127

### Communication Skills

36 Expressing Opinions . . . 128
37 Persuading People . . . 129
38 Agreeing and Disagreeing . . . 130
39 Making Comparisons . . . 131

# Grammar

## ► LP 1 Modal Verbs

Modal verbs are used to say what somebody can or can't, must or mustn't, need or needn't do. Or we can use them to say how certain or uncertain we are. Some modal verbs cannot be used in all tenses. Alternative verbs are used for the missing forms of the other tenses:

***can*** ► *be able to*
***may*** ► *be allowed to*
***must*** ► *have to*
***must not*** ► *not be allowed to*
***need not*** ► *not have to*

**a** Complete these sentences about migrant workers in Europe today.

1 Many migrants ... money to be able to go abroad. *(mussten sich leihen)*
2 They know they ... a new language. *(werden lernen müssen)*
3 Often migrant workers ... longer than a given length of time. *(dürfen nicht bleiben)*
4 Unfortunately, they ... discrimination. *(müssen oft ertragen)*
5 New immigrants ... low-paid jobs and ... long hours in order to earn enough money ... their families. *(werden oft nur finden können – werden arbeiten müssen – um unterstützen zu können)*
6 Many enjoy independence in Western Europe and are happy that they ... on their parents' farms any more. *(brauchen nicht arbeiten)*
7 They ... money to their families at home. *(können schicken)*

**b** Make three more sentences about the situation migrant workers find themselves in, e.g. in Germany. Be sure to include a modal verb in each sentence.

## ► LP 2 Present and Present Progressive

When you use a verb in English, you usually have to decide between the simple and the progressive form. Take a moment to remember when you use which of the forms.
**Remember:** Verbs that refer to a state rather than an activity are normally only used in the simple form.

Complete these sentences with either the simple present or the present progressive. Say which verbs express a state and which express an activity.

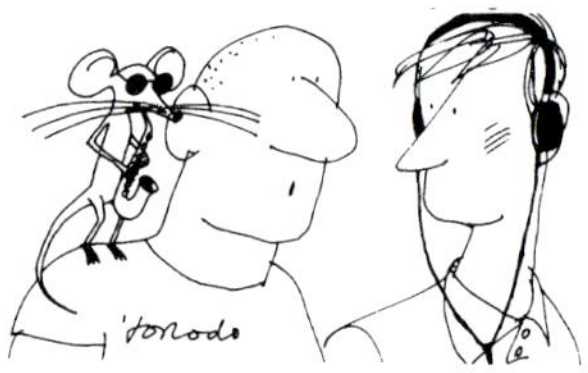

1 'I (prefer) live music.'
2 I (know) the answer, but I can't tell you it.
3 Wait a moment please, can't you see that he (work)?
4 Oh dear, it's broken now, but it (not / matter).
5 Two weeks in the Bahamas? That (not / sound) like a bad holiday!
6 I can't play the piano all the time, but I (practise) whenever I can.
7 The teacher has already explained it five times, but Kim just (not / understand).
8 Oliver won't eat that – he's a vegetarian and that salad (contain) meat.
9 I can see that she (like) the bag, but look how much it (cost).
10 You can't use it because it (not / belong) to you.
11 We (go) now. (You / want) to come with us?
12 Jane, what (you/do)? We're already late!
13 Tim (try) to read his library book as quickly as possible. He (have to) return it in an hour.

## ► LP 3 Simple Present to Talk about Texts

The simple present is often used to talk about texts, e.g. *novels, *short stories, newspaper articles, films or *plays. In summaries the simple present refers to a series of actions or events which happen one after the other. Note, however, that you may have to use different tenses for anything that happens at the same time or that happened before.

**a** Some of the verbs in the following summary of the play *The Pressure Cooker* are wrong. Find thirteen mistakes – either the wrong tense or the wrong form of the tense (simple or progressive) – and rewrite the summary with the correct verb forms.

In the play *The Pressure Cooker* by Steve Skidmore and Steve Barlow, sixteen-year-old Andrea is in trouble. Her mother wanted her daughter to do well at school so she can go to university, but she fails her exams. Her boyfriend Graham did not think success at school was important, and just wanted Andrea to go out with him and enjoy herself.
Things reached crisis point when Mrs X stopped Andrea going out to a party with Graham. Andrea finds out the next day that Graham spends the whole evening with her best friend Dawn.
Desperate[1], she wrote a letter to a magazine asking for advice. A week later in school, Graham takes the magazine out of her hands. He reads the letter out loud and makes fun of it in front of all her school friends. He doesn't realize that Andrea writes the letter herself.
When everybody laughed, Andrea bursts into tears[2] and runs off home. A few days later, Dawn called at her house; Andrea's brother is telling her that Andrea swallows[3] some sleeping pills three days before and that she is now in a coma.

**b** Write four questions about what happens in the play, remembering to use the simple present. Ask a partner your questions.

[1] **desperate** ['despərət] verzweifelt – [2] **burst into tears** in Tränen ausbrechen – [3] **swallow sth.** ['swɒləʊ] etwas schlucken

## ▸ LP 4 Present Perfect and Simple Past

***Have** you **seen** the latest James Bond film? – Oh yes, I **saw** it last weekend when it came out!*

The people speaking here use both the present perfect and the simple past to talk about watching a film. Which tense is used for actions at a particular[1] point of time in the past, and which is used when the exact time is not important?

**a** Put these time expressions into two groups with the headings 'used with the simple past' and 'used with the present perfect'.

in my life • when I was ten • lately • this year • in the spring holidays • ever • never • When ...? • just • at Christmas • the summer before last • already • yet

**b** Read this short interview on reading habits[2] and put the verbs in the boy's answers in the right tense.

- • Now tell me: do you buy the books you read?
- – Well, when I was younger, my parents always (give) me books as a present. But now, well, I (buy) this one with my Christmas money last year, but I (not buy) another one since then. And I (not get) any for my birthday either.
- • So you get them from the library?
- – Some of them, yes. Like this one – I (just take) it out. But more often, I borrow from my friends. I (already borrow) three from my best friend this week.
- • How many books do you get through in a week, then?
- – Well, I (finish) this one last night – and that one I (read) at the weekend. I (not finish) this one yet.

**c** Now the interviewer turns to you. Write your own answers to the following discussion points, talking about your own reading habits in the recent past:

- *Interviewer:* Tell me about any books that you have read in the last year or so.
- *Interviewer:* Compare your reading habits with those of your friends.

## ▸ LP 5 Present Perfect for 'time up until now'

***I've been** a member of Facefriends for two years.* 'Ich bin schon zwei Jahre Mitglied bei Facefriends.'

The present perfect is used to talk about a state or activity in a time 'up until now'. In the corresponding[3] German sentences we normally use the present tense ('Präsens').

**a** Look at this list of time expressions and pick out the nine expressions that take the present perfect, i.e. the ones that indicate[4] a time span that began in the past and continues up to the moment of speaking.

all week • so far • last year • before my driving test • since then • until we moved • all my life • not ... ever • for ages • this school year • How long ...? • since we met • when I was small • while I was in New York

**b** Using the time expressions you listed in **a** and verbs in the present perfect, make sentences about yourself or somebody you know.

1 *I've had a cold <u>all week</u> and I'm fed up with it.*
2 ...

[1] **particular** [pəˈtɪkjələ] bestimmt, speziell – [2] **habit** Gewohnheit – [3] **corresponding** entsprechend – [4] **indicate sth.** auf etwas hinweisen, etwas anzeigen

## ▸ LP 6 Simple Past, Past Progressive and Past Perfect

*When I* ***left*** *Poland, I* ***was hoping*** *to make a new start.*
*I* ***arrived*** *in Britain seven months ago.*
*My brother* ***had*** *already* ***moved here*** *before me.*

Match the verbs in the sentences above with the three past tenses: simple past, past progressive and past perfect. Find the diagram that fits each of the three tenses best and remember what the rule is for using them.

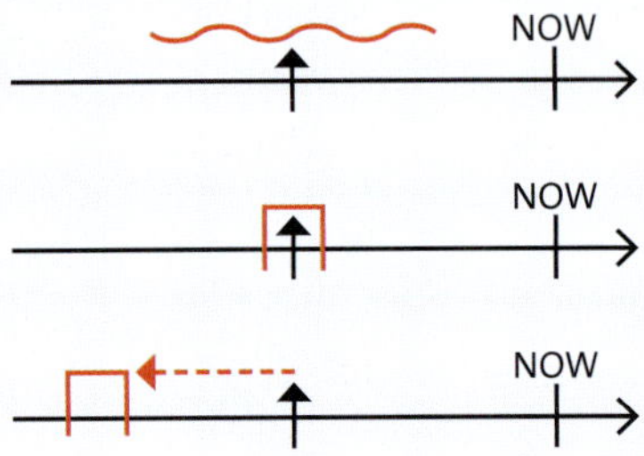


**a** Read this story from *Once*, the musical film about Marketa from Poland who meets a street musician in Dublin, and put in the correct form of each verb.

'I first (meet) Glen as he (play) in a busy shopping street in the middle of town. A few days before then, I (find) myself a job too, so I (sell) roses when I (see) him. He (not want) to talk to me at that time, because he (need) to earn money with his singing. But later, we (discover) that we (can) make music together – me on the piano, him on the guitar, both of us singing. One day while we (practise), we (decide) to record an album in a professional studio.
During the time we (work) together, we (become) good friends – but no more than just friends: Glen always (talk) about the girlfriend who (left) him two years before in London; and me – I (get married) in Poland and (live) in London with my mother and my child.'

**b** EXTRA Speculate on how the relationship – and the music making – might continue. (Try to use some of the past tenses mentioned above.)

## ▸ LP 7 *Will*-Future

There are different ways of expressing the future. The one usually used for prediction[1] or speculation is the *will*-future.

**a** You might speculate on your own future like this:

*'Well, I know I won't look for a job immediately after school. Maybe I'll spend a year travelling around Europe. I imagine I will have some money by then. I'm sure I won't be living at home; perhaps I'll have found a good friend I can share a flat with. In ten years' time, I hope I'll be working in the film industry. Will I have children? – I doubt it!'*

Go through the text and find forms of the *will*-future simple, the *will*-future progressive and the future perfect. How are they formed and what is the difference in use?

**b** Write your own paragraph speculating on the future development[2] of a) cars, b) energy or c) the family. Check the text in **a** for useful phrases like *I imagine*, *maybe*, etc.

[1] **prediction** Voraussage, Vorhersage – [2] **development** [dɪ'veləpmənt] Entwicklung

## ▸ LP 8 Passive

When explaining processes like the greenhouse effect, we often use the passive. This way, we focus on what happens and not on who or what does something.
Find four sentences in the diagram that are in the passive and write down the verb forms. Remember the rule for forming the passive. The examples are all in the simple present. What other forms do you know?

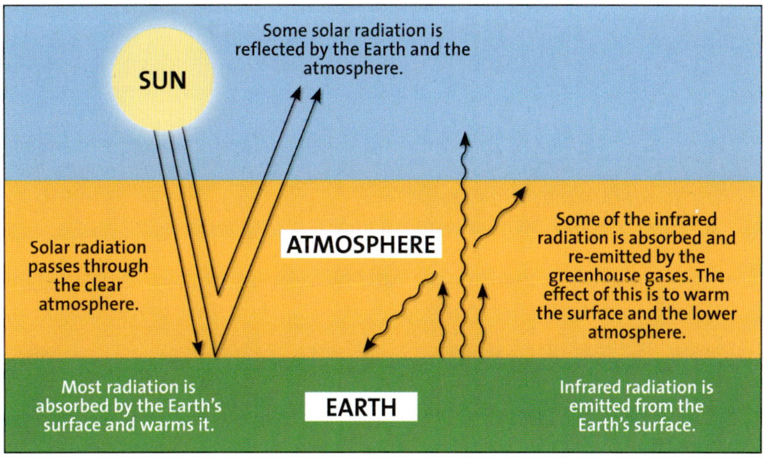


**a** Read the text below about one school's ideas on how to make their school 'greener' – more eco-friendly. Add the verbs in the right form; some are in the passive and some in the active. Watch out for the different tenses.

### 'Greening' school

Solar panels[1] (install) on our roof in 1999. Two years later, we (introduce) waste separation for paper, glass and plastics. A small wind turbine (build) on a hill just outside our school by a Physics class last year.
For over five years now, all lights except those in classrooms (control) by motion sensors[2].
At the moment, some special software (load) onto all school computers to make them shut down automatically at the end of the day.
Drinks that (sell) in our vending machines[3] are cheaper if you (use) your own cup, but the machine also (give) a refund[4] if its plastic cups (return). Snacks which (buy) in the school shop in the break (not normally wrap[5]).
Plans for the future? Hopefully, paper (save) when we (start) sending out letters to parents next year by email only. And before the end of the decade, all school buses should (power) by electricity.

**b** How 'green' is your school? Write down what was, has been or is being done to save resources and protect the environment – or what is not being done, but you think should be. Use the text above and the following list for ideas on how to make schools more eco-friendly.

the playground[6] – redesign to include more grass, plants and water areas
rainwater – collect and reuse
cycle to school – encourage students
chemical products used for correcting mistakes – ban[7]
empty toner cartridges[8] – collect regularly
projects on the local environment – carry out

[1] **solar panel** [ˌsəʊlə ˈpænl] Sonnenkollektor – [2] **motion sensor** [ˈsensə] Bewegungsmelder – [3] **vending machine** (Verkaufs-)Automat – [4] **refund** [ˈriːfʌnd] Rückzahlung – [5] **wrap** einwickeln – [6] **playground** Schulhof – [7] **ban sth.** etwas verbieten – [8] **cartridge** Patrone

## ▸ LP 9 Emphasis: Stress, *do/does/did*, Word Order

When you give your opinion on something, for example on a book, you may want to emphasize[1] certain points to make your view clearer. In English, there are three main ways to do this:

1 Use emphatic *self*-pronouns to stress a noun or pronoun:
*I **myself** have always liked fantasy novels best.*

2 Use *do/does/did* to stress a verb:
*Although I found it rather boring, I **did** finish the book.*

3 Change the word order, for example put a phrase in front position before the subject:
***Three times** I have read that book now. – **For six hours** I was totally lost in my book.*

Using the methods above, place more emphasis on the underlined words and phrases in the text below.

I like novels in which the main character tells the story. Although I don't like my books to be too short, I get impatient[2] when the writer eternally[3] describes things. I'm reading one of those types of books now: the writer has been describing his room for five pages! When I get into a really good book, I would sometimes like to call the writer and chat with them. I have been to book readings twice where the authors have read extracts from their books. If they are good at reading aloud, it's great, but at one of the readings I went to the author read really badly. For tips on books, I listen to friends, but at the end of the day, you have to choose which ones you want to read.

## ▸ LP 10 Emphasis: Inversion

People speaking in public often want to stress an idea that is important to them. In the *speech on pp.14–15 for example, Barack Obama said 'Never again **can we** expect the oceans to keep us safe.' (Without emphasis, the sentence would begin '**We can** never again expect ...'.)
Putting an auxiliary before the subject is called inversion. Speakers often use inversion after negative phrases like *no longer, in no way, under no circumstances, at no time, never before, not until.*

**a** Add more emphasis to the following statements in a debate by using inversion. Check if the meaning of the sentence is still the same after using inversion. You might have to omit words or shift pronouns.

1 Young people have never before had so many opportunities for change.
*Never before have ...*
2 We can no longer say that we did not know what was going on.
3 My generation will in no way support aggressive warfare.
4 We will not allow the pollution of the planet to increase – under no circumstances!
5 We should no longer be destroying our planet's forests.
6 Third World countries have at no time had the chance they deserve.
7 The nations of the world will not make progress until they work together.

**b** Make four more sentences starting with some of the negative phrases used in **a**.

[1] **emphasize sth.** ['emfəsaɪz] etwas betonen – [2] **impatient** [ɪm'peɪʃnt] ungeduldig – [3] **eternally** [ɪ'tɜːnəli] ewig

## ▸ LP 11 Indirect Speech: Statements

*'I was only standing outside this shop yesterday; I still don't understand what the fuss[1] is about,' declared the suspect[2].*
*The suspect declared that he had only been standing outside the shop in the High Street the day before and that he still did not understand what the fuss was about.*

Compare the two versions of the suspect's report. What are the differences with respect to the pronouns, the tenses and references to place and time?

**a** Change the following sentences into direct speech. What did the people actually say?

1 The police officer stated that the suspect would not be taken into custody[3] yet.
2 A witness[4] told the press that he had watched the teenager standing guard[5] on the pavement the day before.
3 The shopkeeper stated that he was going to have a CCTV camera[6] installed the following week.
4 One of the boys' fathers claimed that his son wasn't being given a fair chance to prove[7] himself innocent.
5 The teenagers involved said they were sorry for the trouble but felt they should be left alone now.

**b** Think of some new situations.
Draw four *speech bubbles and write inside them what different people said. Exchange your speech bubbles with a partner and put them into indirect speech.

⚠ **Trouble spot:** When using *told*, always add the person who is told something,
i.e. *she told him that* ... (never: ~~*she told that*~~ ...).

## ▸ LP 12 Indirect Speech: Questions and Instructions

A girl chatting online to a stranger could report the following to a friend:
*My chat partner asked where I lived and whether I was interested in indie rock. Then he told me to come and see him.*
Write down what the actual text was as it appeared in the chat. You should think of a couple of questions and an instruction.

Compare the original with the reported version. What changes are made when reporting questions and what changes are made when reporting instructions?

**a** Report the stranger's further questions to the girl (use *asked, wanted to know, wondered*).

1 When do you finish school?
2 Have you told your parents about this?
3 Can you send me a text message before you leave?
4 How will I recognize you when we meet?

**b** In the end, the girl gets suspicious[8] of the stranger's identity and intentions[9]. Take on her role and report on your last chat, when you finished the online relationship and made it very clear that you wanted no more contact at all:

*I told him (not) to ...; I advised him (not) to ...; ...*

[1] **fuss** Theater, Aufregung – [2] **suspect** ['sʌspekt] Verdächtige(r) – [3] **custody** ['kʌstədi] Haft – [4] **witness** Zeuge, Zeugin –
[5] **stand guard** [gɑːd] Wache stehen – [6] **CCTV** (= **closed-circuit television**) Videoüberwachung –
[7] **prove oneself innocent** beweisen, dass man unschuldig ist – [8] **suspicious** [sə'spɪʃəs] misstrauisch – [9] **intention** Absicht, Plan

## ▸ LP 13 Conditional Sentences: Type I

Possibilities for the weekend
*If my dad lets me borrow the car, I'll drive out to my friend's house. Unless it's really wet, we can organize a barbecue. Her parents won't have any problems with that, provided we don't disturb the neighbours. But I should have a plan B in case it doesn't work out.*

Study the four sentences – each provides a condition and a consequence. For each sentence identify
- the word or phrase that introduces the condition,
- the verb forms used in the *if*-clause and in the main clause.

⚠ Don't use *will* in the *if*-clause.

Think of the options open to you in the following six areas. For each area, write two or three conditional sentences I, considering some alternatives. Use *will, can, could, may, might* or *should* in the main clause.

1 Revising for the next test (Think of meeting in a group, working alone, studying with a coach, ...)
*If we meet to revise in a group, we will probably ... . However, if I ...*
2 Writing your next *essay (Think of writing on the computer, writing by hand, ...)
*Unless I type my essay on the computer, ...*
3 Deciding which film to watch with friends
4 Joining a school club or activity
5 Choosing your next book to read
6 What to spend your last remaining money on before you get your next allowance[1]

## ▸ LP 14 Conditional Sentences: Type II

Compare conditional sentences I and II and answer the questions below.
*If Jeff wins the race tomorrow, he'll be happy.* (conditional sentence I)
*If Pete won the race tomorrow, he'd be happy.* (conditional sentence II)

- What tense is used in the *if*-clause of a conditional sentence II? What form of the verb is used in the main clause?
- Does a conditional sentence II refer to the past, the present or the future?
- Does the speaker think it's probable or improbable that Pete will win the race?

⚠ Don't use *would* in the *if*-clause.

Give a personal answer to the following questions. Use conditional sentences II with *would, could* or *might* in the main clause.

1 If you had a quarrel[2] with a good friend, what form of communication would you use to make up[3] again?
*Well, I wouldn't talk to him face to face, because he might make a scene. If I sent him an email, he might ignore it. But if I called him at the right time, I imagine we could talk things over on the phone.*
2 If you got a nasty[4] email, what might you do?
3 If a stranger you were chatting to offered to meet you, what should you do?
4 If your mobile bill was 200 €, what do you think would be the best thing to do?
5 If you were accused[5] of illegally downloading music and videos, how would you respond?
6 If you were trying to talk to a Frenchman with poor English and no German, how might you resolve[6] the situation?

[1] **allowance** [ə'laʊəns] Taschengeld – [2] **quarrel** ['kwɒrəl] Streit – [3] **make up** sich wieder vertragen – [4] **nasty** fies, gemein – [5] **accuse sb. of sth.** [ə'kju:z] jdn. wegen einer Sache anklagen – [6] **resolve sth.** [rɪ'zɒlv] etwas lösen

## ▸ LP 15 Conditional Sentences: Type III

*If the weather had been better at the weekend, we would have gone to the sea.*
*If Julia's parents hadn't moved the family to Hong Kong, she could have done her 'Abitur' at the same time as all her old friends.*

With conditional sentences III we express what would have happened (or could have / might have / should have happened) if things had been different.

- What tense is used in the *if*-clause of a conditional sentence III? What form of the verb is used in the main clause?
- Does a conditional sentence III refer to the past, the present or the future?

Read more about Julia's move to Hong Kong:

When Julia was 16, her father was sent to Hong Kong by his firm. At first, she was bitterly opposed[1] to the move. She had a boyfriend and she loved going out with all her friends and seeing her grandparents at the weekends; she used to ride her own horse at the local stables[2]. In Hong Kong, the family lived in a high-rise flat[3], she couldn't go riding any more and of course she could only Skype or chat with her friends at home. She broke up with Tim after a while too.

On the plus side, she went to a German International School and made new friends from around the world. She took up sailing and diving – and she grew to love the school trips and family holidays to Thailand and other places around South-East Asia. After a couple of years, she found she could speak English almost like German. In fact, she was not too keen on going back home.

Use conditional sentences III to talk about what would (or wouldn't) have been the case if the family had not made the move.
*If they hadn't moved out to Asia, Julia could still have stayed with her boyfriend. The family should have flown the horse out for her. If … . On the other hand, she would not have taken up … if …*

## ▸ LP 16 Relative Clauses

*The Gulf Stream is a current that supplies Europe with warm water.*
*Al Gore was the man whose film* An Inconvenient Truth *helped change people's views on ecology.*
*The melting ice caps[4] are the image (which) people always remember when they think of global warming.*

Relative clauses are used to define which thing or person we mean. These so-called 'defining relative clauses' do not have commas separating them from the main clause in English.
Identify the relative pronouns in the sentences above. Which relative pronouns are used for things and which are used for people? Explain why the pronoun in the third sentence above is in brackets.

Explain the following using relative clauses.

1 somebody's carbon footprint
*Somebody's carbon footprint is a symbol of the ecological impact (that) their actions have on the planet.*
2 global warming
3 an energy-efficient light bulb[5]
4 an eco-warrior[6]
5 a deposit[7] on a bottle
6 eco-friendly products
7 an endangered species
8 an environmentalist

[1] **be opposed to sth.** gegen etwas sein – [2] **stable** (Pferde-)Stall – [3] **high-rise flat** Hochhauswohnung – [4] **ice cap** Eisdecke, Eiskappe – [5] **energy-efficient light bulb** [ɪ'fɪʃnt] Energiesparlampe – [6] **eco-warrior** ['iːkəʊ] Öko-Aktivist/in – [7] **deposit** [dɪ'pɒzɪt] (Flaschen-)Pfand

## ▸ LP 17 Participle Constructions in Place of Relative Clauses

In English, participle constructions can be used instead of defining relative clauses.
*One very important environmental issue today concerns the different gases filling the atmosphere.*
*(= ... the different gases that fill the atmosphere.)*

*The gases produced help to increase the greenhouse effect.*
*(= The gases that are (being) produced ...)*

Identify the two participles in the sentences above. Which participle is used instead of a relative clause with an active verb, and which participle is used instead of a relative clause with a passive verb?

Look at this list of some of the causes of environmental damage. Imagine you want to shorten the ideas for points on a PowerPoint presentation. Rewrite them using participles instead of the relative clauses.

1 car engines that use too much fuel[1]
*car engines using too much fuel*
2 air conditioners that have been set to low temperatures
3 bottles that were thrown away as rubbish
4 office workers that leave windows open in winter
5 taps[2] that have been left running
6 paper which has been dumped in the landfills[3]
7 tourists who fly to foreign countries
8 people who drive to work instead of taking public transport

## ▸ LP 18 Participle Constructions in Place of Adverbial Clauses

When writing in English, you can sometimes use participle constructions instead of adverbial clauses. Used in the right way, these participles can make your *style more interesting. They shorten your texts too, often saving two or three words per sentence.

Find the participles in the sentences above – two present participles and one past participle. Explain when you use each kind. Now replace the participle constructions with clauses beginning with conjunctions like *when, while, as, after, as soon as, because, since, (al)though* or *and*: *When you write ...*

A participle construction can have its own subject, which is different from the subject of the main clause:
*Nobody having any more to say, the meeting was closed.*

**a** Read the following extract from a summary of Louis Sachar's famous *novel *Holes*. Expand the underlined participle constructions into clauses using conjunctions. Begin like this: *As he is riding ...*

Riding on a bus through a Texas desert, Stanley Yelnats is on his way to a kind of prison camp. He feels this is very unfair, having been sent there for a crime he did not commit. All the prisoners have the task of digging deep holes in the desert, and having dug them, they have to fill them in again. The camp being situated in a hot, dry landscape, Stanley's work is doubly hard.

**b** Continue with the summary of *Holes*. Rewrite the underlined clauses using participle constructions.

Although he tries to fit in at first, Stanley does not trust the Warden[4] who looks after them. After his friend Zero escapes into the desert, Stanley decides to follow him. The two boys need to take care, because they are being chased by the angry Warden. And soon they become quite sure that something was buried in that desert long ago. Since she knows the secret, the Warden uses the boys to find the 'treasure' ...

[1] **fuel** ['fju:əl] Treibstoff, Benzin – [2] **tap** Wasserhahn – [3] **landfill** Mülldeponie – [4] **warden** Aufseher/in, Wärter/in

## ▸ LP 19 *To*-Infinitive and Gerund after Verbs

*Learn **to recognize** the form you need and then practise **using** it.*

Some verbs take a *to*-infinitive *(to recognize)*, others take a gerund *(using)*.
The verbs *begin, continue, hate, intend, like, love, prefer, propose* and *start* can take either a *to*-infinitive or a gerund: *It started **to rain / raining**.*

⚠ Trouble spot: *Stop **looking** at me like that.* ('Hör auf, mich so anzuschauen.')
*He stopped **to look** at the map.* ('Er hielt an, um ...')

**a** Look at the 20 verbs in the box. Eleven take the *to*-infinitive and nine take the gerund. Make a table: 'verbs + *to*-infinitive' and 'verbs + gerund'. It is helpful to get these verbs right. So take five minutes to learn them off by heart[1], e.g. *attempt to do sth.*

attempt • avoid • choose • decide • dislike • enjoy • expect • finish • give up • can't help • imagine • manage • offer • plan • pretend • promise • refuse • risk • seem • suggest

**b** Continue these sentences using ideas of your own.

1 After my 'Abitur', I plan ...
2 I could imagine ...
3 At the weekend, my friends and I enjoy ...
4 I hate it when people pretend ...
5 When I asked her, my mother refused ...
6 Though he/she tries, my friend never manages ...
7 In my opinion, teachers should attempt ...
8 When I think about my English skills, I suppose I need to practise ...

## ▸ LP 20 Gerund after Prepositions

*Thanks for **the interview**.*
*Thanks for **talking** to us.*
After prepositions we use nouns or gerunds (the 'noun form' of the verb), not infinitives.

⚠ Trouble spot: When *to* is a preposition, we use a gerund after it:
*I'm looking forward to **talking** (not: ~~to talk~~) to you again.*

**a** A telecommunications company rings you up to try and sell you something. They want to interview you on the phone. Below are some of the questions they ask. Put in the right preposition (*at, in, like, of, on* or *to*) and use a gerund after it. Check in a dictionary if you are not sure.

1 Do you sometimes dream ... (get ahead) in life?
2 Are you keen ... (hear) all the latest news as it happens?
3 Do you want to succeed ... (solve) software problems on your own?
4 How often do you feel ... (relax) for an afternoon in front of your computer?
5 Would you say you are good ... (keep) in touch with all your friends?
6 Are you used ... (download) music from the web?
7 Maybe you are sometimes a little afraid ... (miss) the latest trends?
8 So, are you interested ... (spend) little money to make a large profit?

**b** You might want to tell the interviewer that you do not want to answer all his questions. What would you say? Make up some sentences with these phrases and a gerund:

tired of • object to[2] • decide against • fed up with • not interested in

[1] **by heart** auswendig – [2] **object to sth.** Einwände gegen etwas haben, etwas ablehnen

## ▸ LP 21 Uncountable Nouns

*Let me give you* | ***some advice.*** / ***a piece of advice.*** / ***two pieces of advice.***

We cannot use *a/an* or numbers (*one, two, three,* ...) with uncountable nouns like *advice*. Uncountable nouns have no plurals. Often you can make an uncountable noun countable by putting a countable noun like *a piece/item of, a glass of,* etc. in front of it.

**a** Read this list of English nouns and put them into two groups: uncountable nouns and countable nouns. Then arrange them in pairs with similar meanings: *vocabulary – words; ...*

vocabulary • furniture • information • step forward • idea • coin • bag • money • luggage • imagination • flat • word • job • news • accommodation • cupboard • article • fact • work • progress

**b** Complete the following sentences with one of these expressions: *an item of, a piece of, a glass of, a bit of, a carton of, a bar of* (sometimes two are possible).

1 Let me give you ... advice.
2 Can you get me two ... chocolate, please?
3 Now, that's a very interesting ... information, Mr Bond.
4 We'll have a Coke and two ... orange juice, please.
5 I returned two ... clothing to the shop.
6 Could you pass me two ... bread, please? I need a sandwich for later.

*a bar of chocolate*

**c** Practise using uncountable nouns in writing. Try to write one paragraph that includes all five of these uncountable nouns: *equipment – furniture – hair – progress – music.*

## ▸ LP 22 Articles

*A, an, the* – or no article at all? English articles are often used differently from the German articles 'ein/eine' and 'der/die/das'.
Translate the following (imaginary) book titles into German and note the difference in the use of articles.

*A Life as an Officer and an Englishman*
*Once an Hour, Twice a Day*
*Quite a Fight*
*At Home in Baker Street*
*Meeting on Mount Everest*
*Double the Trouble*
*Alive Most of the Time*

**a** Imagine you worked for a publishing company and you had to translate the titles of these new German books into English. Remember the differences in the use of articles:

1 Eine ziemlich böse Überraschung
2 Ärger im Buckingham-Palast
3 Sie war Deutsche und Agentin
4 Desaster bei 200 Stundenkilometern
5 Eine halbe Stunde zu spät
6 Der doppelte Spaß zum halben Preis
7 Sieben Tage die Woche Sportler

**b** Try making up new book titles with these phrases:
*a non-smoker; ... times a second; all the time; from Lake Constance.*

## ▸ LP 23 Comparison of Adjectives

Look at the following sentences from pp. 42 and 88 and say how you form the comparative and superlative of short adjectives and of long adjectives.
*For trips of less than 500 miles, the train is usually **quicker** or **more convenient** [than a plane]. (p. 42)*
*... and some dogs were **cleverer** and **more interesting** than some people. (p. 88)*

Make the comparative forms of the following adjectives. All of them are irregular in some way. Try to say how.
*wet • easy • boring • beautiful • bad • good • little • far*

Translating this sentence will remind you of the words and structures used for comparing:
'Obwohl ich so viel gelernt habe wie Leonie, habe ich eine schlechtere Note bekommen.'
*Though I learned ...*

In this exercise, you have two or more alternatives to choose from. Write a couple of sentences for each number to say what you prefer and why (avoiding the word *better* if you can).

1 using a mobile phone – using landlines[1]
*I prefer using landlines because they are cheaper than my mobile – free in fact. But when I send a text message, I use my mobile because I am more familiar with it.*
2 writing by hand – writing on the computer
3 chatting online – phoning
4 cycling to school – taking public transport – driving
5 laptops – desktop computers
6 listening to music on your MP3 player – listening to music on a CD
7 watching a film at the cinema – watching a film on TV
8 shopping on the Internet – shopping in town

"YOU'RE GOING TO GET BIGGER."

## ▸ LP 24 Adverbs of Manner

When describing events, we often use adverbs of manner to say how something happened or was done.
*He spoke to me **very softly**. Because he was talking **fast**, I couldn't understand him **very well**. I could see that he was trying to explain things **in a friendly way**. So he shocked me when he shouted **angrily**, 'Oh, I give up!'*

- How are adverbs of manner formed? What irregular forms do you know?
- Where do adverbs of manner go in the sentence? Put these terms in the correct order: object – main verb – adverb/adverbial – subject.

**a** Form adverbs from the adjectives in the box and add them to the sentences below.

angry • bad-tempered[2] • ironic • nervous • excited • cheerful[3] • kind • silly • nasty • miserable

1 'How d-did you get here?' he stuttered.
2 She picked up the phone, jumped up and cried, 'It's him!'
3 'Oh, shut up!' she said and walked out of the room.
4 'I'm going to have a long, hot, relaxing bath,' she announced.
5 'It's all over now'. – 'Yes, I'm afraid it is', he agreed.
6 She was drunk by now, so she started laughing.

**b** EXTRA Make sentences of your own using the words from the box in **a** that are left over.

[1] **landline** Festnetzleitung – [2] **bad-tempered** schlecht gelaunt – [3] **cheerful** fröhlich, vergnügt

# Vocabulary

## ▸ LP 25 Increase Your Word Power Online

The Internet offers you lots of tools to look up words and learn how to use them correctly. This section will introduce you to some of them.

Webcode: STAR322305-118-1

### a An online dictionary

As you know, a monolingual dictionary does not only give you the meaning of English words or phrases but also shows you how to use them in sentences. You can look up words without having to leave your computer, just by going to an online dictionary and entering the word you need to know about.

Use the *Oxford Advanced Learners' Dictionary (OALD)* website, for example, to look up any unknown words in the following sentences. Then say whether or not the sentences are true.

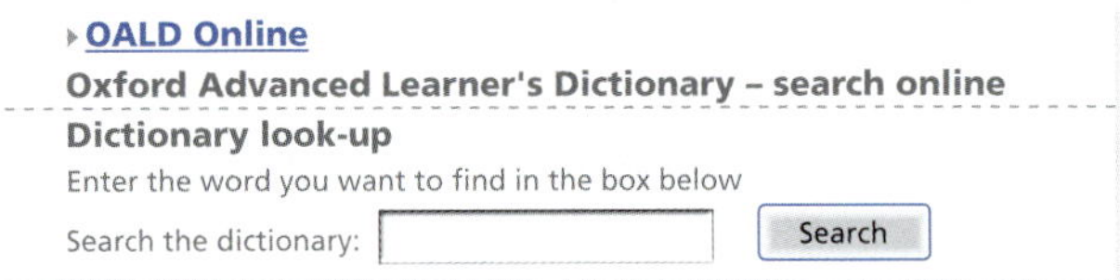


From: www.oup.com/elt

1 Taking snuff is more popular today than it was in earlier times.
2 Traffic on our motorways consumes prodigious amounts of petrol.
3 Somebody who poaches animals is committing a crime.

As with a printed dictionary, it is important to study the full entry, especially the example sentences and the additional information given. Use the OALD website to decide which of the underlined words is best in the given context:

4 He's the best football <u>trainer/coach</u> I've ever seen.
5 The football match <u>starts/kicks off</u> at 7.30.
6 I'm usually quite a <u>fast/quick</u> learner.

Webcode: STAR322305-118-2

### b A visual dictionary online

If graphics and pictures help you understand new language, try using a visual dictionary website. Instead of explaining things, it shows you pictures of all kinds of objects, concepts and activities:

You can enter the word you want to find out, e.g. *exhaust* or *ankle* in these sentences.

1 The *exhaust* on our car was broken, so I was unable to come.
2 She had sprained her *ankle* going downstairs.

Alternatively, you can follow a series of steps to focus on an area of study that you find interesting. Go to the *Visual Dictionary Online*: Click *Sports and games* in the list of *Themes*, then click on *ball sports*, after that *baseball*, and finally *field* – to find a view of a baseball field and the names of its parts.

What steps would you go through to find out about …

- the hat that you call 'Zylinder' in German?
- the seating plan in a court of justice[1]?
- what factors are involved in the greenhouse effect?

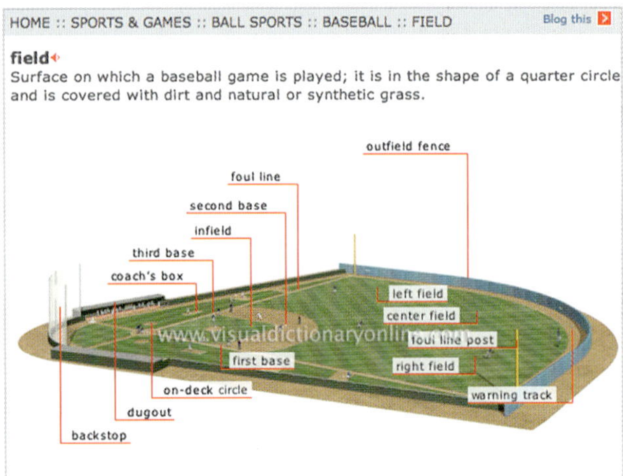


From: *Visual Dictionary Online*

[1] **court of justice** Gerichtshof

### c Search engines[1] as language tools

You probably use Google or another search engine every day. But maybe you haven't yet found out that it can help you check your English and increase your powers of expression.

Let's say you're not sure which is correct or better: *an example of racism* or *an example for racism*? So you run a Google search on each phrase. Remember to put the phrase that you want to check inside quotation marks: *"example of racism"*. What do the numbers of hits for each phrase tell you?

Results **1 - 10** of about **1,960** for **"example of racism"**. (**0.12** seconds)

Results **1 - 1** of about **1** for **"example for racism"**. (**0.10** seconds)

From: www.google.co.uk (Search: pages from the UK)

Try and find out which of the underlined phrases is right in each sentence:

1 Let's discuss the pros and cons / discuss about the pros and cons.
2 You've done a good job / made a good job – thank you, Caroline.
3 How do you call / What do you call a mobile phone in American English?

There is another way Google can help you find collocations. Let's say you know the word *experience* but you aren't sure what verb to use with it. Try using a 'wild card[2]'. In this search, you enter the asterisk* in the place of the word that you want to find out:

Google "* a lot of experience from" Search Advanced Search Preferences
Search: ◉ the web ○ pages from the UK

**Web** Results **1** - **10** of about **24,800** for **"* a lot of experience from"**. (**0.25** seconds)

Marketing Testimonies
I **Gained a lot of Experience from** my Marketing Internship! marketing internships uk «Hello everybody! It is me once again! I am back to New Romney, **...**
www.internship-uk.com/marketing_testimonies2.asp - 59k - Cached - Similar

From: www.google.co.uk

You will find results such as *gained, gathered, got, bring a lot of experience* and you can then decide which fits your text best.

Practice with these phrases:

4 in the * of the picture
5 they faced a * challenge
6 she gave him a * look

⚠ Google has no way of stopping errors appearing in the English of its search results. So you should always double-check the results:

- Look to see if the word or phrase appears relatively seldom (could be an error).
- Look at the context and source of the word or phrase in the search results.
- Go to http://www.google.co.uk and restrict[3] the search to 'pages from the UK'.
- Go to http://books.google.com where you can search the text of (printed) books.
- Look up the word or phrase in a dictionary.

[1] **search engine** ['endʒɪn] Suchmaschine – [2] **wild card** *hier:* Platzhalter – [3] **restrict sth. to sth.** etwas auf etwas beschränken

# ▶ LP 26 Collocations

Collocations are combinations of words that are often used together in English, e.g. *make a plan, a heavy smoker*.

**a** For each group of adjectives choose the right noun from the box.

1 a positive / a possible / a powerful / an unfortunate *effect*
2 a bitter / a salty / a sweet / an unpleasant ...
3 basic / civil / equal / human ...
4 a perfect / an interesting / a permanent / a regular ...
5 the central / an industrial / a rural / an urban ...
6 an angry / a formal / a peaceful / a violent ...
7 accurate / additional / relevant / useful ...
8 an ethnic / a racial / a religious / a small ...

**A** area
**B** effect
**C** information
**D** job
**E** minority
**F** protest
**G** rights
**H** taste

**b** Complete the sentences with the correct English verbs (for the German verb 'machen'). Use a dictionary if you are unsure.

1 Have you ... your bed?
2 Do we have to ... the second task?
3 Let's ... a break.
4 It's your turn to ... the washing-up.
5 We've decided to ... a trip to Paris.
6 Say 'cheese!' – I want to ... a photo.

**c** Work with a partner. Make 'word hands' like the example to show what verbs (and prepositions) go with these nouns: *a book, school, a poem, a job, a decision.* Use a monolingual dictionary or do a Google search if necessary.

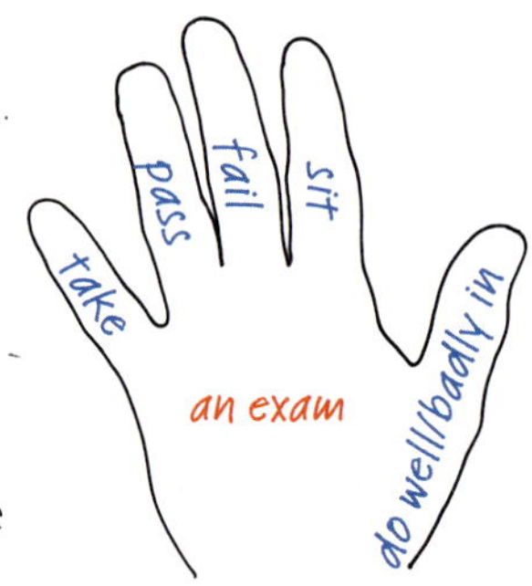


**exam** /ɪg'zæm/ (also *formal* **exam·in·ation**) *noun* **1** a formal written, spoken or practical test, especially at school or college, to see how much you know about a subject, or what you can do: *to* ***take an exam*** ◊ ***to pass/fail an exam*** ◊ *an* ***exam paper*** ◊ *I got my* ***exam results*** *today.* ◊ *A lot of students suffer from* ***exam nerves.*** ◊ (BrE) *I hate* ***doing exams.*** ◊ (BrE, formal) *to* ***sit an exam*** ◊ (BrE) *to* ***mark an exam*** ◊ (NAmE) *to* ***grade an exam*** ◊ (BrE) *She did well* ***in her exams.*** ◊ (NAmE) *She did well* ***on her exams.***

From: *Oxford Advanced Learner's Dictionary,* 2005

**d** Choose one of your 'hands' from **c** and write a dialogue using at least three of the verbs.

*Partner A:* Did you **pass your exam**?
*Partner B:* I haven't **taken it** yet. It's tomorrow. I'm sure I'm going to **fail** because I hate **doing exams** and I always **do badly**.
*Partner A:* Don't be silly, you'll **pass**. You always **do well in exams**.

**e** It is a good idea to learn collocations like vocabulary. A table like this will help you to remember them more easily.

Make three sentences with the collocations from the table that are true for you personally. Then try to make similar collocation tables for *opportunity, challenge* and *responsibility*.

| | | |
|---|---|---|
| gain | experience | ________ |
| have | | in doing sth. |
| learn from | | ________ |
| go through the | | of (doing) sth. |

⚠ **Trouble spot**
Not: ~~make experiences~~

## ▸ LP 27 One German Word, Two English Translations

**a** Match the pairs of words from the two boxes that can be translated using one term in German, e.g. *get up* (**1**) and *stand up* (**L**) – they both mean 'aufstehen'.

**1** get up • **2** ground • **3** bring • **4** recognize
**5** finished • **6** woman • **7** invite
**8** hear • **9** control • **10** mean • **11** difficult
**12** go • **13** sea • **14** if

**A** lake • **B** heavy • **C** think • **D** check
**E** listen to • **F** when • **G** ready • **H** walk
**I** realize • **J** take • **K** floor • **L** stand up
**M** wife • **N** treat

**b** Complete the sentences with the pairs you found in **a**:

1 I would like to ... my CD but I can't ... it because of your noise.
2 Who is that ... over there? – That's my ...!
3 I'm feeling lazy today. Can you ... me a cup of tea? Oh, and ... these letters to the office, please.
4 Swimming in a ... is all right, but it's more exciting in the ... .
5 When you are racing, you always need to be able to ... your bike, so ... it carefully before you start.
6 I ... that your answer is correct, but I am not 100% sure what you ... .
7 Put your hand up ... you've finished. ... you've all finished before the lesson is over, there'll be no homework.
8 Can I ... you out for dinner? I'll ... you, of course.

**c** Invent sentences using the rest of the word pairs.

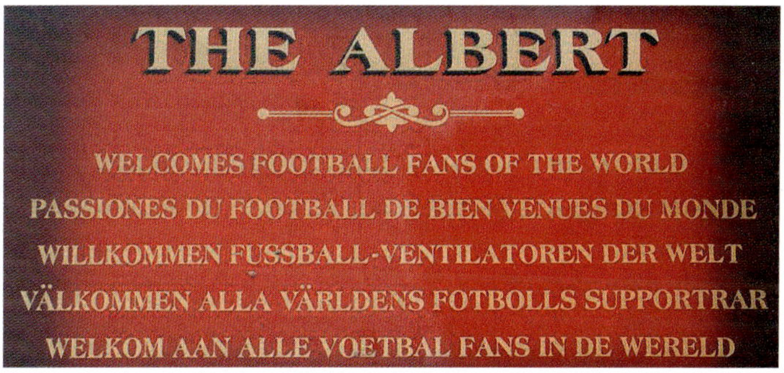


*The people who made this sign (seen on the way to Liverpool's football stadium) must expect German fans to be really cool! Look up* fan *in an English-German dictionary and explain what went wrong.*

## ▸ LP 28 False Friends

**a** The following boxes contain English and German words which sound and look similar, but which have different meanings. Therefore they are called 'false friends'. Write down the correct translations of the English words in blue and of the German words below. Use a dictionary if necessary.

**English words**

I wonder if he's there. • What a lovely gift! • It's open to the public. • I wasn't brave enough to tell him.
It wouldn't be sensible to start again now. • He eventually arrived. • The actual number is much higher.
No means no! • That's a handy little tool. • Your pencil is on the floor. • What was the murder weapon?
He wants to become Prime Minister. • Don't spend too much. • She winked at me knowingly.
I enjoy reading fantasy novels. • He slipped and fell on his backside. • I will survive.

**German words**

sich wundern • Gift • Publikum • brav • sensibel • eventuell • aktuell •
meinen • Handy • Flur • Mörder • bekommen • spenden • winken • Fantasie • Rückseite • (ich) will

**b** Choose at least five of the English translations of the German words above and use them in sentences.

## ▸ LP 29 Confusables[1]

Many English words sound similar (e.g. *advice* and *advise*) or even exactly the same as others (e.g. *break* and *brake*), so it is easy to mix them up.
Do this partner dictation exercise: Partner A reads the first ten sentences, while Partner B writes. Then swap roles for numbers 11–20. Make sure you say all the words very clearly.

1 I need your advice. Please advise me on this.
2 He also came along although he didn't feel well.
3 You will break the brake if you keep pulling it like that.
4 A cool dessert tastes delicious in the hot sandy desert.
5 How does it affect you? What effect does it have on you?
6 I'd like to lie in the sun and lay my hand on her arm; really, I'm not lying.
7 Don't lose this loose button.
8 The show is called *Live a Happy Life* and it's going out live to the nation.
9 I may have won the prize, but I've certainly paid the price for it.
10 There are pandas in that cage, but they're having their afternoon sleep.
11 He was quite quiet.
12 We might have a picnic, but that depends on whether or not the weather stays good.
13 They had to dig deep holes in the ground the whole day long.
14 You simply need more practice – you must practise more.
15 Will you leave me in peace if I give you a piece of the cake?
16 She passed him in the street but she looked straight past him.
17 He was too tired to play two matches at the weekend.
18 Who's the student whose book was stolen?
19 I write with my right hand.
20 I know that I have made no mistakes now.

**EXTRA** If you made a mistake, try to think of a memory aid[2] to help you remember the correct spelling. (e.g. Two o's are not too many.)

## ▸ LP 30 Verbs of Reporting

**a** Don't always say *said* or *tell* or *told*. English has many different ways of describing how people express things in words. Look at the verbs in the box and make sure you know what they mean. You can use most of them with direct or indirect speech.

announce • reply • beg • declare • promise • inquire • command • plead • instruct • claim • maintain • agree • answer • advise • suggest • ask

Find two verbs in the box that generally report:
- a statement
- a question
- an order
- a commitment[3]
- a suggestion
- a response
- a personal opinion
- a request

**b** Choose the best alternative to *said* or *told* in these sentences. You may have to change the sentence slightly:

1 'You will leave and you will leave now', said the officer.
2 The older boy said he had nothing to do with the damage.
3 At the airport, the police told us it was better to take a yellow taxi.
4 After 15 minutes' argument, the receptionist said he would give us our money back.

[1] **confusable** [kən'fju:zəbl] leicht verwechselbares Wort – [2] **aid** Hilfe, Stütze – [3] **commitment** Verpflichtung

# ▸ LP 31 Phrasal Verbs

In the story 'Bread on the Water' (p. 18), the pastor says, 'Depart in peace.' *Depart* is a formal verb which means the same as *go away*, a phrasal verb. Phrasal verbs consist of a verb with a short adverb like *after, away, in, off* after it. They are usually common in informal speech.

**a** Try to match verbs **1–8** with the phrasal verbs **A–H**:

**1** continue • **2** leave/disappear • **3** pass • **4** rise • **5** return • **6** explode • **7** sink, fall • **8** enter

**A** go away • **B** go/come back • **C** go by • **D** go down • **E** go in • **F** go off • **G** go on • **H** go up

**b** The story below contains eight phrasal verbs. Find them and say what they mean by using another verb in their place. (You may have to change the sentences slightly.) You can choose from the following list, but be careful because there is one verb too many:

depress • dress yourself in • escape • find
leave • replace • return • save • switch off

The prisoner decided to get away. The long days alone were getting him down. Luckily for him, he had put away some pieces of rope. He put on some normal clothes. Finally, he put everything back in its normal place and put out the light. 'I hope I never come back here!' he whispered. He glanced back one last time and then he was off ...

*'A guard's coming. Quick, fill in the hole!'*

**c** Complete the dialogues using phrasal verbs from the table on the right.

1 *Rachel:* I'm going to *shut down* the computer. I've been trying to ... about population trends, but I've had no luck.
*Librarian:* Just ... a minute, please. You shouldn't ... so easily. Let's see if I can help you.

2 *Ryan:* You have to behave when you're in the library, or the librarian will ... you ...
*Steven:* I know. She told me to ... my MP3 player last week because she said it was disturbing people.
*Adam:* She made me ... a piece of paper I dropped on the floor.
*Steven:* When Matthew fell asleep in there, she told him to ....
And he certainly did.

| | |
|---|---|
| find | down |
| give | off |
| hang | on |
| pick | out |
| shut | up |
| throw | |
| turn | |
| wake | |

## ▶ LP 32 Word Formation: Prefixes

Like in German, you can expand basic words in English by adding syllables to the beginning of them ('prefixes') or to the end of them ('suffixes').

| prefix | root[1] or stem[2] | suffix |
|---|---|---|
| **under-** | state | **-ment** |

**a** The largest group of prefixes are those that make a word mean the opposite. With a partner, try to find at least two examples of words formed with these negative prefixes.

**anti-** • **dis-** • **in-/im-/ir-/il-** • **mis-** • **non-** • **un-**

Because there is usually no way of telling which root goes with which prefix, you need to check in a dictionary or do a Google search to see if you're right.

**b** Here are some more words with prefixes that you might recognize from German 'Fremdwörter'. Can you explain what idea they add to the root word?

**aqua**planing • **auto**save • **contra**flow • **co-**pilot • **ex-**husband • **hyper**active • **mono**poly • **multi**tasking • **pre-**reading • **re**write • **sub**marine **tele**scope • **trans**atlantic • **ultra**violet

## ▶ LP 33 Word Formation: Suffixes

Suffixes such as *-ly* or *-ness* are added to the end of a word to form a new word, e.g. *friendly* or *kindness*.

**a** You can look up the meaning of suffixes in a dictionary:

**-less** /-ləs/ *suffix* (in adjectives)
**1** without: *treeless* ◊ *meaningless* **2** not doing; not affected by: *tireless* ◊ *selfless*

From: *Oxford Advanced Learner's Dictionary*, 2005

Use a word consisting of a noun + *-less* in each of these sentences.

1 It's ... trying to convince him. He just won't listen.
2 The list of repairs we have to carry out seems to be ...
3 In the last lesson we watched a film about ... people who sleep in parks.
4 I had a ... night. I always lie awake the night before an exam.
5 Our dog is afraid of nothing. He's totally ...
6 The doctor says it won't hurt. It'll be ...

**b** Many abstract nouns are formed by adding a suffix to a verb or an adjective. Sometimes you need to change the spelling or the pronunciation, e.g. *produce* [prəˈdjuːs] ▸ *production* [prəˈdʌkʃn].
Here are six of the most common of these noun suffixes.

| *-ance, -ence* | *-ing* | *-ment* | *-ness* | *-tion, -ation* | *-ty, -ity* |
|---|---|---|---|---|---|
| exist**ence** | warn**ing** | argu**ment** | bright**ness** | pollu**tion** | equal**ity** |

[1] **root** Wurzel – [2] **stem** (Wort-)Stamm – [3] **take advantage of sth.** etwas (aus)nutzen – [4] **dentistry** Zahnbehandlung

Copy the table at the bottom of p. 124 leaving space for a maximum of six more words with each ending. Then use the words in the box on the right to form abstract nouns with the various endings. Use a dictionary if you need to. Write the nouns in your table.

achieve • active • apply • begin • connect • creative • declare • develop • discriminate • happy • human • ill • imagine • meet • pay • punish • react • refer • resist • safe • suffer • willing

Which suffixes are added to verbs and which to adjectives?

**c** There are other, less common suffixes. What abstract nouns can be formed from the words on the right?
Identify the two abstract nouns that are formed from a noun.

arrive • behave • child • citizen • free • injure • mix • serve

**d** Work out the meaning of the underlined nouns and translate the sentences into German.

1 Sickness had reduced the class to half its number.
2 I was dying of boredom in the lesson.
3 I need to give this maths problem my full concentration.
4 Young people need encouragement to work at their studies.

**e** The ideas in the following sentences could be expressed better. Rewrite each sentence using an abstract noun formed from the underlined word.

1 The way I described the scene wasn't very accurate.
*My description of the scene wasn't very accurate.*
2 Being able to read is most important in education.
3 The way your brother performed in the school play was brilliant.
4 The fact that we were excited meant that it was difficult to concentrate.
5 In spite of how friendly the girl was, she never really became friends with anyone.

**f** EXTRA Find German equivalents[1] for these *proverbs.

1 Speech is silver, but silence is golden.
2 Necessity is the mother of invention.

Make up proverbs or sayings of your own. They can be funny ones.
- Education ...
- Happiness ...
- ...

***Education** costs money, but then so does **ignorance**.*

*Sir Claus Moser (British statistician, born 1922)*

*Men are born ignorant, not stupid; they are made stupid by **education**.*

*Bertrand Russell (British philosopher, 1872–1970)*

*Without **education** you're not going anywhere in this world.*

*Malcolm X (an African American leader, 1925–1965)*

*The **excitement** of **learning** separates youth from old age. As long as you're learning, you're not old.*

*Rosalyn S. Yalow (American medical physicist, born 1921)*

[1] **equivalent** [ɪˈkwɪvələnt] Entsprechung

# ▸ LP 34 Word Stress

When you learn new words in English, you need to watch out for the syllables that are stressed. Sometimes the stress patterns[1] change within similar words:

**a** Some words are both nouns and verbs. In nouns, the stress pattern is ['– –], whereas in verbs, it usually is: [–'–]. Practise pronouncing these sentences correctly:

1 May I present you with a present?
2 They can produce a lot, but can they sell their produce?
3 The object I object[2] to is that gun in your hand!
4 It's no good recording everything if you destroy the record.
5 A country shouldn't import more than it can pay for; imports cost money.
6 The rebel village rebelled against the central government.
7 I have contrasted the two colours but I can't see any contrast.
8 We are protesting against your protest!

**b** CD II.07–08 Watch out for stress changes when words get longer. You can listen to a recording of the following pairs of words on the Starter CD.

1 celebrate ['– – –] – celebration [,– –'– –]
2 atom ['– –] – atomic [–'– –]
3 science ['– –] – scientific [,– –'– –]

Continue with the following pairs. Practise drawing the stress patterns.

economy – economic • compete – competition • mountain – mountaineer • identify – identification • electric – electrician • Japan – Japanese

**c** Make a list of the words below, together with similar German words, and underline the stressed syllables: *accent – Akzent*.
Find the three pairs where the English and the German word have the stress on the same syllable.

accent • argument • article • character • culture • electronic • historic • journalist • minister • religion • social • tradition • university • wonderful

Generally speaking, in what way does the stress pattern of the English and the German words in the list differ?

**d** CD II.09 Two- and three-syllable words with prefixes such as *un-*, *dis-*, *in-/im-/ir-/il-*, *sub-*, *pre-* almost always have the stress on the second or third syllable, i.e. prefixes are not usually stressed in English words. Draw the stress patterns for the following words:

inconvenience • submarine • non-smoker • disapprove • mismanagement

**e** CD II.10 As with prefixes, suffixes are not usually stressed. Draw the stress patterns for the following words:

detective • comfortable • democracy • baggage • librarian • explosive

[1] **stress pattern** Betonungsmuster – [2] **object to sth.** etwas ablehnen

# ▸ LP 35 Abbreviations in Text Messages

To save time, many people use the shortened forms of words in text messages and in online chat rooms. There are different ways of shortening words and phrases:

1 You use (the sounds of English) numbers and letters to replace words, e.g. *2 = two/to/too; c = see.*
2 You drop letters, especially vowels from words, e.g. *SPK = speak.*
3 You just write the first letters of the words in a phrase, e.g. *KIT = keep in touch.*
4 You spell words in an easier, shorter way, e.g. *THRU = through.*

**a** Identify what these examples might mean and which of the groups (1–4) above they belong to:

| | | |
|---|---|---|
| B | FYI | ASAP |
| PLS | BFN | RU |
| MSG | BTW | YR |
| Y | ROFL | 2NITE |
| U | COS | F2F |
| RUOK | L8R | MYOB |
| IC | 2DAY | UR |
| CU | B4 | B4N |
| LOL | GR8 | WOT |

**b** In class, collect other English text message abbreviations that you know. But be careful when you use them with people you don't know very well, as some of these forms can offend[1] the reader. You should avoid them in schoolwork too. You can check up the meanings on the Internet.

**Webcode:**
STAR322305-127

**c** Try writing a message in English to your partner that contains a number of these short forms.
You can use emoticons in them too.
Enjoy ☺!

### Texting

- **text message** = SMS(-Nachricht)
- **I'll text you. / I'll send you a text (message).**
  = Ich schicke dir eine SMS.
- **Can you text me the name again?**
  = Kannst du mir noch mal eine SMS mit dem Namen schicken?

*'Just think of it as a long text message.'*

[1] **offend sb.** jdn. beleidigen

## Communication Skills

### ▸ LP 36 Expressing Opinions CD II.11–13

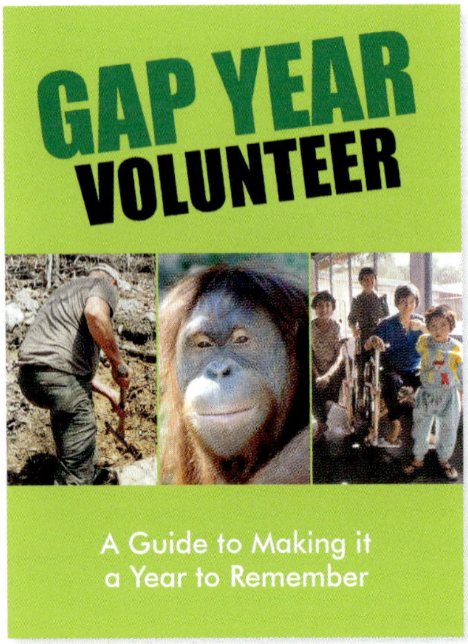


**a** Maddie has just told her friend Jason that she's planning to do a gap year[1] volunteering in Tanzania. Jason has some opinions of his own on that idea.

As you listen to their conversation, try to note down the expressions the two of them use to give their opinions, e.g.: *I think …*

> ⚠ **Trouble spot**
> Ich meine, dass … = **I think that …**
> Not: ~~I mean that~~

**b** Compare your list with that of a partner. If you know any other expressions for giving your opinion, add them to your lists.

**c** Imagine your English friend Samantha – 'Sam' for short – has rung you to announce that she's thinking of backpacking through Spain for three months between school and university. You're worried that she may not know what she's getting herself into. Collect arguments against her taking such a trip, e.g.:

- dangers for a woman travelling alone
- lots of people in Spain don't like the English because of the hooligans
- weather: very hot in summer
- sleeping in a tent
- …

Listen to the dialogue on the CD. In the gaps give your reasons for thinking your friend's plans are not a good idea. Use expressions you collected in **a** and **b** when giving your opinion. Then listen to Track 13 to hear the suggested answers.

**d** **Role-play:** Sam now wants to do the trip to Spain with a friend from school, Pat. Pat likes the idea of taking a trip together, but really wants to go to France. Both have their reasons for preferring one country over the other.
Prepare one of the roles. Then, with a partner, role-play the scene. You can start the conversation like this:

*Sam:* Pat, I really think we'd have a much better time in Spain. Just think of those great-looking Spanish men/women.
*Pat:* Yes, they are nice, aren't they? But I feel I ought to do something for my French. …

[1] **gap year** Jahr zwischen Schule und Universität („Lückenjahr")

# ▸ LP 37 Persuading[1] People CD II.14–16

**a** Henry and his girlfriend Alice are watching a news item about the effects of human activity on the environment. Henry doesn't believe that he alone can do anything to improve the situation, but Alice tries to convince him that he can change his ways[2].

Work in groups of three. Each group member chooses one of the three categories of persuasion[3] in the table below and listens out for phrases that belong in it. Listen to the dialogue at least twice. Then compare your notes and complete the table with all the phrases.

> ⚠ **Trouble spot**
> **persuade sb. to do sth.**
> = get sb. to do sth.
> **convince sb.**
> = make sb. believe sth.

| Asking rhetorical questions and using question tags | Suggesting something / Making somebody think | Showing scepticism[4] |
|---|---|---|
| *You don't really believe that, do you?* | *Just think of all the hot weather we've been having recently.* | *Oh, come on!* |
| ... | ... | ... |

**b** Henry comes to visit you in Germany and tells you and your dad that he's become more 'green'. However, your very environmentally conscious[5] and outspoken[6] dad, who understands but doesn't speak much English, tries to convince Henry that he still has the wrong attitude towards the environment.

Listen to the dialogue on the CD. In the gaps explain to Henry what your dad says. Try to use as many of the phrases from **a** as possible, e.g. *Surely you don't ... / You can't be serious!,* etc. Then listen to Track 16 to hear the suggested answers.

**c** **Role-play:** The new, 'green' Henry is now back at home in England and decides that he needs to make others aware[7] of the effect of their actions. He starts off by trying to persuade his sister Emily to be more caring[8] towards the environment.
With a partner, role-play the scene using the role cards your teacher will give you. You can start the conversation like this:

*Henry:* Emily, I've noticed you left your TV on standby all night. Do you do that often?
*Emily:* Yes, I leave it on standby every night. Why?
*Henry:* Well, because it's a waste of energy – and money. Didn't you realize that?
*Emily:* ...

[1] **persuade sb.** [pəˈsweɪd] jdn. überreden, überzeugen – [2] **ways** *(pl)* Gewohnheiten – [3] **persuasion** Überredung(skunst), Überzeugen – [4] **scepticism** [ˈskeptɪsɪzəm] Skepsis, Ungläubigkeit – [5] **environmentally conscious** [ˈkɒnʃəs] umweltbewusst – [6] **outspoken** offen, direkt – [7] **aware of sth.** einer Sache bewusst – [8] **caring** sorgsam, verantwortungsbewusst

## ▸ LP 38 Agreeing and Disagreeing CD II.17–19

There are many situations, both now and in the future, when you will need to find agreement with somebody, for example in class, with friends, with an employer or colleagues. Remember: agreeing and disagreeing with people can be very different in formal and informal situations.

**a** Listen to the dialogues on Tracks 17 and 18 (between a customer and a salesperson) and decide:
- Is the situation formal or informal?
- Which customer deals best with the situation – the man or the woman?

**b** Work with a partner. Look at the box below with phrases for agreeing and disagreeing. Take three minutes to memorize them (Partner A: Agreeing; Partner B: Disagreeing). Then listen to the two dialogues again and write down the phrases used.

| Agreeing | Disagreeing |
|---|---|
| *I agree (absolutely/100%/...).* | *I'm afraid I don't agree with you.* |
| *I think so too.* | *That's complete/absolute/... nonsense/...* |
| *Me too. / Me neither.* | *I understand what you're saying, but ...* |
| *I couldn't agree more.* | *You've got to be joking!* |
| *That's right/true.* | *That's a good point, but have you thought about ...?* |
| *Good point!* | *I don't think that's right.* |
| *That's exactly what I think.* | *That may be true, but I think ...* |
| *You can say that again!* | *Hang on! / Wait a minute, ...* |
| *Absolutely. / Of course.* | *I agree up to a point but then on the other hand ...* |

**c** Listen to the dialogue on Track 19 and decide whether the situation is formal or informal. Mark the phrases used in a copy of the chart.

**d** EXTRA Listen again to Track 19. Are any phrases used that aren't in your list? If so, suggest why.

**e** **Role-play:** Chris's parents have invited their friends Kate and Andrew to supper. After supper Kate and Andrew talk to Chris and express the view that TV is really bad for young people. They add that they don't allow their children to watch it. Chris, who watches quite a lot of TV, contradicts[1] them.
Role-play the scene with a partner: Partner A will play Chris, Partner B either Kate or Andrew. Before you start, Partner A should collect arguments for allowing young people to watch TV and Partner B should collect arguments against. Both look again at all your agreeing/disagreeing phrases and make notes.

[1] **contradict sb.** jdm. widersprechen

# ▸ LP 39 Making Comparisons CD II.20

**a** Chloe is giving a talk for her Biology class on optical illusions[1]. Look at the illustrations on the right and follow her talk.

1
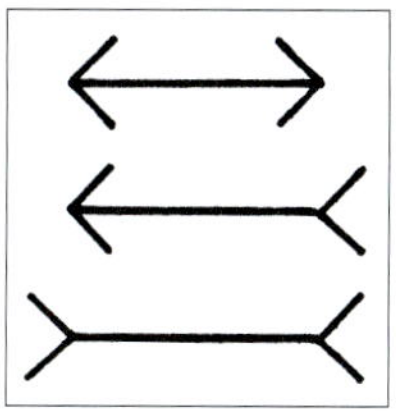

2
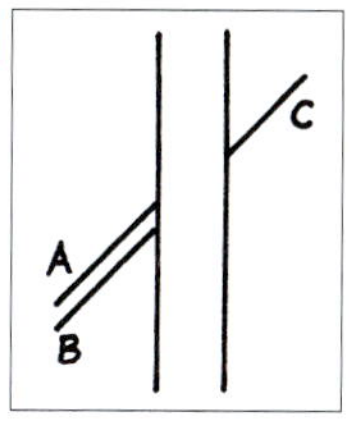


3
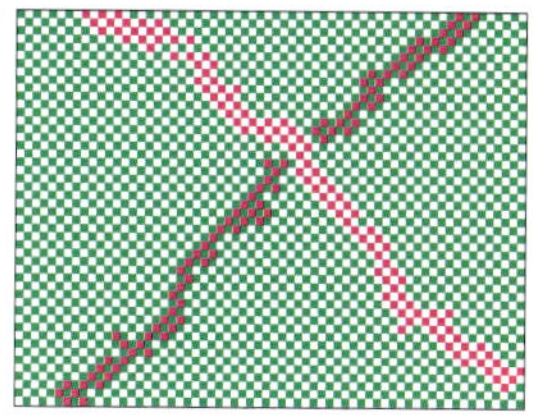

**b** Listen again and note down phrases she uses to make comparisons when talking about the illusions, e.g. *the shortest, a slightly longer one, ...*

**c** Listen to Chloe's talk once more. This time note down phrases she uses to make clear what part of a drawing she's describing, e.g. *at the top, followed by ... in the middle, underneath that, ...*
What other phrases for describing pictures do you know? Add them to your list.

**d** Describe and compare the design of the British flag (the Union Jack) and the German flag using phrases from **b**, **c** and the box below. What additional phrases for making comparisons can you find in the box? Add them to your list from **b**.

**Describing and comparing the flags**

*Both flags have / consist of / are made up of ...*
*The ... is/has ... . The ..., however / on the other hand, is/has/isn't ... / doesn't have any ...*
*While the ... (only) has slanted[2]/straight/thick/thin/horizontal/vertical/diagonal/red/white/blue/black/ yellow bars[3], the ... has ...*
*The ... has bars which run parallel to one another, whereas the ... has a mixture of ...*
*In comparison to / Compared to the ..., which has a cross in the middle, the ... has / doesn't have ...*
*The flags are very similar to / different from each other in that ...*
*The ... appear(s) (to be) longer/darker/thicker than that/those on the ...*
*... is the same length/colour/shade as ...*
*The ... on the ... are not as thick/... as those on the ...*
*The white background of the ... makes it appear much brighter than the ...*

**e** As you can see from the table below, there are some differences between minimum legal age limits[4] in the UK and in Germany. With a partner, compare these limits and discuss whether or not you agree with them. Which differences do you find most surprising? Use phrases from **b** and **d**.

| When can I ... | UK | Germany |
|---|---|---|
| accept criminal responsibility[5]? | 10 | 14 |
| get a job? | 13 | 13 (with parental consent[6]) |
| have sex? | 16 | 14 |
| leave school? | 16 | 16–18 (depending on state) |
| get married? | 16 (with parental consent) | 18 |
| drive a car? | 17 | 18 |
| smoke? | 16 | 18 |
| buy alcohol? | 18 | 16/18 (spirits[7]) |
| vote in an election? | 18 | 18 |

[1] **optical illusion** [ɪ'lu:ʒn] optische Täuschung – [2] **slanted** schräg – [3] **bar** Stange, Stab – [4] **legal age limit** gesetzlich festgelegte Altersgrenze – [5] **accept criminal responsibilty** strafmündig sein – [6] **consent** [kən'sent] Einwilligung, Zustimmung – [7] **spirits** *(pl)* Spirituosen

## Overview

### Study and Language Skills


1 Mind Mapping ... 132
2 Brainstorming ... 133
3 Marking Up a Text ... 133
4 Taking Notes ... 134
5 Making Notes ... 134
6 Dealing with Words You Don't Know ... 135
7 Paraphrasing ... 135
8 Using a Dictionary ... 136
9 Using a Grammar Book ... 137
10 Keeping a Learning Log ... 138
11 Keeping a Portfolio ... 138
12 Working with Pictures ... 140
13 Doing Research ... 141
14 Doing a Project ... 143
15 Mediating ... 144
16 Translating ... 144


### Exam Skills


17 Taking a Test ... 145
18 Answering Multiple-Choice Questions ... 145


### Listening and Viewing Skills


19 Listening for Gist ... 146
20 Listening for Detail ... 146
21 Viewing a Film ... 147


### Speaking Skills


22 Giving a Report on a Book or Film ... 148
23 Giving a Presentation ... 148
24 Taking Part in a Classroom Discussion ... 149
25 Making Conversation ... 150


### Reading Skills


26 Skimming ... 150
27 Scanning ... 150
28 Reading Fiction ... 151
29 Reading Non-Fiction ... 151
30 Keeping a Reading Journal ... 151


### Writing Skills


31 The Stages of Writing ... 152
32 Writing an Outline ... 153
33 Structuring a Text ... 153
34 Linking Ideas ... 154
35 Writing a Formal Letter or Email ... 155
36 Writing a Personal Statement ... 156
37 Writing a Summary ... 156
38 Writing a Characterization ... 156
39 Writing an Essay ... 157


## Study and Language Skills

### ▸ SF 1 Mind Mapping

Mind mapping is useful for brainstorming and for trying to get either a general or a detailed view of a topic. You can also use it to plan a text or talk.

**Step 1:** Write the topic word or phrase in the middle of an empty, unlined piece of paper.

**Step 2:** Using different colours, draw branches and sub-branches out from the central word or phrase. Write words and phrases along these branches (not whole sentences) or use symbols, pictures or icons. You can add ideas at any stage.

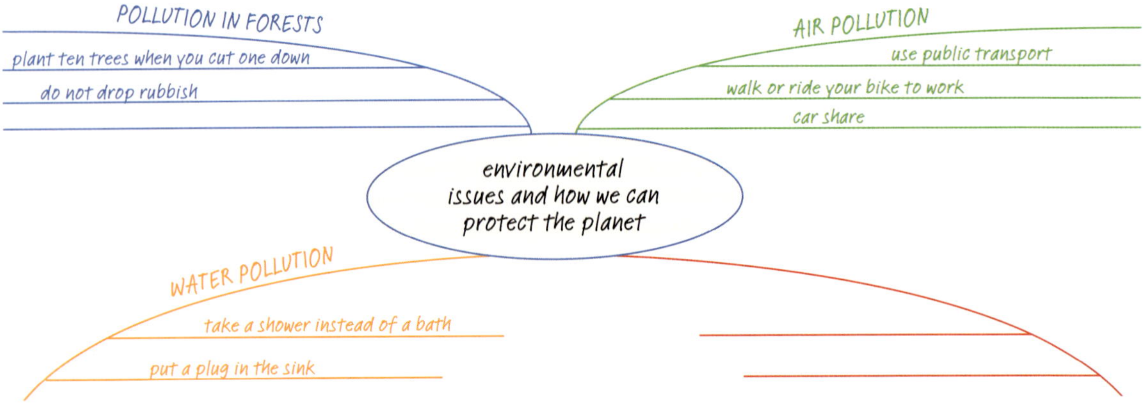


▸ SF 2 Brainstorming (p. 133)

## ▸ SF 2 Brainstorming

Brainstorming is the first step in collecting your ideas. It is useful when you want to write a text or plan a talk. You can brainstorm on your own or in a group.

### Individual brainstorming

**Step 1:**
Write down every idea that comes into your head on the topic you want to write or talk about.

*Environment*

*pollution*
*protect nature*
*WWF / Greens*
*damage → crisis*
*recycling*
*eco-friendly*

**Step 2:**
Choose those ideas you really want to explore further and structure them in a way you find helpful, e.g. in a mind map or in a chart with the 5 W's (the questions who?, what?, when?, where? and why?) and how.

| *Who?* | *What?* | *When?* | *Where?* | *Why?* |
|---|---|---|---|---|
| *WWF (World Wide Fund for Nature)* | *one of the biggest international* | *founded in 1961* | *in Switzerland* | *preserve biological diversity* |

### Group brainstorming

One of many different ways to brainstorm in a group is using the **placemat** method. You can see an example of a placemat on the right.

**Step 1:** Get into groups of four. Each writes down at least three ideas on the topic in one of the four corners of the placemat.

**Step 2:** Together, discuss all the ideas and choose the ones you agree are best or most important. Write them in the middle of your placemat.

▸ SF 1 Mind Mapping (p. 132)

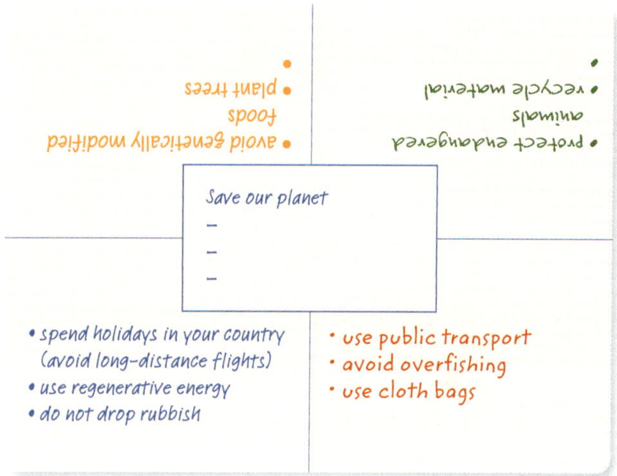


*Placemat activity*

## ▸ SF 3 Marking Up a Text

Marking up a text is useful if there is information in a text you're reading that you may want to look up later. Remember: You can only mark up texts in photocopies or in books that belong to you.

**Step 1:** As you read the text, keep in mind what it is you need to know. When you find that information in the text, mark it by underlining, circling or highlighting it. Mark only keywords.

**Step 2:** When you look over the passages you have marked, you may find it helpful to add keywords in the margins.

**Step 3:** This way, when you need to find the information again, for example while preparing for a test, you only have to read the marked words and your notes in the margins.

**What you can do to save the Earth:**

1. Recycle newspapers, plastic and paper bags, aluminum cans, office and notebook paper, car oil, anything and everything at recycling centres, supermarkets, and petrol stations. It's a bit of an effort but it makes a huge difference. *recycling*
2. Plant a tree. Trees take carbon dioxide out of the air and give us oxygen to breathe.
3. Take cloth bags to the supermarket, especially when you are only buying a few things. Avoid using another plastic or paper bag. Use cloth rags and sponges instead of paper towels. *use bags more than once*
4. Walk if it's close, or take a bus or train or the underground. Cars pollute a lot – if *public transport*

## ▸ SF 4 Taking Notes

Taking notes ('protokollieren', 'mitschreiben') is useful when you want to remember things you read or heard about, i.e. you write down someone else's ideas. It is, for example, helpful to take notes if you need to remember the key points of a classmate's talk or to get information from a recorded message.

**Step 1:** Look or listen for keywords. These are words or phrases that contain the information you need to answer a question or that seem important in a passage.

**Step 2:** Note down the keywords or ideas. Remember:

- Don't write whole sentences:
  NOT: *The world population will increase to 9.2 billion by 2100.*
  BUT: *World pop. → 9.2 bill. (2100)*
- Use numbers, abbreviations and symbols. You can make up your own abbreviations and symbols – but don't overdo it.

**Common abbreviations and symbols**

| | | | |
|---|---|---|---|
| the same as | = | between | *bet.* |
| not the same as | ≠ | for example | *e.g.* |
| about the same as | ≈ | important | *impt.* or *!* |
| and | + | not | *x* or *ø* |
| and so on, et cetera | ... or *etc.* | with | *w.* or *w/* |
| becomes/will be | → | without | *w/o* |

▸ SF 20 Listening for Detail (p. 146) ▸ SF 37 Writing a Summary (p. 156)

## ▸ SF 5 Making Notes

Making notes ('Notizen machen', 'sich Stichwörter notieren') is useful for organizing information, i. e. when you put your own ideas on paper in short form. You make notes, for example, when you're preparing to write a text or structuring your ideas for a presentation.

When you make notes:

- Use keywords, symbols and abbreviations, as in taking notes above.
- Leave room to add more notes later. It is a good idea to leave a wide margin.
- Treat your notes as a process. You can add ideas at any time, preferably in a different colour: use arrows to make connections between ideas, and numbers to put your notes in a different order.

## ▶ SF 6 Dealing with Words You Don't Know

Dealing with words you don't know (or have forgotten) is something you have to do all the time when you're learning and using a foreign language. There are lots of ways to find out what a word means, so don't panic.

- When you're reading / listening to a long text, you do not need to understand every word.
- Watch out for similarities between the unknown word and a word you already know in English, German or another language. But be careful: the words might be 'false friends'.
- Check whether you know parts of the word. Sometimes a prefix or suffix may have been added to a word you already know.
- Use the context, as well as the title or heading, subtitles and pictures. This helps you work out what the meaning of a word might be.

## ▶ SF 7 Paraphrasing

Paraphrasing is useful when you don't know an English word that you need to use in conversation. Paraphrasing is also used in mediating. It allows you to get across the meaning of the word without using the word itself. Here are some tips:

- You can use synonyms: *(to begin) It's the same as 'to start'.*
  and antonyms: *(to win) It's the opposite of 'to lose'.*
- You can use a general word or phrase and then explain what the thing does, what it can be used for or where you can find it. You can also use a relative clause.
  *(A drill) is a machine for making holes in the ground. People use it to get oil.*
  *(A desert) is an area where it's very dry and not much grows.*
  *(A volunteer) is a person who offers to work and help people, but doesn't ask for any money in return.*

▶ SF 15 Mediating (p. 144)

| unknown word | paraphrase | strategy |
|---|---|---|
| *smack* | *= hit* | *synonym* |
| *doubt* | *↔ believe* | *antonym* |
| *trout, pikeperch, salmon* | *different kinds of fish* | *general word* |
| *current* | *movement of water in the sea* | *what the thing is/does* |
| *lawnmower* | *a device for cutting grass in the garden* | *what it can be used for* |
| *exodus* | *a situation in which many people leave a place at the same time* | *relative clause* |

# ▸ SF 8 Using a Dictionary

A dictionary is useful for understanding important words you don't know and whose meaning you can't work out. It tells you the meaning of an English word, how to pronounce it, how to spell it or use it in a sentence. You will probably want to use both a bilingual dictionary and a monolingual dictionary.

## Monolingual dictionary

**Step 1:** Find the word you want in the dictionary and study the full entry, especially the example sentences.
**Step 2:** Check and learn any useful information the entry offers on grammar and *register.

pronunciation — British English — American English — word class — headword — 1st meaning — uncountable noun — example phrase (with collocation in bold type ['fett']) — 2nd meaning — countable noun — idiom — register

**art** /ɑːt; *NAmE* ɑːrt/ *noun* **1** [U] the use of the imagination to express ideas or feelings, particularly in painting, drawing or SCULPTURE: ***modern/contemporary***/*American* ***art*** ◊ *an* ***art critic/historian/lover*** ◊ *Can we call television art?* ◊ *stolen* ***works of art*** ◊ *Her performance displayed great art.* – see also CLIP ART, FINE ART **2** [U] examples of objects such as paintings, drawings or SCULPTURES: *an* ***art gallery/exhibition*** ◊ *a collection of art and antiques* **3** [U] the skill of creating objects such as paintings and drawings, especially when you study it: *She's good at art and design.* ◊ *an* ***art teacher/student/college/class*** **4 the arts** [pl.] art, music, theatre, literature, etc. when you think of them as a group: *lottery funding for the arts* – see also PERFORMING ARTS **5** [C] a type of VISUAL or performing art: *Dance is a very theatrical art.* **6** [C, usually pl.] the subjects you can study at school or university which are not scientific, such as languages, history or literature: *an arts degree* – compare SCIENCE **7** [C, U] an ability or a skill that you can develop with training and practice: *a therapist trained in the art of healing* ◊ *Letter-writing is a lost art nowadays.* ◊ *Appearing confident at interviews is* ***quite an art*** (= rather difficult). IDM SEE FINE *adj.*

**tacky** /ˈtæki/ *adj.* (**tackier**, **tackiest**) **1** (*informal*) cheap, badly made and/or lacking in taste: *tacky souvenirs* ◊ *The movie had a really tacky ending.* **2** (of paint, glue, etc.) not dry and therefore slightly sticky

From: *Oxford Advanced Learner's Dictionary*, 2005

## Bilingual dictionary

- To make sure you have chosen the right English translation of a German word, look up the English word in the English-German part of the dictionary.
- Each number in an entry signals a new meaning. If the translations under 1 clearly don't fit your context, go on to meaning 2, 3, etc.

**Remember:** When using a dictionary, you can save time by first looking at abbreviations. They will tell you:
- in what areas the word is used. If you are reading a scientific article, for example, look first at translations labelled 'Biol' (for Biology), 'Chem' (for Chemistry) or 'Phys' (for Physics).
- what word class the entry deals with.

▸ SF 6 Dealing with Words You Don't Know (p. 135)

# ▶ SF 9 Using a Grammar Book

**Step 1:** Decide what it is you need to look up – something to do with verbs, nouns, sentence structure, etc.

**Step 2:** If you want to revise a problem area, you will find it most easily in the table of contents. To check a very specific point, look in the index.

## Table of contents


*The verb*

| | | |
|---|---|---|
| Summary ............................ | **23** | 21 |
| Modal auxiliaries ........................ | **23** | 22-48 |
| *Be, have* and *do* ........................ | **36** | 49-57 |
| The short forms of the auxiliaries .......... | **40** | 58-60 |
| Full verbs ............................ | **42** | 61-71 |
| Summary: the tenses of the full verbs ....... | **50** | 72-73 |
| The tenses of the full verbs .............. | **54** | 74-94 |
| Simple present ...................... | **54** | 74-75 |


## Index


**indirect object**: 19, 20
as subject of a passive sentence 112
**indirect speech**: 273-280
and direct speech 273
characteristics 274
commands, prohibition 274a, **280a**
questions 274a, **279**
requests, advice 274a, **280b**
suggestions 274a, **280c**
reporting verb **274a/d**, 277a, 278a, **279**, 280


**Step 3:** If you read the rules and the examples together, you will find it easier to understand and remember the rules. Check out all the information in the sample entry below:

chapter — grammar section

The verb **63** **Simple past**

section number — **86** *Use*

grammatical structures —

**a** Tina passed her driving test in 2008.
*Tina hat 2008 ihren Führerschein gemacht.*
I was a cheerleader from 2005 to 2007.
*Ich war von 2005 bis 2007 Cheerleader.*
Did Jeff pay for the concert tickets yesterday?
– No, he didn't. He forgot.
*Hat Jeff gestern die Konzertkarten bezahlt?*
*– Nein, er hat es vergessen.*
When did you last see Nicole?
*Wann hast du Nicole zuletzt gesehen?*

We use the simple past to say that something happened at a **particular point of time in the past** (answering the question *when?*) or in a **particular period of time in the past** (which is now over). The point or period of time can be mentioned, or it may be clear from the context. Some common phrases of time are *yesterday, in 2008, last year/month/week, an hour ago*, etc. We also use the simple past (not the present perfect) after *when ...?*

frequent mistakes — ⚠ *Ich habe meine Uhr gestern verloren.*
**not:** I ~~have lost~~ my watch yesterday.
**but:** I lost my watch yesterday.

In **German**, past events can be reported in the ***Perfekt*** as well as the ***Imperfekt***.

structures you don't need to use actively —

***Notes***

**1** Grandmother would sit at her window for hours, watching the birds.
*Großmutter pflegte stundenlang am Fenster zu sitzen und den Vögeln zuzusehen.*

To express the idea of regularly repeated actions in the past, we can also use *would* + infinitive (without *to*).

**2** It's time we were allowed to do what we want.
*Es wird Zeit, dass wir tun dürfen, was wir wollen.*
I wish he knew how to solve his problem.
*Ich wünschte, er wüsste, ...*

The simple past is used in sentences with *I wish* and *it's time* expressing a wish. In such cases the simple past refers to the present or the future and not to the past.

I wish I were you/I were rich/I weren't here.
*Ich wünschte, ich wäre ...*

Note the special form *I wish I were ...*

▶ *Would* used for typical behaviour: 48

brief summary —

*Simple past:*
*– when we want to say when something happened*
*– when we talk about things in the past or tell a story*

From: *Cornelsen English Grammar*, 2001

▶ SF 17 Taking a Test (p. 145)

## ▸ SF 10 Keeping a Learning Log

Everybody has 'favourite' mistakes – mistakes they make over and over again. One way of dealing with this problem is to keep a learning log.

**Step 1:** Divide an exercise book into sections: Words, Grammar, Spelling.

**Step 2:** Every time you get corrected work back from your teacher or you do a self-assessment test, write down the mistakes you made in the correct part of your learning log book.

**Step 3:** Check each mistake in a dictionary or grammar book. Note down the correct form of the word or phrase.

### Learning log

| Words | | |
|---|---|---|
| **wrong** | **correct** | **remember** |
| *~~an~~ advice* | *a piece of advice* | *advice: uncountable → no indefinite article* |
| *~~spend~~ to charity* | *donate to charity* | *spend money, spend time* |
| *~~Eventually~~ I'll come round tonight.* | *Perhaps I'll come round tonight.* | *eventually – schließlich*<br>*eventuell – perhaps* |

**Step 4:** If you make a particular mistake regularly, do some extra exercises from your Workbook or e-Workbook. That may help you to remember the point.

**Step 5:** Add to your learning log all the time. Always check your 'favourite' mistakes in it before a test.

▸ SF 8 Using a Dictionary (p. 136) ▸ SF 9 Using a Grammar Book (p. 137) ▸ SF 17 Taking a Test (p. 145)

## ▸ SF 11 Keeping a Portfolio

A portfolio has two separate parts:

- The **Dossier** is a good place to keep good or interesting work you have done, which may be useful when you apply for a place on an exchange programme or at university, or when you are looking for a job.
- The **Language Passport** can help you to monitor your progress while learning English.

- You can use any notebook for your Language Portfolio, or you can buy one that already has a structure for you to follow. If you buy one, read the introduction to learn how to use it.
- Assess yourself regularly, and be honest. Like a learning log, the portfolio will help you to identify your strengths and weaknesses.

### Dossier

I did the following at school or elsewhere:

| | I heard, saw | I presented, told, sang | I read | I wrote |
|---|---|---|---|---|
| non-fictional texts on different topics | | | | *an article on environmental issues in my home town for the school newspaper of our partner school in Peterborough* |
| fictional texts (novels, dramas, short stories) | | | *'Looking for Alaska' by John Green* | |
| poems, songs | *several songs* | *several songs in the bathroom* | | |
| films or film snippets | *'Milk'* | | | |

From: *Europäisches Portfolio der Sprachen*, 2007

## Language Passport: self-assessment grid

| Level B2 Date: | 16/9 | 17/11 | 18/1 | |
|---|---|---|---|---|
| **Listening** | | | | |
| I can understand extended speech and lectures and follow even complex lines of argument, provided the topic is reasonably familiar. | | ✓ | | |
| I can understand most TV news and current affairs programmes. | ✓ | | | |
| I can understand the majority of films in standard dialect. | | | | |
| **Reading** | | | | |
| I can read articles and reports concerned with contemporary problems in which the writers adopt particular attitudes or viewpoints. | | | ✓ | |
| I can understand contemporary literary prose. | | | | |
| **Spoken interaction** | | | | |
| I can interact with a degree of fluency and spontaneity that makes regular interaction with native speakers quite possible. | ✓ | | | |
| I can take an active part in discussions in familiar contexts, accounting for and sustaining my views. | | ✓ | | |
| **Spoken production** | | | | |
| I can present clear, detailed descriptions on a wide range of subjects related to my field of interest. | ✓ | | | |
| I can explain a viewpoint on a topical issue giving advantages and disadvantages of various options. | | ✓ | | |
| **Writing** | | | | |
| I can write clear, detailed texts on a wide range of subjects related to my interests. | ✓ | | | |
| I can write an essay or report, passing on information or giving reasons in support of or against a particular point of view. | | | | |
| I can write letters highlighting the personal significance of events and experiences. | | | | |

From: *Europäisches Portfolio der Sprachen*, 2007

- Once you have identified problem areas, develop a plan of action. That might involve:
  - revising grammar points in your grammar book and doing exercises on the topic
  - working with a dictionary or vocabulary help books and computer programs
  - revising your knowledge of skills, e.g. in this Skills File
  - getting more practice in English by watching TV or DVDs in English, listening to English-language radio, reading English-language magazines or newspapers, etc.
- Save work you've done in the Dossier: a test which your teacher gave you a good mark for, a poster you made, or work from a project you did with classmates. A college or an employer you apply to may be interested in seeing the quality and range of your work in English.

## ▸ SF 12 Working with Pictures

Different kinds of pictures (photos, *cartoons, posters, graphs and charts) can help you to understand something you are reading or listening to. They are also useful for getting a message across, e.g. in a presentation.

**1** pie chart

**Sources of greenhouse gas for a typical family in %**

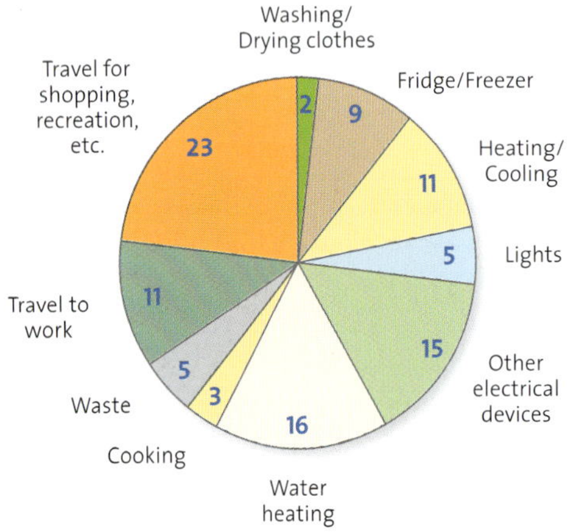

**2** cartoon

**3** photo

**4** poster

### Describing a picture

When you are asked to describe a picture, don't give your opinion.

**Step 1:** Read the title or *caption first. Then look carefully to see what the main theme of the picture material is.
*This picture/photo/poster/cartoon/chart is about ... / shows ... / wants us to ... / provides proof of ...*

**Step 2:** Always describe picture material systematically, e.g. from foreground to background, from top to bottom, from left to right.
*In the centre / foreground of the photo you can see ...*
*The poster shows a picture of ... . Underneath that we see ...*
*In the cartoon there are two ...; one on the left and one on ...*
*The largest slice of the pie chart shows ...*

### Analysing a picture

When you are asked to analyse a picture, you will be expected to draw conclusions about what the picture is trying to do, whether it does so effectively, and how it goes about it.

**Step 1:** The best way to analyse a picture is to ask yourself some questions and note down your answers.

- **For a picture/photo**
  What is the artist/photographer trying to say? How do they say it (technique/colours/...)? What effect does it have on the viewer / me?
  *The picture/photo clearly shows that ...*
  *It's a good example of ...*
  *... is very attractive because ...*
  *... makes the point that ...*

- **For a poster/cartoon**
  Who was it made for (newspaper, charity, political or advertising campaign)? Where and when did it appear? What is it trying to say/criticize/encourage people/me to do?
  *The poster/cartoon was meant to show voters / readers of the paper / ...*
  *It's very eye-catching through its use of ...*
  *It speaks to the reader directly by ...ing ...*
  *The layout / use of colour ...*
  *... is criticizing / making fun of ...*

- **For a chart/graph**
  Who produced it (the government / a political party / a newspaper/ ...) Why?
  *The figures come from ..., so they are quite reliable / so we have to be careful what conclusions we draw from them.*
  *The bar chart / pie chart conveys/indicates an upturn / an increase / a decline in ...*

**Step 2:** Order your notes and ask a concluding question:
Does the picture material achieve what I think it set out to do?
*The poster/chart/... is quite successful at what it is trying to do / ...*
*It doesn't really manage to convince me of ... / that ... / to ...*
*It could have been more effective if it had ...*

## ▸ SF 13 Doing Research

Doing research is a vital part of preparing any talk, report or project.

**Step 1:** Before you start to do your research, brainstorm and list words and phrases relevant to your topic. Rank them from most to least important. Sum up your research goal in just one or two sentences.

**Step 2:** Make a list of keywords (in English) that you can use when checking the table of contents or index in a book. If you're doing your research on the Internet, you'll need to enter these keywords into the search engine. Use only English sources.

▸▸▸

**Step 3:** Before reading whole chapters or articles:

- Check the source.

| General question | Examples |
|---|---|
| Is the source reliable?<br>– Who is the author/publisher?<br>– Whose website are you on? | A respected encyclopedia is more reliable than a daily paper. A university website is more reliable than someone's blog. |
| Does the writer or website have a point of view that you should be aware of?<br>– Is it professional/amateur?<br>– Is it selling an idea/product? | A political party or an activist group may not reveal all the relevant facts. Someone who is trying to sell you something may use emotions instead of facts, or they may even twist the facts. |
| Are the facts and figures based on solid evidence?<br>– Are they proper government statistics?<br>– Is it a poll by a company?<br>– Is it a statement by an anonymous source? | Governments in free societies will provide reliable statistics. A polling agency may ask questions in such a way that the party or company paying for the poll will like what it finds out. Anonymous sources can only be believed if the person reporting can be believed – a trusted investigative journalist, for example. |

- Skim the chapters or articles to make sure they're useful for your topic.

**Step 4:** Read the material you have selected and make notes on it. Make sure to note down the source in case you want to make a direct quote or return to it. In the case of print material, you need the title, the author, the publisher and the date of publication. In the case of an online source, note down the web address. Print out the page with the date on it before it disappears or is changed.

## Tips for Internet research

The Internet is a great tool for doing research. But anyone can publish on the Internet, so the problem of reliability is even greater than with printed matter. It is also easy to 'get lost' in the World Wide Web. This advice aims to help you steer away from these dangers.

- Always check the source of the website before using it.
- Find a search engine you like and use it regularly. Get to know its different features. They can save you lots of time. In some search engines you can:
  - set preferences to show you results in specific languages. This can be very useful when doing a project for English, where you want English results only.
  - use quotation marks to get an exact match for a phrase.
  - use OR for alternatives, an asterisk (*) as a 'wild card', a minus sign (-) before a word to rule out pages containing that word.

| You enter | The result is |
|---|---|
| "John F. Kennedy" OR jfk | pages with either name |
| "reduce your * footprint" | pages with "reduce your <u>carbon</u> footprint", "reduce your <u>personal</u> footprint", "reduce your <u>online</u> footprint", "reduce your <u>paper</u> footprint" and others |
| US President -Obama | pages containing 'US President' are listed, but none which refers to Barack Obama |

– refine your research by putting in more than one word or phrase.

| You enter | The number of results |
|---|---|
| "environmental issues" | 147 000 000 |
| "environmental issues" "reduction of CO2" | 10 100 |
| "environmental issues" "reduction of CO2" "Kyoto Protocol" | 2410 |

**organization responsible for the website**

**contents showing how the words (in bold print ['fett']) occur on the website**

World Business Council for Sustainable Development (WBCSD)
23 Nov 2007 ... **Reduction of CO2** absolute emissions by 8.9% in developed countries (Annex I of **Kyoto Protocol**). Energy consumption in all divisions ...
www.wbcsd.org – 56k – Cached – Similar

Tokyo Metropolitan Government of Tokyo 2007
expected to work positively toward the resolution of such global **environmental issues**. ... Carbon-Minus Tokyo, which aims at a significant **reduction of CO2** emissions, ... Since the **Kyoto Protocol** officially came into effect in February 2005, ... The **Kyoto Protocol**, which was ...
www2.kankyo.metro.tokyo.jp/kouhou/env/eng_2007/ – 35k – Cached – Similar

**other websites that might be interesting to check out**

▸ SF 2 Brainstorming (p. 133) ▸ SF 4 Taking Notes (p. 134) ▸ SF 14 Doing a Project (p. 143) ▸ SF 26 Skimming (p. 150)

## ▸ SF 14 Doing a Project

Doing a project is a good way to understand a topic more deeply. A project consists of several stages such as discussing ideas, doing research, and preparing material.

**Step 1:** After having agreed on the topic of your project, decide who will do which job in your group (e.g. do research on the Internet, write reports, etc.) and by when. Working in a team means that everyone in the group should contribute ideas to the project.

**Step 2:** Plan your work. Make sure you have specific aims and know what the 'product' is going to be, e.g. a display, a presentation, a web page or a class magazine. Always keep in mind your target audience, i.e. who the project is for (other classes, parents, a partner school, etc.)
*A poster would make the point very clear.*
*But we need to present a lot of figures, which aren't very visual.*
*We could present the figures in a visual way, using graphs and charts.*
*A video presentation would be good because we could animate ...*

**Step 3:** Research your topic. When collecting material you could use the Internet, go to a library, borrow a CD or DVD, write to organizations asking for brochures, posters, etc. Check what the others in your group have found. Be selective. Skim the material.

▸▸▸

**Step 4:** Start writing. When you have collected enough material, it is time to start writing your text, draw your map, design your magazine and really get your project up and running. Always make sure you stick to your plan.

**Step 5:** Check your written and visual material. Is it clear? Is the English correct? If not, correct it and then give it to someone else in your group to check again. Then prepare your product. Decide how you can best arrange your information and visual aids, for example, a poster or diagram, to make them clear and attractive.

**Step 6:** Practise your presentation and present your project. Always remember to make eye contact with your audience and to speak slowly and clearly.

**Step 7:** Assess your work afterwards. With your group, discuss how well you think your project went. What could you do better next time?

► SF 13 Doing Research (p. 141) ► SF 23 Giving a Presentation (p. 148) ► SF 26 Skimming (p. 150)

## ► SF 15 Mediating

This skill is useful for helping people who don't share a common language in which they can communicate. Sometimes you will have to pass on information to a German speaker who has little or no English, sometimes to someone who understands English but not German. Mediating can be either spoken or written.

- Mediating is like summarizing: you try to pass on the most important information in your own words. Find your own way of presenting the information but don't include your own opinion or imitate the *style of the person speaking or writing.
- Paraphrase words if you don't know the English equivalents.
- When mediating for a school assignment, you focus on the specific information that is asked for.

► SF 7 Paraphrasing (p. 135)

## ► SF 16 Translating

Translation is a very different skill from mediating. When you translate, it is important to include all information from the original text, and you should try to preserve as much of the original 'flavour' as possible: sentence structure, *tone, *stylistic devices, *register, etc.

**Step 1:** Read through the text a first time, looking up only the most important words. At this point, all you need is a general understanding of the text.

**Step 2:** Go through the text again. This time, make sure you understand every word. If you have any ideas on how to translate parts of the text, note them down right away.

**Step 3:** Write a first translation, leaving room to make corrections later. Mark parts of the text you aren't sure about. You can always correct it later.

**Step 4:** Translate sentence by sentence. It might help you to number the sentences in the original text. For complex sentences start with the main clause and then work on the subordinate clauses. Keep as close as you can to the original. Be careful: the original might use idioms or *figurative language that can't be translated word for word. If possible, try to find a similar image in the target language.

**Step 5:** When you've finished, set your translation aside for a while. After a break, go back and read your translation, but don't compare it to the original. Read it as a piece of work in English or German. If something doesn't sound natural, fix it.

**Step 6:** You will find that the meaning of the title becomes clear only after having worked on the text for a while. Therefore always translate the title or heading last.

► SF 8 Using a Dictionary (p. 136)

# Exam Skills

## ▶ SF 17 Taking a Test

You will be taking lots of tests at school. If you want to do well, prepare well! Here's one way:

**Step 1:** Start early enough to re-read the texts you've worked on since your last test. Learn the vocabulary and grammar in them. If you're unsure of anything, look it up in a dictionary or grammar book. Pay special attention to your 'favourite' mistakes.

**Step 2:** A few days before your test, make sure that you know keywords from the sort of questions you might get (see 'Language for Tasks: Operatoren', pp. 168–169). They might include:
*analyse* • *assess* • *comment* • *compare* • *describe* • *discuss* • *explain*
If you're not sure about any of these, look them up.

**Step 3:** Check all texts, vocabulary and grammar again a couple of days before the test. If you're finding it difficult to remember words, try writing a short text in which you use them. If you're finding it difficult to deal with a grammar point, try explaining it to a friend. That often helps you to fix it in your own mind.

**Step 4:** During the test remember to read all the questions all the way through before you start to answer the first one. Keep an eye on the time – you should leave a few minutes for checking and correcting.

▶ SF 8 Using a Dictionary (p. 136) ▶ SF 9 Using a Grammar Book (p. 137) ▶ SF 10 Keeping a Learning Log (p. 138)
▶ SF 39 Writing an Essay (p. 157)

## ▶ SF 18 Answering Multiple-Choice Questions

More and more tests are written in the multiple-choice format. If you apply the following techniques to a lot of multiple choice tests, you'll probably find them easier than traditional tests.

**Step 1:** Read the questions – or statements with missing words – carefully before you start to answer.

**Step 2:** Before you read the choices, try to come up with the correct answer in your head. If your answer is the same as one of the alternatives given, it's probably correct.

**Step 3:** Read all the alternative answers before deciding on one of them (or several of them, if the question can have more than one answer).

**Step 4:** 'Say' the sentences with the different solutions in your head. Often you'll find that one of them simply 'sounds' right, or that several definitely sound wrong.

**Step 5:** If you aren't sure of an answer, mark the question and go back to it later.

# Listening and Viewing Skills

## ▸ SF 19 Listening for Gist

Listening for gist is the skill you need when you're trying to a get a general picture quickly. Maybe you want to find out if something really is of use or interest to you.

**Step 1:** Before listening, make notes on
- what you need to find out
- what you expect to hear in the text
- what words might help you.

If you want to know the end of a story, you could make notes on the names of key *characters and events. If you want to find out what the speaker's general attitude to a specific topic is, you could make notes on keywords to do with that topic.

**Step 2:** While you are listening, just concentrate on the areas you want to know about. You don't need to understand every word. The atmosphere, sound effects and tone of voice may help you. Take brief notes.

**Step 3:** As soon as you've finished listening, complete your notes.

▸ SF 4 Taking Notes (p. 134) ▸ SF 5 Making Notes (p. 134)

## ▸ SF 20 Listening for Detail

When you have to listen for detail, you need to be able to pick out specific information and understand it completely.

**Step 1:** Before listening, make notes on the exact questions you need to answer and note down vocabulary that might help you. For example, if you need to find out from a radio interview in which year someone won an award, note down the person's name and the name of the award.

*Kate Winslet*
*Oscar:*

**Step 2:** While listening, focus on the names or keywords you have written down. Take notes on the specific information you need. If you're listening to a long text, interview or *speech, watch out for signal words that might alert you to the information you need.

| | |
|---|---|
| list of items, reasons: | *and, another, too* |
| counter arguments: | *although, but* |
| reasons for something, consequences of something: | *because, so, so that* |
| comparisons: | *bigger / older / more often / ... than* |
| chronology: | *before, after, later* |

**Step 3:** Check that you've got and understood the details you need. Listen again if you need to. Check your notes and complete them.

▸ SF 4 Taking Notes (p. 134) ▸ SF 5 Making Notes (p. 134)

## ▸ SF 21 Viewing a Film

More and more information is to be found in the visual media: films, documentaries and video clips. Learning viewing skills will help you follow or analyse a *plot, or extract information you need or find interesting.

**Step 1:** Before viewing, make sure you know what sort of visual material you'll be watching. In a feature film you need to cope with music, loud sound effects and quick cuts. A documentary is likely to be slower, but there will probably be a lot of facts to absorb in the commentary. If it's a video clip from the Web, the visual or sound quality may make it harder to follow.

**Step 2:** Make notes on what it is you want. Write down any questions you need to answer or any keywords you're looking for.

**Step 3:** While viewing, watch for gist, just as you would read or listen to a text for gist.

**Step 4:** Prepare a viewing log to help you focus on aspects of film content and film technique. Watch a second time and fill in the log. These film terms may be useful:

**1 Wide shot (WS)**
A view from a distance that shows the whole scene/place. It gives you an impression of the setting.

**2 Close-up (CU)**
A full-screen shot of one person's face or one object. It helps you see details and focuses your attention.

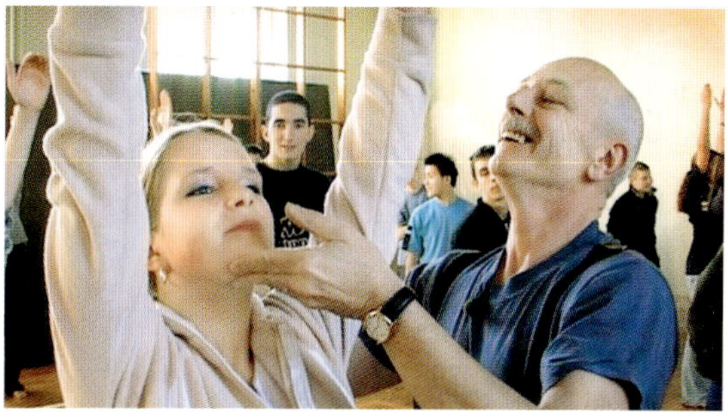

**3 Cut**
The point at which one shot changes (cuts) directly to another.

**4 Zoom**
A shot which goes from a WS to a CU (or a CU to a WS) without a cut.

### Viewing log for: BE THE CHANGE

| Who? | What? | When? | Where? | Why? |
|---|---|---|---|---|
| *Jennifer* | *started 'Unite for Sight'* | *seven years ago / as a student* | *Yale University, USA* | *Everyone should be able to receive eye care even if they aren't able to afford it.* |

| Camerawork | Sound | Acting |
|---|---|---|
| *CUs of Jennifer*<br>*WSs of Africa* | *voice, music* | *documentary style – real people* |

**Step 5:** After viewing, you will probably need/want to write or talk about what you have seen.
*The film/... is about ... . He/She is ... . It's a very interesting ...*
*It tells the story of ... and how he/she ... / It follows the lives of ordinary people and shows ...*
*The wide shot of the village square shows how many people come for help / ...*
*The close-ups of the ... make it much easier to understand ...*
*There is no music in the clip/film. That is good because it makes it easier to understand.*
*The music is very dramatic – it makes the film even more exciting.*
*It seems as if the actor is really feeling ...*

# Speaking Skills

## ▶ SF 22 Giving a Report on a Book or Film

A good way of telling others about a book you've read or a film you've seen is to give a report on it.

**Step 1:** At the beginning, state briefly what the book or film is about. Give the title, say who it is by, and when it was published or produced.
*The film is about environmental issues connected with global warming.*

**Step 2:** Give a short summary of the book/film, focussing on the main ideas or actions. Say what makes it special, e.g. the topic it deals with, the *setting, the *characters.

**Step 3:** You can also read aloud or show a short extract that is typical of the book or film. Provide any information that the class may need to follow.

**Step 4:** At the end, you can give your opinion on the book or film and recommend it to others, or not, as the case may be.

## ▶ SF 23 Giving a Presentation

Giving a presentation is a skill that you need both at school and in later life (work, college, university, etc.).

**Step 1: Preparing your presentation**

- Research your subject, making notes in English.
- Check your English and look up words that you find difficult to pronounce in a dictionary.
- Think of ways to make the talk more interesting, e.g. by using visuals, jokes.
  Visualizing facts and figures can be a big help to your audience. When you are presenting statistics, a bar chart or pie chart may make them more attractive and easier to understand.
- If you want to offer your audience a handout prepare it now too. The handout should include the main points of your presentation and can offer additional material (statistics, sources, pictures, etc.). You should structure the handout clearly. Headings and tables can help here. Leave room for your audience to write notes on it.
- You can also use electronic media, e.g. a presentation program.
  – Make sure the font you use is large enough to be read at the back of the room.
  – Only write one idea on each slide.
- Check that all the equipment you need is available.
- Practise your presentation in front of a friend or mirror.

**Step 2: Giving your presentation**

- Start by explaining the topic and structure of your presentation.
  *I'm going to talk about ...*
  *I've divided my material into three parts. The first is about ..., the second is about ..., and the third is about ...*
  *Here are some handouts to help you with my presentation. You can make notes in the margin.*
  *But don't worry, I won't just be talking – I also have some photos and some charts to show you.*
- Keep your presentation simple. Speak slowly and clearly.
- Make sure you don't overload transparencies.
- Stand up straight and face the audience, always keeping eye contact with them.
- At the end summarize the important points.
  *So/Just to remind you, here are the main points again: Firstly / Number one ...*
- Ask your audience if they have any questions.
  *That's the end of my presentation. Thank you for listening. Have you got any questions?*

▶ SF 5 Making Notes (p. 134) ▶ SF 8 Using a Dictionary (p. 136) ▶ SF 13 Doing Research (p. 141)

## ▶ SF 24 Taking Part in a Classroom Discussion

Having classroom discussions is a great way to exchange ideas and opinions with your classmates and to practise your English at the same time. A good discussion needs to be well-prepared and well-conducted.

**Step 1:** Each person collects information on the chosen topic in order to back up their opinion. Research aspects that interest you in books, on the Internet, in newspapers and magazines, etc. Make notes.
**Step 2:** Organize your notes. Maybe you want to have material ready to show during the discussion.
**Step 3:** Choose a discussion leader.
**Step 4:** Start the discussion. Remember to listen carefully to what other people say. Whenever you can, refer to their points when you speak.
**Step 5:** At the end of the discussion, the discussion leader summarizes the conclusions you have reached. Listen carefully and correct the summary if necessary.

### Useful words and phrases

**Making a point:** Before the discussion begins, make notes on your reaction to the topic. When the discussion starts, be ready to express your opinion. Make your own view clear.
*I think ... / I feel ... / In my opinion ... / I (can't) believe ...*
*The fact is that ... / The point is that ...*

**Adding a point:** Follow up what has been said before.
*I think ... is right because another thing that happens is that ...*
*What's more, ... / Furthermore, ...*
*We shouldn't forget that ...*

**Backing up a point:** When you make an argument, give reasons for your opinion, offering evidence – facts, quotations, figures, ...
*I thought people were exaggerating, but look at ...*
*I really don't think you can argue with these facts. Look ...*
*I agree with ... / That's true. / That statement is right because ...*
*Here's an example of what I mean: ... / These figures prove my point: ...*
*The Chancellor has just said in an interview that ...*
*Firstly, ... . Secondly, ...*

**Disagreeing:** Remember to be polite when you wish to express a different opinion.
*I'm afraid I don't agree with ... / Sorry, those facts aren't correct.*
*I don't accept ... / I think it's wrong to say ..., because ...*
*... talked about ..., but what about ...?*

**Expressing uncertainty:** Say you're unsure about what someone else has said.
*I'm not clear about ..., but I think that ...*
*..., you said ..., but surely all ... think ..., don't they?*

**Asking for clarification:** If you have misunderstood or not heard what has been said, ask the person to repeat it.
*I'm sorry, ..., I didn't understand that – can you say it again, please?*
*Could you repeat that, please? I'm not sure I understood what you said.*
*Excuse me, but did you mean that ...?*

**Summarizing:** At the end of the discussion, summarize your views.
*So, to sum up, ...*
*That's why I think ...*
*So there can't be any doubt that ...*

▶ SF 5 Making Notes (p. 134) ▶ SF 13 Doing Research (p. 141)

## ▸ SF 25 Making Conversation

One of the most important skills you will need whenever you're talking to people in English is the skill of making conversation. If you just remember a few points, you'll come over as polite and friendly and you'll find that you can avoid a lot of the stress in meeting new people, whether in a formal or an informal situation.

**Step 1:** A friendly start
formal: *Hello! / Good morning. / How do you do? / I'm pleased to meet you.*
informal: *Hi! I'm new here. My name's ... / Hi there! Is it OK if I sit here?*

**Step 2:** Keeping the conversation going
- Avoid one-word answers.
  *It's nice to meet you too. / My name's ...*
  *Yes, of course you can. / No, I'm sorry but ...*
  *Yes, thank you./ Fine, thank you.*
- Follow an answer or a statement with another question wherever you can.
  *What about you? / And you? / What do you think? / Do you like ...? / Have you ... yet?*
- Respond to questions
  *Well, I'm interested in ... too. / I often ... too. / I like ... a lot.*

**Step 3:** A friendly end
formal: *Well, I hope to see you at the ... then. / It was nice talking to you.*
informal: *Bye, then. / See you later.*

# Reading Skills

## ▸ SF 26 Skimming

This skill is useful for quickly finding out what a long text is about, i.e. reading for gist. Use it to decide whether or not to read a text more closely. Skimming will also help you to get an overview of a text's structure so that you'll understand it better when you read it.

**Step 1:** Look first at the title, any words in bold print, pictures and their *captions.
**Step 2:** Then look at the first and last sentences of each paragraph. The first sentence of the paragraph is usually the topic sentence and will give you the main idea of the paragraph.
**Step 3:** Don't read every sentence in detail.

## ▸ SF 27 Scanning

This skill is useful for finding specific information in a longer text without having to read the whole text, i.e. reading for detail.

**Step 1:** Decide which keyword or short phrase might help you to find the parts of the text that contain the information you are looking for.
**Step 2:** Make a mental picture of the keyword or phrase as it would look on the page.
**Step 3:** Keeping your mental picture in mind, move your eyes quickly over the printed page. You can use your finger to guide your eyes. Don't try to read the text. You will find that the words you're looking for will 'jump out at you'.
**Step 4:** After you have located relevant parts of the text, read them for the information you need. Scan the text again if you have to – either for the same keyword or phrase or for different ones.

## ▸ SF 28 Reading Fiction

Reading a long text like a long *short story or a *novel can be a challenge. But it's also a pleasure, especially if you remember different techniques to make the task easier.

**Step 1:** Before you start reading a long text, think about why you're reading it. Do you want to enjoy a story, learn about the author's *style, find out more about a country and its customs, ...?

**Step 2:** Don't even try to read a long text the same way you would read a short text – you'll never finish! Read at a speed you feel comfortable with, and don't worry about unknown words. Use your techniques for working out meaning. If that doesn't help, you can look up the words in a dictionary.

**Step 3:** Stop every now and then. Close your book and think about what you have just read. Summarize it in your head or ask yourself questions about it, e.g. using the five W's. If you're clear about what's happening in the story, read on. If not, you may have to go back.

▸ SF 6 Dealing with Words You Don't Know (p. 135) ▸ SF 10 Keeping a Learning Log (p. 138)

## ▸ SF 29 Reading Non-Fiction

Lots of what you read is non-fiction, i.e. the texts contain facts that can be checked and verified.

**Step 1:** Before you read a text closely, skim it. You may find that the text isn't relevant to your purpose. But you will also have a much better idea of what the text is about when you actually read it.

**Step 2:** Think about what you have already learned from skimming the text. What questions does it leave open or raise? It might help to write them down.

**Step 3:** Read the text carefully. Try to work out the meaning of words you don't know; if you can't work them out yourself, look the words up in your dictionary. While you're reading, take notes or highlight important information in the text.

**Step 4:** Organize the information you've noted down or highlighted in the text in a way that will help you to remember it. Outlines or mind maps usually work best. Use the method that works best for you.

**Step 5:** You may need/want to present your information in a new form: a summary, a diagram, a chart. This can help you to remember the information and give you something to look at later.

▸ SF 3 Marking Up a Text (p. 133) ▸ SF 4 Taking Notes (p. 134) ▸ SF 6 Dealing with Words You Don't Know (p. 135)
▸ SF 8 Using a Dictionary (p. 136) ▸ SF 26 Skimming (p. 150) ▸ SF 32 Writing an Outline (p. 153)

## ▸ SF 30 Keeping a Reading Journal

A reading journal helps you to structure the thoughts and ideas you have while reading, as well as to gain insight into the story, the topic(s) it deals with, its *characters and its narrative *style.
The six R's can help you to make the most of your reading experience.

**Step 1:** While reading, just 'go with the flow'. Use different strategies to work out the meaning of unknown words **(read)**.

**Step 2:** After having read a few chapters or part of a chapter, think about what you've read, and, if you find it helpful, write a brief summary of it **(recap)**.

**Step 3:** To make the most of your reading, write down questions or ideas that come up when you read **(reflect)**.

**Step 4:** If you want to, you can use your notes/reflections as a basis for further research or to answer questions on the text **(react)**.

**Step 5:** After reading, it may be useful to write down your thoughts on the book to help you structure them better and to be able to judge the book better **(review)**.

**Step 6:** If you want to share your reading experience and your opinion of the book with others, you can present the results of your reading journal **(report)**.

▸ SF 1 Mind Mapping (p. 132) ▸ SF 5 Making Notes (p. 134) ▸ SF 6 Dealing with Words You Don't Know (p. 135)

# Writing Skills

## ▸ SF 31 The Stages of Writing

Writing involves many different skills. Following these steps will help you to produce better written texts.

### The planning stage

**Step 1:** Brainstorm your topic. It's better to have too many ideas than too few.

**Step 2:** Define your topic. It's important that you know what it is you want or need to write about. Be clear in your mind who you are writing for and why. Do you want to convince your readers of something, inform them or simply entertain them?

**Step 3:** Organize the ideas you've collected. Now is the time to decide which ones you will include in your text. Decide on an order for presenting your ideas and then write an outline or make a mind map with numbers to show the order.

### The first draft stage

**Step 1:** Do your research. What do you need to know more about? Find out about it. As you learn more about your topic, you might have to adjust your plan.

**Step 2:** Write a first, rough draft. Following your outline or mind map, write down what you want to say. Don't worry at this stage about correctness or even the best way of saying something. You can even write a word in German if you can't think of the English expression. Leave lots of room on the page to make corrections later.

**Step 3:** Write out your first draft. Read what you have written and make first improvements. Use your dictionary to find the English expressions for things you've written in German. Write out your text again clearly, leaving room for adding and correcting later.

**Step 4:** Do something else if possible. Go for a walk or listen to music. The main thing is: take your mind off your writing. When you come back, you will see things you didn't see before.

*'We GOTTA GO to Disney World this summer! It's already in my rough draft of "What I Did on My Summer Vacation"!'*

### The revision stage

**Step 1:** Read your work. Read what you have written without making any changes to it. When you have finished, think about it: Is it logical? Does it say everything you want to say? Is everything in the right order? Go back and make any necessary changes.

**Step 2:** Proofread your work. Read your text slowly and carefully. Check the content, *style, grammar, spelling and punctuation. Use your learning log to help you look for your 'favourite' mistakes. You may have to read the text several times, looking for only one or two things each time. Asking a partner to check your work is a good idea too.

**Step 3:** Rewrite your piece. Make a clean copy of your work.

▸ SF 1 Mind Mapping (p. 132) ▸ SF 2 Brainstorming (p. 133) ▸ SF 10 Keeping a Learning Log (p. 138)
▸ SF 13 Doing Research (p. 141) ▸ SF 32 Writing an Outline (p. 153) ▸ SF 33 Structuring a Text (p. 153)

## ▸ SF 32 Writing an Outline

This skill is useful for organizing information. It's a more formal way of making notes. You can use it to examine the structure of a text you have read or to plan a presentation or a text that you want to write.

### The structure of an outline

- An outline is arranged so that you can quickly see what's most important. The most important ideas are farthest to the left.

Title
I. Main idea 1
    A. Important fact
        1. Supporting fact
        2. Supporting fact
            a. Example or detail
            b. Example or detail
    B. Important fact
II. Main idea 2

- All 'main ideas' are of equal importance, as are the 'important facts', etc.
- The 'main ideas' often correspond to whole sections of the text, the 'important facts' to individual paragraphs.
- Use keywords when writing an outline.

▸ SF 5 Making Notes (p. 134)

## ▸ SF 33 Structuring a Text

This skill is useful for writing any kind of text. Your readers will be able to follow your thoughts better if you structure them logically.

- Different kinds of texts require different structures. For example, to tell a story or to report on something, you might want to relate events in the order they occur, i.e. in 'chronological order'. To convince others of something, you might want to give your best arguments first, then the less important ones.
- There are a few general rules for ordering a text. Every longer text should have a clear beginning, middle and an end.
  - The **beginning** needs to state clearly what the text is about. It can consist of one or more introductory paragraphs and should awaken the readers' interest. Some examples from different kinds of texts:
    *In the course of this essay I intend to prove that ...*
    *There are many possible reasons for migration. Here we will examine ...*
    *Yesterday Tottenham Road was the scene of a terrible accident in which many people were injured. ...*
    *When Jane woke up last Saturday, she knew it was going to be an unusual day. ...*
  - The **middle** develops the ideas or relates the events.
    *An example of the problem I'm talking about can be seen ...*
    *The most common reason for leaving one's home country is ...*
    *A witness reported having seen ...*
    *After several minutes of this, Jane decided it was time to ...*
  - The **end** brings the text to a conclusion, usually in a paragraph or two. It is here that readers find out what conclusions you draw from the facts presented in the text, where they find out what happens to the main *character in the end, or where they are reminded of what you are trying to convince them of.
    *In conclusion, I believe it is clear that ...*

▸▸▸

*To sum up our survey of national and international migration, ...*
*Considering the damage done to the cars involved, the victims are lucky that ...*
*At the end of this amazing day, Jane ...*

- When you write your text, follow your outline.

### What else helps the reader?

- Start a new paragraph for every new thought.
- Use topic sentences in your paragraphs. The first sentence should state what is important; the other sentences should add to that thought or illustrate it.
- Connect your sentences logically. Do not just write one sentence after another.

  *There's a lot of unrest in the country. People are worried about the economy.*
  BETTER: *There's a lot of unrest in the country because people are worried about the economy.*

▸ SF 32 Writing an Outline (p. 153) ▸ SF 34 Linking Ideas (p. 154)

## ▸ SF 34 Linking Ideas

This skill is useful for making your writing easier to follow and, at the same time, more interesting. It allows you to improve your *style of writing.

### Types of connectors

The connectors are used:

- to show how your text is organized:
  *In the article, the writer describes how ...*
  *Firstly, he states that ... . Secondly, ...*
  *Then he goes on to say that ...*
  *Another point he makes is that ... . Finally, ...*

- to give reasons for something:
  *Due to / Because of / As a result of increased immigration, ...*
  *... numbers rose sharply. Therefore, the government felt that it had to ...*
  *... had been in trouble with the law, so ...*

- to add ideas:
  *The author thinks her characters ... . In addition, / Moreover, she has given them ...*
  *In addition to / Besides / As well as finding ..., the main character becomes ...*

- to contrast two or more thoughts:
  *Although one could argue that ..., I believe ...*
  *Whereas / While most people would ..., the Prime Minister has said ...*
  *Serious scientists all agree that ... . However,/But some politicians still claim ...*
  *On the one hand, there is a feeling that ... . On the other hand, it's clear that ...*

- to give examples:
  *This is true in a number of cases, for example / for instance / e.g. ...*

- to explain results and consequences:
  *As a consequence, / All in all, / Consequently, it is fair to say that ...*
  *To sum up, / To conclude, / In conclusion, I would like to say ...*

# ▸ SF 35 Writing a Formal Letter or Email

Formal written communication is useful in many contexts, including applying for a place on an exchange programme or at university, applying for a job, or requesting information from a company or organization about their product or service.

## How to write a formal letter

- Use the proper format (cf. below).
- Keep your language formal, i.e. don't use slang or colloquial expressions and avoid using contractions where possible (e.g. use 'do not' instead of 'don't').
- If you know the name of the person you are writing to, start your letter with 'Dear Mr X' or 'Dear Miss/Mrs/Ms Y' (AE: followed by a colon, ':'). Close the letter with 'Yours sincerely' (AE: followed by a comma).
- If you don't know the name of the person who will be reading your letter, open with 'Dear Sir or Madam' (AE: followed by a colon) and close with 'Yours faithfully' (BE) or 'Sincerely,' (AE).

### addressee unknown

Your
address
here

Date

Recipient's
address
here

*Dear Sir or Madam*

Body of letter

*Yours faithfully*

Your signature
Your name

### addressee known

Your
address
here

Date

Recipient's
name and address
here

*Dear Ms Jones*

Body of letter

*Yours sincerely*

Your signature
Your name

## How to write a formal email

- It is not necessary to include the recipient's address or the date in the body of your email, as they appear automatically in the header.
- Open and close your formal email the same way you would write a formal letter.
- Type your name and contact details at the bottom.

▸ Glossary: register (p. 164)

## ▸ SF 36 Writing a Personal Statement

If you apply for a place on an exchange programme, at university, or for a job, you will probably be asked to write a personal statement. A good personal statement as well as your CV can help you to get to the next stage of the selection process: the interview.

### What's important?

- Find out as much as you can about the organization or university you want to apply to or the company offering the job: What are their goals? What kinds of people are they interested in? What are they looking for?
- Write your statement in the first person. It should explain how you would fit in, based on your research.
- Follow directions carefully, especially if they say they want your statement to be in a certain format or of a particular length.
- Keep your language formal, but allow your personality to shine through.
- Even though you must try to show yourself in a good light, do try to be modest.
  NOT: *I know everything there is to know about being a graphic designer.*
  BUT: *I have experience in the field of graphic design, but am always keen to learn more and to build on / to further my current knowledge.*

▸ Glossary: register (p. 164)

## ▸ SF 37 Writing a Summary

Writing a summary is effective for passing on the content of a long text, film, *play or listening piece. You need to include the most important information, but also to be brief.

**Step 1:** Read / Listen to the text, or watch the film clip you want to summarize at least once. Then state in one or two sentences what the piece is about. Use the present tense.
*The article is about the problems facing immigrants just after their arrival in their new home country.*

**Step 2:** Use the five W's (the questions who?, what?, when?, where? and why?) to make notes or a mind map about the text. Write down only the things you think someone needs to know about your text in order to understand what it's about.

**Step 3:** Use your notes to write a first draft of your summary. Don't use quotes or examples from the original. Use your own words, but don't give your opinion on anything.

**Step 4:** Revise your draft. If you have been told to use a certain number of words for your summary, count the words. In case you need to reduce the number of words, make sure you have explained things rather than giving examples from the text.

**Step 5:** Prepare your final draft. It should contain all the important points and read well.

▸ SF 5 Making Notes (p. 134) ▸ SF 31 The Stages of Writing (p. 152)

## ▸ SF 38 Writing a Characterization

This skill is useful when you're analysing a literary text. Writing a characterization can help you to understand a narrative text better, and you can use it to demonstrate your understanding.

### Understanding a character

- To produce a characterization, you will probably have to read the text or parts of the text again. Make notes on:
  - what the *narrator or other characters in the story say about the character. Be sure to include physical features as well as personality traits.
  - what the character says or thinks about him- or herself.
  - what the character says and does. This is often more reliable information than others' observations about the character.

- Think about what conclusions you can draw about the character by what they do. If the character is shown helping someone else, for example, does it mean they're a helpful person, or are they trying to impress somebody? Make notes.

### Writing the characterization

Proceed as you would with any other text, from first draft to final draft, but consider these special points:

- Start with your character's name and a general statement about him or her. The opening paragraph should include a statement about why the character is important in the story. Use the present tense.
  *Andy, one of the two main characters and the narrator's best friend in the story 'Bread on the Water' by David Lubar, is a typical teenage boy with a big mouth and a big heart.*
- In the middle of your profile, add details about the character. This information should support what you have said in your opening statement.
  *In church, Andy makes puns on the quotes from the Bible. This shows him to be a very clever boy with a good sense of humour. But the fact that he doesn't stop, even after he and Tommy are thrown out of the church, shows that ...*
- Back up every statement you make about your character with examples.
  *Andy is caring and tries to help the homeless man by buying him something to eat.*
- Finish by restating your main claim about the character followed by a few concluding sentences.
  *As we have seen, Andy is very generous and, although he misbehaves in church at the beginning of the story, he is the only one who ...*

▸ SF 5 Making Notes (p. 134) ▸ SF 31 The Stages of Writing (p. 152) ▸ Glossary: character (p. 158)

## ▸ SF 39 Writing an Essay

This skill is useful for expressing your opinion in a formal context. Essays are often required in tests, where you have limits on both time and on the number of words you're allowed to write.

**Step 1:** Read the task carefully and make sure you understand what is expected of you. Form your opinion on the question.

**Step 2:** Proceed as you would with any other text, from first draft to final draft, but consider the following points:

- In your introductory statement, restate the problem from the task:
  *In the following, I will look at the question of whether ... / I would like to discuss ...*
  *I intend to show that ... / to present arguments in favour of ... and against ...*
- Each paragraph that follows should deal with a single argument. If you are dealing with the pros and cons of something, take one of these approaches:
  - Discuss all the arguments in favour first, then all those against.
  - Discuss one argument in favour, directly followed by what speaks against it, then do the same with the next argument, and so on.
- Illustrate your ideas with examples.
  *The more people get involved in an action, the more impact it will have, as the 'Hands up for peace' initiative proves. / What Kierra Box showed us is that it is possible to achieve anything as long as you are determined to see it through.*
- Your concluding statement should sum up your arguments in some way and restate your opinion:
  *All in all, it can be said that ...*
  *In conclusion, I would like to say that ...*
  *I would like to finish by saying that ...*

▸ SF 31 The Stages of Writing (p. 152)

## Alphabetical List of Terms


act ... 161
advertisement ... 161
atmosphere ... 158
byline ... 162
caption ... 161
cartoon ... 161
character ... 158
characterization (direct, indirect) ... 159
column ... 162
column title ... 162
device (stylistic) ... 165
dialogue ... 161
drama ... 161
essay ... 162
feature story ... 162
fiction, fictional text ... 158
figurative ... 165
free verse ... 160
headline ... 162
humour ... 163
imagery ... 165
irony ... 165
layout ... 164
letter (formal, informal) ... 163
line ... 160
literal ... 165
metaphor ... 165
narrative prose ... 159
narrator (first-person, third-person, omniscient) ... 159
news story ... 163
non-fiction, non-fictional text ... 161
novel ... 159
play ... 161
playwright ... 161
plot ... 159
poem ... 160
poetry ... 160
point of view (limited, unlimited) ... 160
proverb ... 164
pun ... 165
register (formal, informal, neutral, slang) ... 164
rhyme ... 160
rhyme scheme ... 160
rhythm ... 160
scene ... 161
setting ... 159
short story ... 159
showing ... 159
simile ... 165
speech ... 163
speech bubble ... 161
stage directions ... 161
stanza ... 160
style ... 163
stylistic devices ... 165
symbol ... 165
telling ... 159
tone ... 164
wordplay ... 165


# Fiction

A fictional text is one that does not deal with facts in the real world, but rather creates its own world or tells an invented story. This world 'exists' and this story is 'true' only in the context of the fictional work.

**Language help**
- a work of fiction
- light/popular/romantic/science fiction

A work of fiction can take just about any form. The main types are:

- **narrative prose:** Short stories, novels, etc.
- **poetry:** Poems can tell a story (narrative poems), describe a mood, etc.
- **drama:** Plays are usually fictional, although sometimes based on actual events, and may even use authentic dialogue (e.g. a historical drama).

## Atmosphere ['ætməsfɪə]

The writer creates a feeling or mood in his or her work in order to evoke the reader's or listener's emotions.

## Character ['kærəktə]

Characters are the people in a fictional text. They are usually presented through their actions and thoughts as well as by description.

**Language help**
- the main character / protagonist [prə'tægənɪst]
- a central/major character
- a minor/secondary character
- hero ['hɪərəʊ] / heroine ['herəʊɪn] (the main male/female character)

## Characterization [ˌkærəktəraɪ'zeɪʃn]

Characterization is the way in which the author of a fictional text presents his or her characters to the reader or, in the case of a play or film, to the audience. There are two main ways of presenting a character:

**Language help**
- ... is shown/presented/characterized as somebody who ...
- ... is characterized by his/her actions/speech, which ...

- **direct characterization ('telling')**
  Somebody tells the reader what sort of person a character is. This can be:
  – the narrator
  – another character in the story
  – the character him- or herself
- **indirect characterization ('showing')**
  The reader has to draw conclusions about a character based on what the character says and does.

## Plot

The plot is the structure of the action in fictional texts. It is a set of events that are connected by cause and effect and are often centred around at least one conflict. A plot is composed of several elements.

# Narrative Prose

A narrative ['nærətɪv] prose text is a fictional story told by a narrator and written in a continuous flow of sentences, i.e. not as a poem or drama. Typical examples of narrative prose are novels and short stories.

- **novel:** A novel is a long fictional work of narrative prose. Most novels are divided into chapters. A novel often has lots of characters and several storylines running parallel to one another. The **setting** (place and time of the action) can vary: the story often takes place in different locations and over a long period of time.
- **short story:** Like a novel, a short story is also a fictional work of narrative prose, but shorter and less complex. Short stories typically have only a few characters, and the setting doesn't change much, if at all: the story usually takes place in only one or two locations, and the relative time period is fairly short. Short stories usually only have a single storyline, and they can normally be read in just one sitting.

## Narrator [*BE:* nə'reɪtə; *AE:* 'næreɪtər]

The narrator is the person who tells the story in a narrative text. There are two main types of narrator:

- The **first-person narrator** is a character in the story and refers to him- or herself as 'I'.
- The **third-person narrator** isn't a character in the story and refers to all the characters as 'he', 'she' or 'they', or by their names.
  A third-person narrator with an unlimited point of view is known as an **omniscient** [ɒm'nɪsiənt] **narrator**.

Note that the narrator isn't the same as the author of a story. That's easiest to understand if you remember that a female author can write a story with a male narrator and vice versa. A narrator can say things the author would never say him- or herself.

**Language help**
- The author uses a ... narrator.
- The story is told/narrated by a first-person narrator / the main character's mother / ...
- The narrator tells/relates the story ...
- The author uses the narrator to ...
- The author has his/her narrator say ...

## Point of view

The point of view of a narrative is the perspective the story is told from. The point of view of a first-person narrator is easy to identify: the narrator tells the story from his or her own perspective. By concentrating on a particular character and the things that character can see, hear and maybe even think, a third-person narrator can still tell a story from that character's point of view. The concepts of narrator and point of view are closely related:

A first-person narrator can only have
- a **limited point of view:** A character in a story can't possibly know everything that's going on. The reader's view is limited by what the character sees and wants to tell.

A third-person narrator can have
- a **limited point of view:** The narrator may be limited to the experience of one or more characters in the story, or maybe he or she doesn't know the characters' thoughts and feelings.
- an **unlimited point of view:** This omniscient narrator doesn't follow any one character, but moves around, entering into characters' minds whenever he or she wants.

# Poetry

A **poem** is a piece of creative writing structured by **lines** and **rhythm** (the arrangement of stressed and unstressed syllables in a line). The lines of a poem are often arranged in groups called **stanzas**. To emphasize the structure and to create certain effects, traditional poets often use rhyme, whereas many modern poets use **free verse**, i.e. poetry without a regular rhyme or rhythm.

## Rhyme

Rhyme is the similarity of the sound of two or more words or parts of words.

'Just fancy that!' my parents say
At anything I mention.
They always seem so far away
And never pay attention.

**Language help**
- The word ... rhymes with ...
- The two words rhyme.
- a perfect / an imperfect rhyme

**⚠ Trouble spot**
**They rhyme.** = Sie reimen sich.
Not: ~~They rhyme themselves.~~

## Rhyme scheme

Poets arrange their rhymes in different ways – this is the rhyme scheme. If you need to find out the rhyme scheme, you give each new sound a new letter. In the above poem *say* and *away* would be **a**, *mention* and *attention* would be **b**. So the rhyme scheme is **a**, **b**, **a**, **b**.

**Language help**
- The rhyme scheme stays the same / changes in the last stanza.

## Drama

A drama or **play** is written to be performed by actors in a theatre, in a film, on TV or on the radio. The actors take the part of the characters.

A play is usually divided into **acts**; the acts are divided into **scenes**. In its written form, a play consists of two main elements:

- **dialogue**
  The dialogue is what the characters say.
- **stage directions**
  The stage directions are the **playwright's** description of how he/she wants the stage to look and what he/she wants the actors to do when they perform the play. This can include how they are to be dressed, how and where they move, what objects (props) they are to use and how they deliver each line of dialogue.

**Language help**
- a one-act/five-act play
- a play in two acts
- The writer/playwright gives detailed / very few stage directions.
- The stage directions leave little / lots of room for the actors to develop the characters themselves.

## Non-Fiction

Non-fictional texts (advertisements, letters, news stories, speeches, etc.) are different from fictional texts in that they normally refer to the real world, whereas fictional texts create their own world. Some works of non-fiction are meant to inform, others to persuade people of something, still others to express an opinion or even to sell something.

### Advertisement [*BE:* əd'vɜːtɪsmənt; *AE:* ˌædvər'taɪzmənt]

An advertisement – also known as an 'advert' *(BE)* or 'ad' – is a text that tries to sell a product (e.g. a new soft drink), a service (e.g. shoe repairs), an idea (e.g. to use less energy) or a candidate (e.g. to vote for a certain person in an election). The purpose of an advert is to persuade people to do something. Advertising can be printed, as in a newspaper, magazine or brochure; spoken, as on the radio; or it can be filmed, as in a cinema or in a TV commercial.

**⚠ Trouble spot**
**advertisement** *(n)* [əd'vɜːtɪsmənt]
**advert** *(n)* ['ædvɜːt]
**advertise** *(v)* ['ædvətaɪz]

speech bubble

cartoonist's signature

### Cartoon

Cartoons are expressions of opinion on the part of a magazine or newspaper, or at least of the cartoonist. They are visual and usually humorous. To achieve a humorous effect, cartoonists often exaggerate the physical features of people they are portraying and use wordplay in their **captions** (words underneath a picture) or **speech bubbles**.

**Language help**
- a humorous/political cartoon
- The cartoon portrays ...
- The cartoon criticizes / makes fun of ...
- The cartoonist has drawn ... in a very cruel/funny way.

## Column ['kɒləm]

A column is an article that appears regularly in a newspaper or magazine. Columns can be humorous or serious, and they can deal with any subject, e.g. lifestyle, personal problems, home repairs or politics. Any opinion expressed in a column is the opinion of the writer, or 'columnist', and not necessarily the official opinion of the newspaper or magazine it appears in. The columnist is named in the **byline**, i.e. the line which says who the column is by.

**Language help**
- a daily/weekly column
- an advice column

headline

column title

byline

# In a recession, head for the mall where you can buy seven Crunchies for £1.49

**STATUS ANXIETY**

**Toby Young**

I was awestruck. As a long-term resident of west London, I had been looking forward to my first glimpse of this emporium, but it was even better than I imagined. I simply had no idea shopping centres could be this good. From now on there would be no need to go anywhere else. It was the answer to all my prayers.

I am not talking about Westfield, obviously, but the Oaks Shopping Centre in Acton. The new £3 billion retail park in Shepherd's Bush may boast a branch of Tiffany, but the Oaks has a branch of Netto, the Danish-owned discount chain where you can buy a two-litre bottle of diet cola for 19p. If you cannot find what you're looking for in Netto, you can try your luck in Poundstretcher, which offers a 16-piece dinner set for £9.99. It is credit crunch-tastic.

When I first moved to Acton a year ago, I was too snobbish to set foot in the Oaks, dismissing it as a retail substrata that even Kerry Katona would steer clear of. In fact, there is a branch of Iceland in the Oaks, the frozen food chain that Katona's a spokesperson for. Having combed the aisles of Iceland, I now realise you can [illegible]

However, in Iceland you can buy a bag of seven Crunchies for £1.75 and in Poundstretcher you buy seven for £1.49. If there's a better bargain to be had in Britain, I'd like to know what it is.

My favourite shop is 99p Stores — which, needless to say, is only one store in spite of the 's' on the end. Its motto is 'quality prod- [illegible]

when you consider that it is the size of a sack of potatoes.

Don't get me wrong. I have got nothing against Westfield. I went there on the opening day and stood, mesmerised, in front of the window of La Senza as three models paraded up and down in their underwear. The fast food on offer is particularly good and scarcely a Sunday passes without me dragging my wife and four children down there to get stuck into the burgers at Byron.

But there is something reassuringly British about the window displays in the Oaks. My favourite this week is the one in Savers, another discount store. It consists exclusively of toilet rolls piled on top of each other: '6 rolls for the price of 4', boasts the sign. How could anyone resist? Iceland contains an array of party food accompanied by the slogan: 'Proud sponsors of *I'm a Celebrity … Get Me Out of Here!*'

The other great thing about the Oaks compared to Westfield is that it is much less crowded. This is surprising, given that we are now in the midst of a full-blown recession, but that may be about to change.

From: *The Spectator*, 6 December 2008

**⚠ Trouble spot**

**headline**
= Schlagzeile

**heading**
= Überschrift

## Essay

An essay is a text in which the writer discusses a topic or expresses his or her personal views on it. It discusses, describes or analyses one topic. Essays can be any length and on any subject matter; they are written for different purposes or occasions. Their tone is entirely up to the writer: some essays are serious, others light-hearted and entertaining.

## Feature story

A feature story is an article in a newspaper or magazine that concentrates on (or features) one or more individual cases in order to make a general point. An article on poverty, for example, is more emotional and interesting to the reader if it shows how one or two people deal with their poverty rather than only discussing statistics.

## Letter

We distinguish between **formal** and **informal** letters, which differ according to format and style. Today most informal correspondence is done by email. Thank-you letters and letters of sympathy, however, are best done by post. There are various kinds of formal letters, for example business letters or covering letters (in American English 'cover letters'), which you attach to your CV when you're applying for a job.

## News story

News stories – also called news items or news reports – are reports on recent events found in newspapers, magazines, on television or on the radio. A news story must never directly express an opinion, but should present the facts of an event as objectively as possible. A good report answers the five W's, i.e. the questions who?, what?, when?, where? and why?.

## Speech

A speech is a spoken text delivered to an audience. The speaker (or his or her speech writer) normally uses different stylistic devices to make the speech more interesting. One effective way of appealing to the audience is to address them directly or to use the first-person plural 'we' (which shows that the speaker and the audience are alike and must therefore want the same things). The quality of a speech depends not only on the choice of words, however, but also on the delivery.

**Language help**
- make/give/deliver a speech
- ... is a good/gifted/poor speaker

**⚠ Trouble spot**
Not: ~~hold a speech~~

# Style and Stylistic Devices

Style is a particular way in which a fictional or non-fictional text is written. Features such as register or tone that make a text typical of a particular author constitute his or her style.

## Humour ['hju:mə]

Humour is when something, e.g. a character, or a character's behaviour, makes you laugh. A writer may use humour in a gentle way that makes you smile at a character's weakness:

'Turn with me to Romans twelve,' Pastor Donald said. Andy started to snicker. 'Romans twelve, Christians nothing,' he whispered. (p. 18, ll. 8–11)

**Language help**
- The author uses humour to ...
- The humour of the text comes from ...
- ... sets the humorous tone of the piece.
- The ... is written in a humorous tone.

Or he/she may use it in a cruel or angry way to make you laugh at something terrible.

'Either that wallpaper goes or I do.' (Oscar Wilde on his deathbed)

Humour is one of the most difficult things to translate as different people and cultures see things differently and may not laugh at the same jokes.

## Layout ['leɪaʊt]

How and where you place all the different elements on a page is called the layout. The layout includes the font, size and colour of the letters, the relationship of print to visual materials, etc. You can judge how good or bad a layout is by whether it serves the aim of the page: If the page is from a novel, it should allow the reader to read smoothly and easily – the layout should be calm, the letters not too small, the chapters clearly marked. An advertisement or poster, on the other hand, wants to get over a message very quickly, so it has to be clear and eye-catching. Newspapers and magazines are different again: they want to sell, but also to inform and amuse, so they usually need a variety of layout elements.

**Language help**
- a clear / a modern / an attractive layout
- The layout is well-structured / crammed / full / confusing / busy.
- The layout guides the reader.
- The page is well/nicely/attractively laid out.

Briefing

**Verbatim**

'I don't really feel like I need to respond to people that view it that way.'
LAURA BUSH, First Lady, on critics who say that her husband's presidency was a failure

'I hid in a bush near the church and heard people wailing as they were being cut with machetes.'
ABEL LONGI, of Kampala, Uganda, accusing rebels of hacking to death scores of people seeking refuge at a Catholic church

'It was not one of my choosing, but as a storyteller, what could make a better story?'
KETZEL LEVINE, who launched an NPR series about the economic struggles of Americans, on using the final episode to tell how she was laid off halfway through the project

'We don't want to start our government's work with violence.'
SUTHEP THAUGSUBAN, Thailand's new Deputy Prime Minister, on telling police not to use excessive force against protesters

'Everything indicates she won her crown through the intervention of her boyfriend, a drug lord.'
CARLOS PUIG, writer for the *Milenio* newspaper, on Mexican beauty queen Laura Zuñiga, who gave up her title after being detained for drug and weapons violations

'We wish one day to play a concert in the center of Baghdad. We hope.'
AKHLAD, of UTN1, a band formed in Iraq that models itself after the Backstreet Boys

'Last year, we warned a mocking world that 2008 would be horrible compared to 2007, and we were right.'
MARIE GABRIEL, founder of the French group Funacon, on its annual anti-New Year protest

Back & Forth:

Politics

Environment

Internet

From: *Time*, 12 January 2009

## Proverb ['prɒvɜːb]

A proverb is a well-known, commonly used phrase or sentence that contains advice or a generally recognized truth. It is often used to achieve a humorous effect or to show that something is important and profound. Don't judge a book by its cover. (Meaning: Do not judge by appearances.)

## Register ['redʒɪstə]

Register is the level of language used in a text. It could be formal, neutral or informal, depending on the nature of the text.

**Language help**
- The text is written in a very high/formal/low/informal/neutral register.
- The author uses a lot of slang to show that he/she is ...
- The author has his/her characters use a lot of slang to make them ...

- **formal:** Formal style is used in texts that are serious and/or official. Often the sentence structure is complex and the vocabulary quite difficult, e.g. information from ministries, laws, etc.
- **neutral:** Neutral style is the usual style used by normal, educated people. It's the style you'd see in most novels, articles, letters, etc.
- **informal:** Informal style uses simple sentence structure, short forms (e.g. *don't*, *can't*, etc.) and easy-to-understand vocabulary. It is used between friends and in relaxed situations and may include slang.
- **slang:** Slang is very informal language mainly used between people of the same age or from the same background. The dictionary will indicate when a word is slang.

## Tone

Tone can reflect the writer's attitude to the topic he or she is writing about and/or to the reader. The writer's tone may be serious, humorous, angry, etc.

**Stylistic devices** are methods and techniques used to produce a particular effect in a text. Here are a few of them:

## Imagery ['ɪmɪdʒəri]

When a writer uses language in a way that goes beyond the normal dictionary definition, i.e. that is not **literal**, but **figurative**, then he/she is using imagery. Images are meant to stimulate the reader's imagination, giving him or her a new angle on a particular topic. Images can come in many different forms:

**Language help**
- an original / a surprising metaphor/simile
- The metaphor/simile illustrates/shows ...
- The author uses this simile/metaphor/symbol to ...

- **metaphor** ['metəfə], **metaphorical** [ˌmetə'fɒrɪkl] *(adj)*
  A metaphor is a comparison between two things which are not really like each other. Metaphors don't use the words 'like' or 'as' (cf. simile). They are meant to create a picture (image) in your mind that sheds more light on a topic.
  Earth's Clock (p. 37)
- **simile** ['sɪməli]
  A simile is a comparison between two things that are not really like each other. Similes use the word 'like' or 'as'.
  '... his silver hair sticking up like an old-age porcupine.' (p. 70, ll. 6–7)
- **symbol** ['sɪmbl]
  A symbol is a concrete object that stands for something else.
  A clock is a symbol of the passing of time.
  A pendulum is a symbol of a regular reversal of a trend.

⚠ **Trouble spot**
ein Symbol **für** die Zeit
= a symbol **of** time

## Irony ['aɪrəni], ironic [aɪ'rɒnɪk] *(adj)*

When a writer or speaker wants to make fun of a person or thing, but doesn't want to do this openly, he or she may use irony. Irony often works by using words in a meaning opposite to the one they really have. The English are particularly fond of irony – the tone of voice can help you to spot it when someone uses it in conversation.

## Wordplay

Wordplay (also called **pun**) is when an author deliberately plays with words that have two different meanings or with two words that sound the same. In the cartoon the words *hair* and *hare* ('Hase') sound the same, but their meaning is different.

*'No, no, no, Rapunzel. Your hair, your hair! Not your bloody hare ...'*

**Language help**
- make a pun
- use wordplay
- play with words
- The author makes extensive use of wordplay/puns.
- The headline is a nice play on words.
- The writer plays with the different meanings of the word ... / makes a pun on the different meanings of ...

⚠ **Trouble spot**
**Pun** is countable:
*a pun, lots of puns.*
**Wordplay** is uncountable:
*He uses wordplay.*

## Texts

**Chapter 1, pp. 14–15**: From: Barack Obama: 'University of Massachusetts at Boston Commencement Address', June 2, 2006; **p. 17**: 'If I Can Stop One Heart from Breaking' by Emily Dickinson, first published 1924; **pp. 18–22**: From: Destination Unexpected by Donald R. Gallo (Ed.), Candlewick Press, 2003 / © David Lubar; **p. 25**: From: *New Statesman*, October 17, 2005 (http://www.newstatesman.com/200510170017); **Chapter 2, p. 30 / B**: From: The Works 2, Brian Moses & Pie Corbett (Eds.), London: Macmillan Children's Books, 2002; **p. 31 / E**: University of Bath, Bath, U.K.; **p. 34**: From: WHY IS SNOT GREEN by Glenn Murphy, London, Pan MacMillan, 2007; **p. 35**: From: 'The Science behind the News' by Terence Wood, from: *The Gamma Series of the Royal Society of New Zealand*, Issue 03/05 Juni 2005; **p. 37** Earth's Clock: From: The Works 2, Brian Moses & Pie Corbett (Eds.), London, Macmillan Children's Books, 2002; River Runs Red: © Sprint Music, für D/CH/A / Osteuropa: Sony / ATV Music Publishing (Germany GmbH), Berlin; **p. 40**: From: *National Public Health Week*, USA, April 7–13, 2008, p. 7 www.apha.org / APHA American Public Health Association, Washington, DC; **p. 41**: From: Change the World 9 to 5: 50 Ways to Change the World at Work, We Are What We Do (Ed.), London, Faber & Faber, 2006; **p. 42**: From: 50 Ways to Greener Travel (Green Series), by Siân Berry and Aaron Blecha, London, Kyle Cathie Ltd, 2008 (© text: Siân Berry, © artwork: Aaron Blecha, © book design: Kyle Cathie Limited); **p. 44**: 'Klimaveränderung ist beispiellos', *Der Tagesspiegel*, Berlin, 7. November 2008; 'Die nächste Eiszeit steht bevor', Ralf Nestler, *Der Tagesspiegel*, Berlin, 13. November 2008; **Chapter 3, p. 47 / B**: From: *Northwestern News Network (NNN)*, April 19, 2006 (© Mari Fagel / Northwestern University / McCormick Tribune Center, Evanston, IL); **pp. 50–51**: From: The New York Times, 2008 © 2009 The New York Times. All rights reserved. Used by permission and protection by the Copyright Laws of the United States. The printing, copying, redistribution, or retransmission of the material without express written permission is prohibited; **p. 52**: From: The New York Times, 2007 © 2009 The New York Times All rights reserved. Used by permission and protection by the Copyright Laws of the United States. The printing, copying, redistribution, or retransmission of the material without express written permission is prohibited; **pp. 54–55**: From: BLACK SWAN GREEN by David Mitchell, London, Hodder & Stoughton, 2006, © David Mitchell, 2006; **p. 60**: © From: A SKY FULL OF POEMS by Eve Merriam. © 1964, 1970, 1973, 1986 by Eve Merriam. Used by permission of Marian Reiner; **Chapter 4, pp. 68–69**: From: Newsweek, 2008 © 2009 Newsweek, William Underhill. All rights reserved. Used by permission and protection by the Copyright Laws of the United States. The printing, copying, redistribution, or retransmission of the material without express written permission is prohibited; **pp. 70–72**: © Marina Lewycka, 2007. All rights reserved; **p. 73**: 'Migration Tide Turns As East Europeans Head Back Home' by Gareth Jones and Kuba Jaworowksi, from: *The Scotsman*, June 17, 2008; **Chapter 5, p. 85**: list of top ten 'loves and loathes': © National Literacy Trust, London, 2008; **p. 86**: © 2003 by Mark Haddon. All rights reserved; **p. 87**: © 2007 Sherman Alexie. Reproduced by permission of Hachette Book Group USA; **p. 88**: © 2003 by Mark Haddon; **p. 90**: © From: LOOKING FOR ALASKA by John Green, copyright © 2005 by John Green, text. Used by permission of Dutton Children's Books, A Division of Penguin Young Readers Group, A Member of Penguin Group (USA) Inc., 345 Hudson Street, New York, NY 10014. All rights reserved; **pp. 92–93**: © 2007 Sherman Alexie. Reproduced by permission of Hachette Book Group USA; **pp. 96–97**: © Nick Hornby, 1998; **p. 99**: © 2007 Sherman Alexie. Reproduced by permission of Hachette Book Group USA; **Partner B, p. 102**: Based on: 'African Adventure' by Ian Ludgate, from: *Times Online*, October 30, 2007, www.timesonline.co.uk; **p. 103**: From: The New York Times, 2008 © 2009 The New York Times. All rights reserved. Used by permission and protection by the Copyright Laws of the United States. The printing, copying, redistribution, or retransmission of the material without express written permission is prohibited; **p. 104**: © From: LOOKING FOR ALASKA by John Green, copyright © 2005 by John Green, text. Used by permission of Dutton Children's Books, A Division of Penguin Young Readers Group, A Member of Penguin Group (USA) Inc., 345 Hudson Street, New York, NY 10014. All rights reserved.

## Photos / Illustrations

**A1PIX**, Taufkirchen: p. 110 (top); **action press**: p. 141 (© bildstelle / LEHTIKUVA OY) **Alamy images**: pp. 3 (top, 2nd image from right: © Danita Delimont / Russell Young), 4 (left, 2nd image from right: © Danita Delimont / Russell Young), 10 (2nd image from right: © Danita Delimont / Russell Young), 17 (2: © JUPITERIMAGES / i2i / BananaStock), 20 (© Jeff Greenberg), 22 (© Enigma), 25 (© Philip Wolmuth), 27 (© Jacky Chapman), 53 (© Steven May), 68 (© Anthony Eva), 69 (left: © Alex Segre, right: © Stan Kujawa), 76 (left: © Ed Eckstein / PHOTOTAKE Inc.), 81 (God bless the Queen: © Stan Kujawa, girl with painted face: © Peter Marshall), 88 (Sherlock Holmes: © ACE STOCK LIMITED), 90 (bottom: © avatra images), 107 (© Image Source Black), 108 (bottom: © Geoff du Feu), 109 (bottom: © David Taylor), 115 (© bilderlounge / Andreas Böckel), 128 (bottom right: © Charles Stirling / Travel), 140 (3: © Philip Wolmuth); **www.anfield.de**: p. 121 (© www.anfield.de / Uwe Kaiser); **ASSOCIATED PRESS (AP)**: pp. 14 (© STF), 15 (© STF), 16 (© Elise Amendola), 52 (top right: © Tom Gannam, bottom left : © Nick Ut), 140 (4: © Mannie Garcia / Shephard Fairey); **Blickwinkel**: pp. 3 (bottom and top, 3rd image from right: © McPHOTOs), 4 (left, 3rd image from right: © McPHOTOs), 10 (3rd image from right: © McPHOTOs); **Boomtown Media**, Berlin: pp. 58, 59, 147 (© Die Bilder aus dem Kinofilm RHYTHM IS IT! von Thomas Grube und Enrique Sánchez Lansch werden mit freundlicher Genehmigung von Boomtown Media, Berlin, zur

Verfügung gestellt. © 2004); **Candlewick Press**: pp. 8, 83 (7: © Cover illustration © 2002 Candlewick Press. From FEED by M. T. Anderson. Reproduced by permission of Walker Books Ltd on behalf of Candlewick Press); **Caro Fotoagentur**: p. 134 (bottom: © Andree Kaiser); **CartoonStock.com**: pp. 35 (backdrop: © Chris Grosz), 49 (© Wilbur Dawbarn), 117 (© Roy Nixon), 123 (© Naf), 124 (© Piero Tonin), 127 (cartoon: © Dave Carpenter), 130 (© Carroll Zahn), 140 (2: © Rex May Baloo), 152 (© Chris Wildt), 161 (© Jose Neves "Nemo"), 165 (© Jason Love); **Cinetext**: pp. 36 (right: © Sammlung Richter), 57 (bottom: © Cinetext Bildarchiv), 63 (right: © CINETEXT), 79 (bottom: © Neue Visionen), 97 (bottom right: © CINETEXT); **CNN**: p. 26 (all: © CNN / Unite for Sight / Jennifer Staple); **Commonwealth Copyright Administration**, Australia: pp 32, 140 (1: © Global Warming – Cool it – pie chart. Copyright Commonwealth of Australia, reproduced by permission); **Corbis**: pp. 3 (top, 3rd image from left: © Hola Images), 4 (left, 3rd image from left: © Hola Images), 10 (3rd image from left: © Hola Images), 18 (© C. Lyttle / zefa), 28 (© James Marshall), 46 (8: © Fancy / Veer), 57 (top: © Bettmann), 102 (© GILBERT LIZ / SYGMA), 143 (© LWA-Dann Tardif), 145 (top: © Gabe Palmer); **Cornelsen Verlag**: pp. 8, 82, 83 (1, 3, 4, 6), 86 (cover), 87 (cover), 90 (cover), 96(cover), 114, 148; **Creators Syndicate**, Los Angeles: p. 24 (© 1991 FarWorks, Inc. All Rights Reserved / Dist. By Creators Syndicate); **Paul Cumes**, Long Beach, CA: p. 38 (top); **Defd Deutscher Fernsehdienst**: pp. 36 (left), 79 (top), 108 (top: © Kinowelt Film / defd); **dpa Picture Alliance** GmbH: pp. 6 (5: © dpa-Zentralbild / Wolfgang Thieme, 7: © dpa-Zentralbild / Soeren Stache), 45 (© Carl-W. Röhrig / OKAPIA), 46 (5: © dpa-Zentralbild / Wolfgang Thieme, 7: © dpa-Zentralbild / Soeren Stache), 135 (© dpa-Zentralbild); **Ellen Forney**, Seattle, WA: pp. 93, 94; **Das Fotoarchiv**: pp. 6, 46 (1: © John Powell); **Getty Images**: pp. 7 (crowd: © Scott E. Barbour / The Image Bank), 37 (right: © Redferns / GAB Archive / Kontributor), 50 (binoculars: © rubberball, students: © White Packert / Iconica), 64/65 (crowd: © Scott E. Barbour / The Image Bank), 71 (© VEER Rob McGowan), 73 (pendulum: © Gary S. Chapman), 104 (© Image Source); **Glasbergen Cartoons**, Sherburne, NY: pp. 6, 47 (C: © Randy Glasbergen); **Greenpeace**: pp. 5, 31 (D: © Greenpeace); **HarperCollins Publishers**: pp. 8, 82 (2: © 2009 HarperCollins Publishers. All rights reserved. Reproduced by permission of HarperCollins Publishers, New York); **Gabriele Heinisch**, Berlin: p. 131 (1, 2); **The Henry Moore Foundation**: p. 17 (4: © photo: The Henry Moore Foundation archive. Reproduced by permission of the Henry Moore Foundation); **InToon.com**: p. 44 (© Mike Keefe, The Denver Post and InToon.com); **iStockphoto**: pp. 54 (silhouette left: © rangepuppies, silhouette right: © Leontura), 62 (dog: © antony84), 110 (bottom: © Viorika), 116 (© leva); **Keystone Pressedienst**: p. 17 (3: © KEYSTONE Pressedienst); **laif**, Agentur für Photos und Reportagen: p. 51 (© Michael Nagle / NYTs / Redux); **Matthias Luedecke**, Berlin: p. 73 (top); **mediaskill OHG – Bildmaschine**: p. 129 (© Robert Kneschke / Bildmaschine.de); **MGM** Metro-Goldwyn-Mayer Studios, Inc.: p. 63 (left, middle left); **Office for National Statistics (ONS)**, U.K.: p. 33 (© Crown Copyright. Reproduced under the terms of the Click-Use License); **Penguin Books (USA)**: p. 101 (cartoon: from: *It's a teacher's life* by David Sipress, © 1993 by David Sipress. Used by permission of Dutton Signet, a division of Penguin Putnam Inc.; **Photolibrary**, London: pp. 6 (2: © Richard B. Levine, 3: © Charlie Abad, 6: © S. Meltzer / PhotoLink), 46 (2: © Richard B. Levine, 3: © Charlie Abad), 47 (6: © S. Meltzer / PhotoLink), 70 (bottom: © britain-onview / Flight Images LLP), 78 (right: © Bay Hippisley); **Picture Desk**: p. 98 (© MAVERICK FILMS / THE KOBAL COLLECTION); **Pitopia**: p. 56 (bottom: © Marco Menne); **www.planestupid.com**: pp. 5, 31 (F); **Political Cartoons.com**: p. 75 (top right: © 2005 Andy Singer – All Rights Reserved); **Random House, Inc.**: pp. 8, 82 (5: © Jacket Cover from GIRLS IN LOVE by Jacqueline Wilson. Used by Permission of Laurel-Leaf, an imprint of Random House Children's Books, a division of Random House, Inc.); **Report Digital**: pp. 7 (image in magnifying glass: © Jess Hurd), 17 (1: © Roy Peters), 43 (© Roy Peters), 64 (image in magnifying glass: © Jess Hurd), 74 (© Philip Wolmuth), 74/75 (© Philip Wolmuth), 75 (top left: © Jess Hurd), 76 (right: © Howard Davies), 78 (left: © Sam Morgan Moore), 81 (street scene and children: © Howard Davies); **Reuters Pictures**: p. 19 (© REUTERS / Tim Wimborne); **Anita Roddick**: pp. 4 (right), 11, 12, 164 (right); **Crispin Rodwell**: p. 66; **Steve Rotman**, San Francisco, CA: p. 101 (bottom); **Shutterstock images**: pp. 6 (A: © Natalia Siverina), 37 (left: © jirkaejc), 41 (© Barbro Bergfeldt), 47 (A: © Natalia Siverina), 72 (Ukrainian flag: © Fenton, Union Jack: © John Rawsterne), 84 (© Vladimir Melnikov), 86, 87, 88, 90, 92, 93, 96, 97, 99, 104 (backdrop empty book: © Svetlana Pritmova), 95 (© Christopher Dodge), 97 (bottom left: © Orla), 113 (© Louise Cukrov), 127 (top: © Natalia Siverina), 131 (flags: © Adam Golabek), 145 (bottom: © Chad McDermott); **Matthias Stolt**, Hamburg: p. 72 (passport); **Summersdale Publishers Ltd.**: p. 128 (top left: © Summersdale Publishers Ltd. / Matrix Media); **Superbild**: pp. 6, 46 (4: © ORE Oredia Patrick Carl); **Nora Tschepe-Wiesinger**, Berlin: p. 62 (all, except dog); **unicef**: pp. 3 (top, logo and images left, 2nd from left, right: © unicef), 4 (left, logo and images left, 2nd from left, right), 10 (logo, images left, 2nd from left, right: © unicef); **WaterAid** (www.wateraid.org): pp. 5, 30 (C: Flyer: © WaterAid / www.wateraid.org / Photo: © WaterAid / Caroline Penn); **Rainer Weisflog**, Cottbus: p. 134 (top); **Writer Pictures**: pp. 89 (© Geraint Lewis), 92 (© Mathieu Bourgois); **Youth Speaks Inc.**: p. 61 (The Brave New Voices International Youth Poetry Slam Festival, which is produced by Youth Speaks Inc. www.bravenewvoices.org, www.youthspeaks.org); **Zazzle.com**: p. 85 (© photo courtesy of ZAZZLE®).

**Cover:**
**Getty Images** (© Bongarts / Alexander Hassenstein)
**Map (inside front cover):**
**Carlos Borrell**, Berlin

# Language for Tasks ('Operatoren')

*Context 21 • Starter* uses the same special vocabulary ('Operatoren') for tasks that is used in standard tests, including the Abitur. Be sure you understand what's required of you when you come across one of the verbs below.

AFB I (= Anforderungsbereich I) refers to text comprehension and definition.
AFB II focuses on text analysis and comparison, and stylistic devices.
AFB III concentrates on discussion, comment, evaluation and text production.

| The instructions say: | What's expected: |
|---|---|
| **analyse** *(BE)*, **analyze** *(AE)* ['ænəlaɪz] (AFB II) | Look at something in detail and explain its meaning and/or structure. ('analysieren')<br>*Analyse the main elements of the poster.*<br>► examine |
| **assess** [ə'ses] (AFB III) | Show the pros and cons of something in a balanced way, and then give an opinion on it. ('auswerten, beurteilen, bewerten')<br>*Assess the effectiveness of the government's approach to fighting poverty.*<br>► evaluate |
| **characterize** *(usu. AE)*, **give/ write a characterization of** ['kærəktəraɪz, ˌkærəktəraɪ'zeɪʃn] (AFB II) | Look closely at the typical features of somebody or something, giving examples and explanations. ('charakterisieren')<br>*Give a characterization of the mother in the story.* |
| **classify** (*also:* **put into context**) (AFB I/II) | Arrange different things in groups and explain how the things in each group are similar to each other but different from the other groups. ('einordnen, zuordnen')<br>*Identify the different jobs discussed and classify them according to the type of tasks involved.* |
| **comment on** ['kɒment] (AFB III) | Express your opinion on something, giving evidence to support your view. ('kommentieren')<br>*Comment on the speaker's belief that ...* |
| **compare** (AFB II/III) | Explain similarities and differences between two or more things. ('vergleichen')<br>*Compare how the characters are portrayed in the film and in the novel.* |
| **contrast** [kən'trɑːst] (AFB II/III) | Show the differences between two or more things. ('kontrastieren')<br>*Contrast the rights of African Americans in the 1960s and today.* |
| **define** (AFB I) | State the nature and/or meaning of something. ('definieren')<br>*Define the term 'racism' as it is used by the writer.* |
| **describe** (*also:* **give/write a description of**) (AFB I/II) | State what something or somebody is like, including all the relevant details. ('beschreiben')<br>*Describe the writer's invention and what it is used for.* |
| **discuss** (AFB III) | Look carefully at something from all sides before stating your opinion. It should be clear from what has gone before, how and why you arrived at this opinion. ('diskutieren, erörtern')<br>*Discuss how education influences attitudes towards immigration.* |
| **evaluate** [ɪ'væljueɪt] (AFB III) | Show the pros and cons of something in a balanced way, and then give an opinion on it. ('einschätzen, bewerten')<br>*Evaluate the author's view of the impact Obama's speech had on his audience.*<br>► assess |